BREAK FREE FROM ADDICTION

Using the **TWELVE-STEP PROGRAMME**

DR ROBERT LEFEVER M.A., M.B., B.Chir.
Founding Director of the PROMIS Recovery Centre

Foreword by **CLARISSA DICKSON WRIGHT**

CARLTON
BOOKS

Break Free from Addiction reports information and opinions of medical and other professionals which may be of general interest to the reader. It is advisory only and is not intended to serve as a medical textbook or other procedural guidebook for either physicians or patients. The information and opinions contained herein, which should not be used or relied upon without consultation and advice of a physician, are those solely of the author and not those of the publishers who disclaim any responsibility for the accuracy of such information and opinions and any responsibility for any consequences that may result from any use or reliance thereon by the reader.

The case studies herein are all taken from real life. Names and personal details have been changed in order to protect privacy and confidentiality.

THIS IS A CARLTON BOOK

This third edition published in 2008 by Carlton Books Ltd
20 Mortimer Street
London
W1T 3JW

10 9 8 7 6 5 4 3 2 1

Text copyright © 2008 Dr Robert Lefever
Design copyright © 2008 Carlton Publishing Group

First published by Carlton Books Ltd in 2000

A CIP catalogue record for this book is available from the British Library.

ISBN 978 1 84732 085 8

Production: Lisa Moore/Janette Burgin

Printed and bound in the UK by CPI Mackays, Chatham, ME5 8TD

Contents

To Robin

"We should take care not to make the intellect our God."
– Albert Einstein

"Great perils have this beauty,
that they bring to light the fraternity of strangers."
– Victor Hugo

"To be alive is Power
Existence in itself
Without a further function
Omnipotence enough."
– Emily Dickinson

"Two roads diverged in a wood, and I –
I took the one less travelled by,
And that has made all the difference."
– Robert Frost

Foreword

On 10th August 1987 I was delivered three parts drunk to the door of PROMIS, Dr Robert Lefever's treatment centre at Nonington in Kent. Due to my chronic alcoholism, my life was in ruins, I was destitute, homeless and probably dying. The only thing that kept me off the streets was my ability to cook but my drink-induced behaviour meant that any jobs I obtained were of increasingly shorter duration. While I recognized that I could not stop drinking, I was, however, like so many alcoholics, in denial of the fact that my life was a total mess or that I needed to change my outlook and behaviour.

PROMIS had been open less than a year at this date. While following the Minnesota Method, it was very much Robert's brainchild and was revolutionary in many of its methods. Perhaps most important for me, and probably alone among the treatment centres of the time, it allowed one to recover with dignity. Robert had sat down with his staff and devised a programme which combined confrontation and rigorous honesty with attention to the spiritual void in the addictive personality. There was no religious buzz or Deistic bent but we as patients were encouraged to look within the emptiness inside ourselves and recognize that it was as important a part of our illness as the drug of our choice itself.

I remember my first meeting with Robert very well. I had been in PROMIS for several days when he took us for a lecture on the physical effects of addiction with a discussion afterwards. He has a mild manner which disguises his enormous energy and positivity. He always wore a scarf in the colours of his old college, which revealed much about his own self-image. Someone once said of Robert that everyone builds castles in the air but he turns them into bricks and mortar; he is a very practical visionary.

When I left PROMIS I moved into the Halfway House which at that time was the upper part of Robert's home. Realizing that a number of patients needed residential aftercare and that many would not make it without such a facility, Robert and his wife Meg moved down into their own basement. Robert would take us for morning meditation every day and it was during my six months there that I learnt more of his philosophy. Robert does not see problems: he sees solutions, which he then works towards whatever the cost to himself. If he believes something he will not bow to force or material pressure.

Today, others in the field of eating disorders are adopting the theories Robert has advocated for so long without acknowledging his contribution. In my time at PROMIS they mocked him but he stuck to his principles.

When I went into treatment I believed I could stop drinking but I had no belief that life would ever be enjoyable again; it would be something I had to live through. I owe to PROMIS my life, but to Robert I owe the fact that I enjoy it! His parting words to me were "Remember to jump off the precipice and trust the process". I trusted him and jumped and the rest is public history.

Clarissa Dickson Wright

Introduction

I don't like pills. I don't think they ever make people happier. They can stabilize the frankly psychotic but they have nothing to offer the sad or frightened. They give to today at the expense of tomorrow. Nor do I have any time for psychoanalysis: I see no point in trying to prove that I am cleverer than my patients. In any case, why look backwards? Patients learn through new experience rather than through ponderous reflection. What if someone's mother did this or that or if a particular patient was abused or abandoned in some way? That was then, not now, and heaping self-pity on to blame and self-justification isn't going to get anyone anywhere.

Working with patients who have addictive or compulsive behaviour (there's no difference apart from how we react to the words) must be among the most rewarding of all branches of clinical practice. Other doctors presumably choose a speciality because it suits their minds and temperaments. Surgeons like fixing things, physicians like thinking, and psychiatrists who prescribe drugs or electro-convulsive therapy…God knows what those psychiatrists like. I like humanity, not *en masse* but singly. I love the challenge of helping someone to be happier.

Imagine someone systematically destroying himself or herself, knowing that something is desperately wrong, but unable to work out what it is, while hanging on for dear life to the substance, activity or person that makes life worth living. That's addiction.

Now imagine him or her truly happy, free from all counterfeit mood-altering substances and processes, accepting life's challenges and making the best of them, concentrating on creativity and spontaneity and on the potential beauty of each new relationship. That's recovery.

I try to help people to move from the first state to the second. Could anyone be more fulfilled than I am in my work?

To be sure there are times of exhaustion, frustration, even loneliness – but this must be true for any worthwhile human endeavour. Also there are risks of becoming (in my own mind at any rate) a saviour or guru. Counselling is very seductive for the counsellor. Protecting myself, and more particularly my patients, against that has been a major challenge. Getting rid of "the burden of self" (a concept taken from the literature of Alcoholics Anonymous) does not mean destroying my mind and personality, far from it. It means doing my best in my professional work, focusing on improving my skills as the best way of showing my care for patients, and recognizing that I do not help them by doing their work for them.

Further, I have to "let go" (another phrase from the Anonymous Fellowships) of the short-term end result of my work. Some patients get better and that is to their credit. Others don't (yet) and that is their sadness. I do my work, caring for them, loving them even, but acknowledging that each patient has his or her own process and timetable of recovery. Some see the relevance of the ideas and the need for immediate change. Perhaps they were in so much pain that any idea or change would be better than none. Thereby they run a fearful risk of capture by a cult. Others take much longer to accept that their own perceptions and determination simply dig them further into the pit of destruction and despair.

And some others drag on and on. For them the prospect of change seemed too fearful, too unattainable. This sense of hopelessness does not constitute a reason for prescribing mood-altering drugs. Prescription drugs simply institutionalize the hopelessness, writing off the patient forever, while claiming to "provide a window of opportunity to sort out their problems".

All patients need to pass through this phase of personal despair and all counsellors have to let them do it. The same process, or a whole range of similar processes, are an essential part of helping young children to develop their own personalities and learn through their own experience.

Yet the analogy with parenting brings another risk for the counsellor. I am not a parent to my patients. My professional work with them is no less and no more than exactly that. I have enough trouble and reward with my own children: I don't need any more. My function is to do my work. I do this partly in order to release the patients' families from being their therapists. None of us can be counsellors to our own families; we get too close and we are too easily manipulated. We may even take on their pain and that doesn't help them or us.

But disengaging myself from the outcome of an individual patient's treatment does not mean that I can disregard the overall consequence of my work for all patients. If ideas don't work in practice then they don't work at all, regardless of how worthy or even how obviously right they might initially appear to be. Independent academic studies (done by someone outside my own organization) on the outcome of patients' treatment are the driving force of further refinement of ideas and clinical practice.

Naturally, it is hurtful when patients don't get better, and especially when they relapse after an initial period of recovery, but this is an experience I share with all doctors. What makes counselling failures (or postponements) particularly difficult to bear is the intensely personal nature of the work. My patients are not interesting cases, nor are they fodder for research, they are John and Mary, people whom I know well on a personal basis, often along with close members of their family, and it does matter to me when things don't work out as we all hoped.

Furthermore, in working with addicts, disappointments and even disasters are an all-too-frequent occurrence. Yet, if I am to be any use to my next patient, I have to let go of the outcome of treatment for the last one. I do not believe this to be possible if one works on a one-to-one basis with patients and thinks of them at all as "my" patients. All my work, and that of my counselling staff, is done in groups, never one-to-one with patients, and we work alongside each other, rarely by ourselves.

Working in a genuine team of individuals, each with his or her own skill, is enormously rewarding. We learn from each other and support and challenge each other. Counsellors who believe that they, or some other therapist, have unique insight and skill can become a menace, clinging to one truth at the expense of all others. In any case, patients differ in their preferences of personality and no single counsellor can be all things to all men and women. Recognizing our own and each other's skills and weaknesses is vital to the constructive working of a counselling team. Further, we guard the team jealously: counselling isn't a game, or simply common sense, although that constitutes a large part of it. It's a professional skill that has to be learned and practised. I myself have had to work harder at developing my counselling skills, such as they are, than at any aspect of my medical work or, for that matter, anything in life.

Gaining an insight into the specific nature of addictive or compulsive behaviour is theoretically possible for anybody but it comes naturally to those of us who ourselves suffer, in one way or another, from addictive disease. But therein lies yet another danger: recovering addicts don't know everything about addiction, and how to treat it, simply by being recovering addicts. We have a great deal to learn professionally as counsellors and there is a great deal that we can learn from other professions. Nonetheless, it is inevitable that we gain some specific insights when we have shared an experience ourselves. Madness has a particular poignancy for those who have been there.

"O! let me not be mad, not mad, sweet heaven;
Keep me in temper; I would not be mad!"

says King Lear. Yet mad he was. We watch in grim, sad, fascination as he destroys his family and himself.

Oliver Sacks' man who mistook his wife for a hat also fascinates us, but more with curiosity than sadness. Naturally we feel sad for the man, and indeed for his misapplied wife, as we would for any family struck with such a macabre cerebral affliction. But we watch from outside, as spectators at the zoo. Lear's tragedy is closer to home, more likely to happen to us, but mercifully sufficiently distant in Shakespearian time and probability of personal experience for us to be moved with compassion, but not truly frightened for ourselves.

The threat of addiction in contemporary society is, by contrast, very real. Those of us who suffer from it try to shut it out, as Lear tried to shut out his madness, but we fail as surely as he did. As with Oliver Sacks' benighted character, we also suffer from disordered perception and cannot ourselves see what is wrong even – and perhaps especially – when those about us are most emphatic in pointing to our delusion. And those who do not suffer from it, even those with medical training, commonly watch not with compassion nor even with fascination, but with disgust and contempt mingled with fear. And, to compound this, we abuse ourselves, thinking ourselves to be weak-willed, stupid and pathetic.

That's the way it is. But it need not be so ...

Dr Robert Lefever

Part I

Addictive Disease

Denial; Compulsory treatment; Family enmeshment; Ecosystem of madness; Psychiatric or addictive?; Medical education; Failure to control; Spiritual parasite; Drug education; Genetics; Compulsive helping; Physiological addiction; Matching study; Minnesota Method; Other approaches; Higher power; Neuro-transmission; Environmental influences; Childhood influences; Fixed viewpoints; Medical attitudes; Monitoring counsellors; Paradoxes; Terminology; Dry Drunk; Depression or addiction?; Early diagnosis; Heart-sink patients; Damage from addiction; Disease of the human spirit; Religion; Rational approaches; Addictive nature; Addictive characteristics; Risks to treatment centres; Dispelling shame; Accurate diagnosis; Intervention; Family intervention; Love, education and punishment; Compulsive helper counsellors; Addictive relationships; Psychopathology.

How do we get inside the madness of behaviour that is obviously self-destructive? If we can't understand it, we can't treat it. We try in vain to use rational approaches to correct irrational behaviour. We try love. We try education. We try punishment. They don't work. There's nothing wrong – and everything right – with love, education and appropriate punishment; but they don't work in changing addictive or compulsive behaviour. Of course they should – but they don't.

Denial

Douglas (45) is a city insurance broker. He drinks to the point of damage. His wife is dependent upon his income and therefore wants him to change his ways, but she has long since given up on any personal relationship. His son still loves him and hopes that he can help his parents to stop fighting. Maybe that would influence his father to stop drinking or, at least, learn to drink sensibly. Douglas loves both his wife and his son and believes that his real problem is that he is in the wrong job. He is therefore training to become a bereavement counsellor. He is convinced (utterly and absolutely) that the solution to all life's problems is to "live in the here and now" and he loses no opportunity to share this profound insight with anyone and everyone.

After a particularly heavy bout of drinking (it had been a depressing day in the office) he fell over and smashed his face into the ground. He was grazed and bruised and his nose bled but there was nothing more obviously seriously damaged. The next day his wife told him that she had finally had enough and that unless he went for treatment, she would leave him and learn to survive somehow without him.

Faced with the prospect of being on his own, he agreed that he would at least talk to someone about controlling his drinking – but not yet: he wasn't bad enough. After all, he certainly wasn't an alcoholic.

By nightfall he was paralytically drunk again and his wife simply bundled him into the car and drove him to our treatment centre. The admitting doctor examined him and found no abnormality apart from the obvious signs of years of "social" drinking and the recent facial injuries. Nonetheless the doctor's sixth sense made him instruct the nursing staff to monitor Douglas every half hour. This they did – and found by the end of the next day that his conscious level was worse rather than better, as one would expect if his problem was solely due to a drinking binge. Something was now obviously wrong and he was transferred to a general hospital.

A CT scan of the brain revealed a blood clot (a sub-dural haematoma) and he was transferred to a neuro-surgical unit, where they released the clot by drilling burr holes into his skull.

Within three days his brain, relieved of the pressure, was back to its normal philosophical self and he informed the doctors that he needed to leave the hospital and go about his business because, as he said, he had to "live in the here and now". The surgeons called in the psychiatrists, who responded that they had no power to detain him against his will (which is true, because the damaging use of alcohol or drugs is generally seen by doctors as a personal choice, rather than as due to a mental illness).

Douglas left the neuro-surgical unit and went straight to a bar. By nightfall he was paralytically drunk again. His wife wouldn't let him in the house (by now she had learnt from us that no addict chooses to seek help until the perceived pain of change is less than the pain of continuing as he or she is). So he turned up at his son's home. Within two days his son became unable to cope with his father's mood swings and with his continuing "need" for a drink. He couldn't understand how his father had suddenly become like this. After all, he was still in full-time work so he couldn't be an alcoholic. Nonetheless, Douglas asked for our help again and we sent a car to bring him back to the treatment centre. Hospitals, even psychiatric hospitals, generally don't take in drunks unless they have something else wrong with them. His wife wouldn't have him back. His son had to go to work and couldn't cope with him as well. So Douglas really didn't have much choice. He didn't want help from us - because, as he said, he didn't need it; all he needed was a different job and for his wife to be more understanding - but at least we provided warmth and shelter and, though he wasn't much interested in it, food. (We have several clever people on our staff, but only one genius - our chef Patrick, who was himself formerly one of our patients.)

After five days Douglas was a new man. His "military" bearing had reasserted itself, his facial grazes and bruising had gone, his charm had returned and he was again giving advice to all within earshot, counsellors and fellow patients alike, that we should "live in the here and now". He thanked everyone for their kindness, reassured us all that he had no intention of drinking, despite denying that his neuro-surgical adventures had had anything whatever to do with previous drinking, and left.

The chances of Douglas surviving are not good. We recommended him to stay for the full treatment programme - he had hardly begun it, having only just emerged from detoxification in the nursing unit. (Getting off addictive substances or processes is relatively straightforward and quick; learning how to stay off - and be comfortable doing so - is the difficult bit and that takes a lot longer.) But we can't force him.

Compulsory treatment

In some cases patients are referred to us on probation from the courts and it may be a condition of their sentence that they stay in treatment with us until we say they are strong enough to move on. Follow-up studies show that these "compulsory" patients do just as well as those who are voluntary, some of whom may simply be coming for "treatment" in order to get out of trouble of one kind or another but may have no real intention of changing. We can't force Douglas to stay because we have no power to make him do so. Until the Mental Health Act formally acknowledges alcoholism, drug addiction and other forms of compulsive behaviour as various aspects of a disease that is beyond the control of the sufferer, we cannot detain Douglas against his will, even for what we perceive to be his own good.

Politically, as a libertarian, I am generally concerned about the prospect of increasing the powers of doctors to confine people against their will, let alone enforce "treatments" upon them, perhaps especially "for their own good". Yet how do we help Douglas? How do we get inside the madness that is driving him to self-destruction?

Family enmeshment

Isobel (32) was brought to our out-patient counselling centre in London by her mother and sister, who said with one voice, "She refuses any treatment for her anorexia that involves feeding regimes. That's why we brought her to you for counselling." My staff are quite used to patients and families insisting on dictating the terms of treatment (understanding the fear that drives them to do so is a necessary part of counsellor training) but they were simply frightened by Isobel's appearance: she was five foot six inches tall and weighed just 68 pounds. They called me over from my medical practice.

Perhaps I was too abrupt. Perhaps if I had taken more time to win their confidence before stating the obvious, the story would have had a happier ending. Perhaps if I did addiction work full-time rather than in addition to my general medical practice (in the hope that people will see that addiction work - and care for people's human spirits, not just their bodies and minds - is a part of general medical practice) then I might have been in less of a rush to get back to my office.

"You're too thin. You're going to die", I said, trying to be both gentle and firm at the same time. "It would be totally irresponsible of us to offer you anything other than an emergency re-feeding regime. When your body is safe from terminal risks of malnutrition - and your brain less parched and shrivelled, as a CT scan would show it to be now - then we can counsel you, but not before."

The family left; upset. Two weeks later they drove to the treatment centre, without our foreknowledge, parked the car and carried her into the nursing station. Isobel had eaten nothing since I had seen her in London and was now too weak to walk. The family's faith in us was touching but irrelevant. Helping people involves caring for them, rather than worrying about one's own reputation.

Michael, our nursing director, was polite and concerned, as always, but equally adamant that our treatment centre is no place for emergency treatment. Yes, we treat anorexia, but our therapeutic programme is spiritual (restoring hope) rather than primarily dietetic (restoring the body). He arranged for her to be transferred to a private hospital under the care of a Consultant Physician.

The nurses hovered over Isobel, supervising her every moment, particularly at meal times, in the hope of persuading her to eat anything at all. They could not. The only thing that she would allow was an intravenous drip containing a salt solution similar in content to body fluid. She refused permission for glucose to be put into it. Isobel and her family said that they did not want psychiatrists to be called in and the family would not support an application to be made to the courts under the Mental Health Act for her to be fed against her will. "She's had so much suffering at the hands of doctors", they said. "It's never helped. She's got to be allowed to do it her way now." The Consultant Physician did not overrule this.

One member of our counselling staff used to visit her in the hospital each day in order to try to give her some insight into our therapeutic programme. She tried to give Isobel confidence that she really could take the risk of giving up control and then learn how to get better. The counsellor chosen for this responsibility was herself only slightly heavier than Isobel when she came to us eight years previously for treatment of her own anorexia. On the principle that it takes one to understand and help one, we tend as a general rule to select our counselling staff from former patients.

She tried but failed. I myself tried and failed. After running the treatment centre as usual at the weekend, I called into the hospital to spend some time with Isobel. "I've had a lovely lunch", she said, cheerily, "roast beef, potatoes and carrots." The nurse shook her head in contradiction. It wasn't a lie: Isobel really believed what she said. It is just that her truth is incorrect.

One rather odd feature about Isobel was that on some relatively short occasions she seemed not just "mad" in the anorexic sense but mad in a more general sense: wild or high, as if she had taken amphetamines. It would not have been the first time that family members had given drugs to patients (I remember one mother getting heroin from a dealer – how she did that still amazes me – and bringing it to her son in the treatment centre "because he told me on the telephone that you were detoxing him too quickly"!) but there seemed no evidence of that mischief in this case.

After ten days in hospital Isobel did indeed get her wish to do things her way and perhaps, macabre though this thought may appear, her family also got their wish. She died.

After death a phial of lighter fuel (the presumed inhaled cause of her transient additional madness) was found hidden in Isobel's vagina.

What could we have done to get inside Isobel's madness? Or, for that matter, to break the collusion of her family in her madness? Bearing in mind that we met them only at the end of Isobel's life (quite often people only come to us when they have exhausted every other approach), it was perhaps unreasonable to expect them to listen to our suggestions – to separate the madness from the girl herself and confront the madness while loving the girl – after they have been brutalized by all sorts of harrowing experiences for years.

Ecosystem of madness

Addictive or compulsive behaviour drags surrounding people into the madness. One may be sympathetic and helpful when someone has cancer or a heart attack or even just influenza, but one does not usually see the condition as a challenge to one's own belief system. Where addictive or compulsive behaviour is concerned, however, everyone (the addicts themselves, the family members, people at work, doctors and nurses, social workers, teachers, politicians and the public at large) has firm opinions on the cause of this type of behaviour and on what should be done about it. When you take an addict into treatment you take on his or her entire ecosystem of associated madnesses.

Psychiatric or addictive?

Belinda (35) had spent eight years wandering between the general hospital neurology department and the specialist psychiatric hospital in her local area. Doctors and nurses, and every paramedical professional you could name, had done everything possible to help her, yet still she remained "depressed" and "agoraphobic". Her eating disorder was undiagnosed and therefore untreated. She still lived at home with her parents and very rarely left home except to go to one or the other hospital. She had never worked and she had no friends apart from other patients whom she met during in-patient treatment. She was good with her hands and, predictably, had had years of hospital experience at basket weaving, such was the limited vision of occupational therapy in those days. She was equally familiar with all other hospital routines such as ward rounds, medicine times, visiting times (not that her family ever bothered to visit Belinda; they had given up) and so-called exercise times. She knew the nurses, the chaplains, the orderlies and porters, the general doctors and the psychiatrists, but never felt that any one of them knew her. She took her medicine because she was told to do so and because she had no idea what else to do.

She came to us through one of the other patients who had been in the same psychiatric hospital. That patient, Joan (33) had also spent years wandering between the two hospitals. The general hospital said that Joan's fits must be psychological, rather than due to epilepsy, and the psychiatric hospital said the opposite. When Joan came to us we had no doubt that her fits were psychological (quite apart from any other clinical observation, she had never actually hurt herself, however dramatic her gyrations might be) and we gradually took her off all psychotropic medication. At the same time we persuaded her to give up alcohol and cannabis, despite the fact that she had previously used both, not only in the presence of the staff of the psychiatric hospital but actually with them. When Joan developed a new drug-free personality, and felt genuinely happy for the first time in her life, she wondered whether we might help Belinda in the same way.

We have always provided a few free beds (until recently when financial pressures have been more acute) and Belinda was given one of these. Altogether she was with us for a year: three months in the in-patient programme in the treatment centre and then nine months in the "halfway house" that my wife and I used to run in our own home in London. Belinda was one of the last patients in the halfway house and I have to say in retrospect that the whole financially disastrous experience was worth it just to have helped her (and also the other patients, including another overeater patient who once fell asleep on top of the upright piano: no mean achievement!).

Once Belinda was free from the medication that had been prescribed to help her, she got better. Many patients with specific psychiatric conditions such as schizophrenia or manic depression are helped considerably by appropriate medication – although even in these cases one needs to be absolutely sure of the diagnosis before wading in with the prescription pad. In Belinda's case she needed no medication whatever. In fact she needed the opposite: in addition to her eating disorder she had become a prescription drug addict.

It would be easy to argue that Belinda had been made into a prescription drug addict by careless prescribing but I do not believe this to be true. Addicts are more probably born than made. She would have discovered some other form of "treatment" for her sense of inner emptiness if she had not discovered the mood-altering effects of prescription drugs. Her friend Joan discovered alcohol and cannabis (and several other addictive substances and processes) but Belinda only ever had two outlets for her addictive tendency, and her doctors genuinely had nothing else to offer.

Belinda now has a small home of her own, provided by the State, she has a paid job as a child-care assistant, and she is still good with her hands. On my office desk in London is a glass paperweight with a crocheted lace mat, made by Belinda, stuck to the underside. It is one of my most treasured possessions. She now has lots of friends through her contacts in Overeaters Anonymous and she regularly introduces new "hopeless cases" to us.

If only I could say that I myself behaved substantially differently from Belinda's doctors before I became aware of the nature of addictive disease and recovery.

Rachel (23) is the daughter of a Cambridge University contemporary of mine. I have been the doctor to her family for as long as I have been a doctor and since before she was born. She bounced into my office one fine spring day asking for some medication for hay fever – but she wanted me to check on whether it was mood-altering.

"What does that mean?", I asked in all innocence.

"I'm a recovering heroin addict", she replied without any sense of shame or need for further explanation. She simply assumed that I

would know what she meant and what her statement implied for safe prescribing. I didn't.

*"How on earth did someone like you become a heroin addict?",
I asked incredulously, "and, come to that, how did you get out of it?
Anyway, what do you mean by 'recovering'?"*

*"It means that I don't use any mood-altering substance (including
alcohol) because I would tend to become addicted to it. I can't speak for
other people: they might not. But I know I would, so I need to be careful
to check on what I take."*

She looked at my blank stare of continuing incomprehension.

*"As for coming off drugs and staying off them", she went on, "I go to
meetings of Narcotics Anonymous."*

*"What on earth is that?", I scoffed. "I suppose it's like Alcoholics
Anonymous where they hold hands in cardboard city and talk about God."*

*"How many meetings have you been to, in order to form this
judgement?"*

"Not a lot... well... er... none."

Medical education

She had certainly got me there. In six years of medical training I had
never once been taught about alcoholism or drug addiction or any form
of addictive or compulsive behaviour as such. The only things I had been
taught were their medical consequences and what to do about them. I
had been taught how to deal with drug overdoses and had been taught
to encourage people to live healthy lives and not take drugs. I had been
taught how to examine for liver damage and the various other ravages of
high alcohol consumption and I had been taught to encourage people to
drink sensibly, within a recommended number of "safe" units a day. But I was
taught nothing about alcoholism or addiction as illnesses in themselves.

I "knew", from my own clinical experience in hospital accident and
emergency departments and in general medical practice, that alcoholics
are a damn nuisance: they keep coming back in for one thing after another
and they don't listen to what you say, however much time and care you
give them. I "knew" that they are simply not worth the bother. The same
is true for drug addicts, compulsive gamblers, sex addicts (whatever they
may be, if anything), bulimics and so on and so on. Why couldn't they just
pull themselves together, use a bit of will-power, get a sense of personal
responsibility like the rest of us, and simply sort themselves out and stop
being a nuisance to everybody else?

Yet here was Rachel; one of my own kind; not a member of my family
– but not far off. She took me (very definitely as a visitor and not as a
participant member) to a meeting of Narcotics Anonymous, where I
immediately recognized three other patients of mine. I had no ideas that
any of them had ever been addicts or that they were members of Narcotics
Anonymous. I asked them why they hadn't told me.

"You wouldn't understand: you're a doctor", they replied.

I suppose that was a red rag to a bull. I'm not "a doctor": I'm me. Anyway, my first love was, and still is, music. I have always considered myself more an artist than a scientist, although by now I'm equally committed to being both.

I became determined to find out more about addiction and recovery. After finishing work in my medical practice in the evenings I began to go to a local "Minnesota Method" (using the principles of Alcoholics Anonymous) hospital-based treatment programme. By that time of day the counsellors had gone home so I learnt from the patients. I remember trying to persuade one of them that drinking a small amount of alcohol was more normal – and less fanatical – than giving up altogether.

"Real control", I said pontifically, "comes from learning to do things sensibly."

"I can't", he replied, "I've tried."

"Try harder."

"I did."

That conversation wasn't going anywhere but it did make me wonder about countless similar conversations going on between other doctors and patients (or family members and their disastrous black sheep; or employers and their employee failures who had shown so much initial promise; or teachers and their favourite pupils who had simply gone off the rails; or magistrates and the troublemakers back in front of them yet again) at the same time.

Failure to control

We express surprise that alcoholics, drug addicts, sufferers from eating disorders, compulsive gamblers and other addicts of one kind or another, fail to learn from experience. So do we. When the addict says "I can't do (whatever it is) sensibly; I've tried", he or she is telling the truth. We ourselves need to learn from that experience.

I remember making exactly that point to a distinguished Consultant Physician friend of mine to whom I refer patients for chest problems. "That's absolute nonsense", he said angrily, "I know plenty of people who have given up smoking. Everyone can do it." I replied that, in general, the people who can stop (and be at peace with themselves and not return to further use of an addictive substance or process) weren't addicts in the first place, whereas he, of all people, must have many people suffering, or even dying, from illnesses related to cigarette smoking who nonetheless continued to smoke. Furthermore, was it not true that his own hospital had found it necessary (even in one of the top hospitals for heart and lung diseases in the country) to provide smoking areas for their staff because otherwise they could not recruit sufficient nurses? Isn't that proof of their addiction, when nursing staff, particularly those in a heart and lung hospital, would give up their jobs rather than give up smoking cigarettes?

Far from agreeing my point, this exceptionally clever and normally mild-mannered man simply got more angry.

Spiritual parasite

I tell this story not in criticism of him but in awareness that addiction puts up barriers to its own treatment. Addicts do their very best to upset the medical profession along with everyone else. At the very time that they ask "Help me", they also say "Get away from me". At the very time they beckon you on, they push you away. It's as if there are two people inside the same head – and that is exactly the image that I myself find most helpful in understanding the nature of the madness of addictive disease: the human being says "Help me" while the disease says "Get away from me". How devastating a disease it is that pushes away its own treatment! How much more devastating that the basic psycho-pathology of addictive disease is "denial": the disease "tells" the sufferer that he or she does not have it!

Joe (38) is one of the most talented and delightful people I have ever known. He is naturally funny. I remember in one of the patient "shows" that we put on periodically at the treatment centre (in order to remind the staff that we are not the only ones with ability: it is very easy to fall into that trap when one is in an all-powerful role as a counsellor), Joe came on stage wearing a white coat and with a sprig of parsley sticking out of his flies. I can't explain why that should be funny. Perhaps it was just our fondness for Joe – and our awareness of his particular madness – that made us cry with laughter. "Oh, excuse me," he said, "I must be going now: I've got a train to catch." Again we cried with laughter. Joe had finally stuck in the treatment centre after running away no less than nine times! He always found it necessary to climb out of the bathroom window and "escape" across the fields, despite our repeatedly pointing out to him that the door was open (we have no locks) and that the driveway is far less muddy.

On the last occasion, he arrived in the main line terminus in London wearing only his pyjamas and an overcoat. His feet were bare. He begged the price of a drink, or more probably a drug, from passing passengers. The thing about Joe is that, as I have said, he is exceptionally talented. He earns his considerable living as a commodity broker in the city (some might say that it is a step up from there to begging barefoot in a station) but he could just as easily have been a concert pianist, or definitely an actor or entertainer of some sort. Yet this same talented, lovely, individual couldn't stay away from alcohol and cocaine or anything else he could lay his hands on (most recently heroin, which is becoming disturbingly fashionable in smart circles).

Joe's father died of alcoholism. The obituaries didn't say that: they rarely do except for jazz musicians, for whom it is almost a badge of honour. Joe's mother is still what she would call a "comfort" drinker. She appears to need a lot of comfort. Joe's sister may have a problem but I'm not sure, although I do believe that his wife may come our way one day. At present she is running hard in the opposite direction, getting as far away from us and from Joe as possible. Joe and his wife both sought solace elsewhere, hence all the agony and the running away from the treatment centre. Joe couldn't bear the pain and shame that his drugs caused him – but he couldn't live without them either. Most of all, despite his family history and despite all his personal disasters and humiliations, Joe still didn't believe that he was an addict.

"Everyone in the city is on something," he said, educationally, rather than defiantly. "All my friends take drugs." Well, indeed they might – but is that perhaps why Joe makes them his friends in the first place?

This capacity to blend into the background is very important to addicts of any kind. If you find that your life is getting out of control in some way or other, it helps to feel more "normal" by surrounding yourself with people who behave in a similar manner. People who drink too much stick together for mutual reassurance. They often seek employment in trades or professions in which their excesses will not be noticed: the army, the media, the breweries and so on. It is often thought that these professions and others have a high risk of alcoholism. The true picture is the reverse: they have a high attraction for alcoholics. Similarly, people who habitually use drugs develop a whole language and culture of their own. Sex addicts refer to themselves as "swingers" in order to "normalize" their excessive (and dangerous) behaviour. Compulsive gamblers dress up (or down) according to circumstance in order to make out to themselves, and to each other, that what they are doing is part of normal social behaviour. Girls with anorexia join the ballet, or become athletes or gymnasts, or they go into the fashion industry or even, defying all challenge, work in some way with food. In each case the addict plays chameleon, hiding the true problem from public view in a desperate attempt at self-conviction that all is well.

Tammy (15) is an experienced drug addict. She is a pupil at one of the top private girls' schools in the country. She has everything – but she throws it away. What sort of madness is this? She doesn't need anything. She isn't deprived. She resents her stepfather's existence but he has never abused or abandoned her in any way. She might more reasonably resent her real father who has expressed no interest in her whatever and who has had no contact since walking out when Tammy was one year old. In fact, Tammy idolises the fantasy that she has of him. But would that be sufficient reason in itself to get her into drugs? There are vast numbers of children who come from broken homes, or who live in deprived social circumstances (which Tammy definitely does not), or who have been physically or even sexually abused (which again Tammy has not) and yet they do not take drugs. Tammy is clever and pretty: she has everything going for her. Why the madness of drugs?

Was she led into bad ways by other girls at school? Well, there certainly are other girls with drug problems in that school – just as there are in any school – but there is no reason why Tammy in particular should have been led astray. Did she forget the slogan "Say no to drugs", and make one foolish experiment and then, accidentally, get hooked?

Drug education

Drug education is a very popular idea – in fact a number of popular ideas: Firstly, that children can all be influenced by slogans (in fact the ones who are influenceable may never have been at risk in the first place, other than in the general sense that any drug can be potentially dangerous, just as alcohol could impair one's driving or any prescribed medication could possibly cause an allergic reaction). On the same basis, the common assumption is that drugs are "pushed" on to children. The truth is that children most commonly get drugs from each other and from other members of their own families. As with alcohol and nicotine in adult society, drugs are primarily shared rather than pushed at school or at home, even though, in both cases, there is an ultimate supplier. Yet, remove that ultimate supplier and the pressure of demand will soon create another. But the idea that school children become drug addicts because of peer pressure, fearing that they will be laughed at or ostracized by their friends if they do not, is erroneous. The majority of schoolchildren do not take drugs, whatever the peer pressure. I doubt that they were influenced by slogans: they probably didn't want drugs in the first place. Conversely, I believe that the children who are addicted may well think that the slogans are silly and over-exaggerated.

Secondly, that drug addiction comes initially from foolish experiment. That must be true in so far as one cannot become addicted to a substance one has never taken but it doesn't mean that Tammy would never have become addicted to any other substance, such as alcohol or, for that matter, sugar. Alcohol and sugar may be thought to lead to "lesser" addictions than drug addiction but, in my clinical experience of treating over two thousand addicts of all kinds as in-patients in the last fourteen years and nowadays also seeing 350 new out-patients each year, there is no such thing as a "lesser" addiction in terms of human suffering, but only in terms of some specific risks.

Thirdly, that one can become "accidentally" hooked. Even crack cocaine, ecstasy and the "designer" drugs, chemically manufactured as variants of existing drugs, take repeated use for addiction to become established.

I fully understand why people want to believe these things and I fully understand people's fear that we must present a united front in educating and advising our children, but children are not fools: they deserve to be told the truth. The truth is that the major damage by far from addictive substances in our society comes from alcohol and nicotine. One in five of all hospital beds is occupied by people with conditions related to their use of alcohol. Twenty times as many people die from the effects of alcohol, and sixty times as many people die from the effects of cigarette smoking, as from the use of all illegal drugs put together. I do not condone the use of illegal drugs – I spend much of my professional life dealing with the consequences of drug addiction – but I do believe that we should speak the truth about all addiction in our society instead of focusing simply on the illegal drugs and on concern for problems in our children. We have addiction problems everywhere in our society and we should examine our own behaviour first of all.

Perhaps the clue to Tammy's addiction comes from the fact that her real (genetic) father is an alcoholic. Is there an addictive gene or, more probably, a group of addictive or potentially addictive genes? Perhaps there is such a high incidence of addiction in broken homes not because the home is broken as such but because there may have been good reason (such as parental alcoholism, eating disorder or drug addiction) for the home to have become broken.

Julia (30) came through in-patient treatment with us for drug addiction eight years ago. Hers had been a wretched story of social decline. She came from a wealthy Italian family who had international business interests. Everything seemed to be going well for her, despite the early death of her mother, when she qualified as an accountant and was married in a magnificent social blaze. But "la dolce vita" didn't last: it never does on cocaine, the greatest fraudster known to pharmacology, promising so much but in fact taking away everything. Julia lost everything: her job, her husband, the love and support of her family, her health, her looks – the lot. In that state she came to us. There is no rule that says that people must inevitably lose everything before they seek help – but it was certainly true in Julia's case. She worked hard on the recovery programme, dragged her self-esteem up from the gutter, went a bit crazy temporarily when she fell for an American guru and all his claptrap on the nature of human relationships (he has certainly had plenty of experience: he is currently on his sixth wife!), but then got herself back on an even keel.

As a result of her success, we were asked to look after her younger brother Claudio (24). He had no apparent addiction but was profoundly depressed. The inner emptiness of addictive disease (the neurological and psychological state that exists before the sufferer discovers mood-altering substances and processes to "treat" it) is often misdiagnosed as depression or even manic depression. We therefore admitted Claudio for assessment. He spoke good English, as do all the members of his family (this is not a requirement for admission: some patients learn English while in treatment with us, so they get that benefit irrespective of what they learn on the recovery programme) but for the first week we heard not a word out of him. He sat, sad and silent for hour after hour, day after day. He responded monosyllabically when asked questions. He was always polite but he contributed nothing spontaneously. In those days we used to do one-to-one counselling sessions as well as group therapy but those became a trial of endurance for both Claudio and the counsellors.

Nonetheless, a gradual change did occur – not during the daytime when the counselling staff were doing their very best to help him, but in the evenings when he was with the other patients. By design, all our bedrooms are shared (addiction is a disease of emotional isolation) and

Claudio gradually began to talk to his room-mate. Later he came out of his protective shell with other patients. Eventually he made contributions to the group therapy sessions when he could see that another patient needed help. This process (reaching out to help others) gradually restored Claudio to health. Some of the people he tried to help benefited from the experience, others did not – but the process of taking his mind off himself and putting it on to other people (the fundamental principle of recovery from any addiction, because it provides a substitute mood-altering process) got Claudio better. It turned out that he had in fact been drinking and using all sorts of drugs without anyone knowing. He hid it all very successfully behind his "depression".

One thing we couldn't influence was his cigarette smoking. He refused point blank to let go of that. I personally believe that it is best for patients to give up all addictive substances and processes at one go – but I can't force people (other than my staff: I do not recruit counselling staff who smoke; they need to be free from all addictive substances and processes so that they develop the sensitivity of feeling and intuition necessary to do their professional work effectively) to do things that they don't want to do. Although nicotine addiction is ultimately the most damaging of all addictions (and we do everything possible to support those who do give up and we make life just that bit uncomfortable – no smoking anywhere in the house, only by the dustbins, whatever the weather – for those who don't), nonetheless, we have to focus primarily on those addictions that are most likely to cause immediate damage or even death. Claudio was functional by the end of our treatment programme, despite his continued smoking, and he went on to train as a lawyer and is now an assistant in a major international firm.

*By this time things at home were getting hot for their father, **Silvio (56)**. He had been happy to pay for treatment for his children but he had not anticipated that they would promptly turn round and point the finger (in love but perhaps with a tinge of revenge!) at him. I have a lot of sympathy for Silvio on this issue because my own son had done exactly the same to me. My own eating disorder (it happens just the same in men as in women but we tend not to be noticed) and my workaholism (we hide that as a "necessary" part of supporting the family) and my compulsive risk-taking, most recently on the treatment centre (my risk-taking is the ultimate desperation of my wife, who pointed out recently that we lose our home – or at least its financial value – every ten years) only came out into the open after our son got better from alcoholism and drug addiction and pointed the finger at me.*

Silvio came to us for just one week. He didn't like sharing a room, he didn't like group therapy and he didn't like the counselling staff, whom he felt were too big for their boots. (I think in retrospect that at that time he was right on the last issue.) He came off alcohol completely and went back to Rome. We anticipated that he would go straight back to drinking – but he didn't. He has remained contentedly dry from that day to this.

He hasn't followed our suggestions - but so what? If he and his family are happier and he is free from the problem that previously tortured him, that's what matters to me. If he gets better by painting his toenails blue or by standing on his head - or whatever - then that's fine by me. I have no monopoly of solution: I only know what works for me and, in my clinical experience, works best for most people like me. I also know, mostly, what doesn't. On that knowledge, I base my clinical work. But the plain fact is that 35 per cent of our patients do not get better so I still have a lot to learn, and some patients, like Silvio, get better (at least for a time) in other ways, so I may have a lot to learn from them as well.

Genetics

A genetic predisposition to addiction does not mean that everyone in the family will necessarily inherit that particular gene or set of genes. Nor does it cast the black spot of eternal damnation: there is a great deal one can do in learning to live with a potential condition once one is aware of it. People with allergies learn to avoid the substances to which they are allergic. People with short sight wear spectacles or contact lenses, yet behind them are still as short-sighted as before. People with addictive tendencies learn to put down the addictive substances or processes that particularly affect them and, on a day-to-day basis, learn to work the Twelve-Step programme of recovery, first formulated by Alcoholics Anonymous.

There is as yet no proof that addictive or compulsive tendencies other than anorexia are genetically inherited, but there is considerable interest in genetic influence on the development of dopamine receptors in the mood centres of the brain. Professor Ernest Noble of the University of California, Los Angeles, found that people with a particular "allele" (genetic alternative) on chromosome eleven tended to have an increased appetite for alcohol, cocaine, nicotine, caffeine and sugar. I like the look of this work, because it bears out our own clinical observation that all addictive processes are the same in their nature, even if the particular substances or processes of addiction may differ.

Many studies focus on one substance - commonly alcohol - and, I believe, thereby miss the true picture by having too narrow a focus. In my own family my father's father married the barmaid whose father owned the place, thus guaranteeing every alcoholic's dream: free drinks for life. My mother's mother (a distinguished headmistress) died of alcoholism and my mother, I believe, had an eating disorder (my father would deny it, saying that she must have had something wrong with her glands - but, one way or another, she was certainly spherical). I myself have several addictive outlets (as do most addicts) and our son is alcoholic and drug-addicted, although now mercifully "in recovery", working the continuing recovery programme, as I do myself, on a day-to-day basis. My wife's father committed suicide from his alcoholism (it is estimated that at least one third - I would guess significantly more - of all suicides are committed by people with an addiction of one kind or another) and his father, a church organist, was also an alcoholic (which must have been fun at times for the congregation, if not for his family).

I give this family history not out of pride or bravado but simply as a matter of fact. My reason for repeatedly using examples from my own family are that I know them and can write confidently about them; that I wish to emphasize that addiction runs in families and that it is most probably genetically inherited; that I want to encourage others to put down any sense of shame in coming from an addictive family; and that I wish to encourage other doctors to diagnose and treat addictive disease in its broad manifestations appropriately. Doctors will resist diagnosing their addicted colleagues, let alone patients, while any sense of disgrace, depravity or failure of will-power is attached to the diagnosis of addictive disease. I have no shame in being an addict, nor in coming from a family of addicts (although I have to express some concern over one of my close relatives who does not appear to have any addictive tendency and is not like the rest of us at all!); it is just the way we are. I have considerable guilt over some of my behaviour, particularly towards my wife, and I try to make appropriate amends to the people I have harmed and not to do those things any more.

The interesting question about my wife, Meg, is this: Why, when she came from the absolute carnage of her own addictive family did she marry into mine? The majority of families have no addiction at all. Why did she marry me? Why did her previous boyfriends, and the people she finds attractive now, all have some addictive tendency? Why, when she has absolutely no addiction of her own, does she find herself fatally attracted to addicts? I even use her as a diagnostic instrument: if I am unsure as to whether a man has an addictive tendency I ask Meg and she either says, or does not say, "Yes, I think he is rather nice!".

Is this just familiarity: is it the type of relationship (since her childhood conditioning) that she understands? Personally I think it is rather more than that. I think she does have an addictive tendency: compulsive helping. When we look at the particular addictive characteristics that differentiate addicts from the non-addictive population, we find that some people have exactly these same characteristics on the need to be needed. The primary addict needs to be "fixed" in some way: he or she wants something or somebody "out there" to fill up the emptiness "in here". As the exact mirror-image, the compulsive helper, like Meg, wants to gain a sense of self-worth through being needed. These two, the addict and the compulsive helper, fit together perfectly in a co-dependent (a term which has too many different meanings to have any meaning at all other than in this defined instance) relationship. The literature of Addictions Anonymous refers appropriately to the relationship between an addict and a compulsive helper as "a dreadful dance". It is.

Compulsive helping

It might be thought that compulsive helping is a nice, healthy, even kind and compassionate, addiction but it isn't. It's a curse. It gets in the way of normal relationships. The compulsive helper does too much, taking on too much responsibility for other people so that those other people don't learn from their own experience. Further, the compulsive helper gets progressively damaged, while saying "Oh, that doesn't matter: don't worry about me". There is a limit to appropriate selflessness – and compulsive helpers go beyond it, just as there is a limit to sensible drinking, or sensible anything, and addicts go beyond those limits. Compulsive helping is as progressive and destructive as any other addictive tendency, although it is the mirror image, and it needs to be treated just as seriously.

So where did Meg's compulsive helping come from? The answer to that is easy for anyone who knew her mother. She was indeed a dear, kind, lady who never had a harsh word for anyone, who never grumbled for herself despite an exceedingly difficult life before and after her husband's suicide, and who richly deserved (appropriately) the mayor's award for "Helper of the Year", for looking after the elderly when she herself was in her eighties. (Not everything a compulsive helper does is necessarily an act of compulsive helping, just as not everything an addict does is necessarily addictive: sometimes it is simply an act of human kindness.) But there was a darker side to my mother-in-law, as there is to Meg and to any other compulsive helper. There is an appropriate time to say "no". There is an appropriate time not to keep the peace. Other people, particularly young children, can be significantly damaged if the people whose function is to care for them do not do so because they cannot stand up to the demands, or confront the appalling behaviour, of the addicts in their families.

This may sound as if I am blaming Meg and her mother for my behaviour and that of my father-in-law. I do no such thing. Speaking for myself, I accept that I am totally responsible for my own behaviour, past, present and future. I may, through my genetic inheritance, not be responsible for being an addict but I have always been, am now, and will always be, responsible for my behaviour towards other people. I would say exactly the same for Meg and her mother and for any other compulsive helpers: they may not be responsible for being compulsive helpers (I believe that also to be most probably genetically inherited), but they are responsible for their behaviour towards other people.

As it happens, some people are both addicts and compulsive helpers. I am myself. In my relationship with Meg I tend to be the addict to her compulsive helper but in my relationship with my son, and in my relationship with some of my staff and some of my patients I tend to be the compulsive helper to their addict. In fact, reflecting over my own life, it is my compulsive helping that has caused me most damage and pain, and often damaged other people as well, when I have not put my foot down, or when I have not walked away from a relationship, when it would have been most appropriate to do so.

I suspect that the genetics of addictive behaviour, when they are finally all worked out will show that there are three principal addictive pathways. The first is "hedonistic" (eat, drink and be merry for tomorrow we die). This leads people towards "recreational" (street) drugs, some prescription drugs, nicotine, caffeine, gambling and risk-taking, addictive sexual activity and "dominant" relationships (aggressively using other people as if they were drugs and "threatening" to hurt them in some way if they don't do what one wants). The second addictive pathway is "nurturant" (doing something to soothe one's self). This leads people towards bingeing or starving in their relationship with food, exercise, shopping and spending (and shop-lifting if the money runs out, although stealing as such is a hedonistic addictive outlet), compulsive exercise, workaholism (using work not for any productive purpose but to give one a previously lacking sense of being worthwhile) and "submissive" relationships (manipulatively using other people as if they were drugs and "threatening" to hurt one's self if they don't do what one wants). The easiest way to distinguish between the emotional blackmails of dominant and submissive addictive relationships is that in the dominant relationship the addict implies "Do as I say or I shall hurt you", whereas in the submissive relationship the addict implies "Do as I say or I shall hurt myself". (Incidentally, self-mutilation is often seen in people who have eating disorders or other "nurturant" addictions. This may seem bizarre but they say it makes them feel better.)

It will be noticed that alcohol does not appear in either the "hedonistic" or the "nurturant" pathways. This is because we find that it appears in both, acting as both a stimulant and as a tranquillizer.

The third addictive pathway is "compulsive helping" (using one's self as a drug for other people).

Physiological addiction

I'm not saying that environment and exposure play no part in the development of addiction but I am saying that I believe that genetic predisposition is a necessary prerequisite. Some people have particular addictive tendencies and others do not. It is on exactly this issue that I need to be especially careful, so that I am understood precisely. I am not saying that some people can use addictive substances without risk. The obvious example is that drinking alcohol and driving a car can lead to dreadful accidents and death, whether one is an alcoholic or not. (It is just more probable that the alcoholic, as opposed to other people, will drive under the influence of drink.) The important distinction is this: if one injects morphia into anyone on earth on a regular basis, he or she can be made physiologically dependent upon it so that withdrawal symptoms will occur when the injections are stopped. Most people will go through these withdrawal symptoms, being very uncomfortable – like having a bad 'flu – for a few days, but after that will have no great wish, and certainly no sense of compulsion, to return to using morphia or any other addictive substance or process. They will be able to drink alcohol without it triggering a craving for morphia. Other people (the people whom I believe have the genetic predisposition to addiction) will find it much harder to get off the morphia, will have cravings to return to drug use, and will commonly find that these cravings are triggered by drinking alcohol or by using other mood-altering substances or processes.

There are a number of significant implications that come from the concept that addictive tendencies might be genetically inherited.

Firstly, as previously hinted, we need to look at all addictive substances and behaviour simultaneously and not at any particular addictive substance or behaviour in isolation.

Secondly, we need to target those families who are most at risk (by observing the incidence of addictive behaviour in the family) just as we target those most at risk of any other clinical condition. It is more important to identify those who are most at risk than it is to educate everybody on the subject of addiction. (Exactly this mistake was initially made in trying to deal with a potential AIDS epidemic.) The people most at risk should be targeted first. They need to be told about their particular risks and given all appropriate education and help. In the case of addiction they do not need to be told repeatedly about the nature, or the dangers, of drugs or alcohol or nicotine: potential addicts know most if not all about that already – and it still makes no difference to their behaviour. They need educating on the nature of addictive disease and recovery.

It is worth repeating that one cannot combat a genetic predisposition with education, punishment or love, the three approaches that are most commonly applied. Addicts need to be identified and told about the nature of addictive disease and recovery because this is what affects them. Other people can learn about addiction later (after we have first targeted the addicts themselves) – and it is important for these other people to understand addiction because the problem affects so many people (at least 10 per cent of the population) that absolutely everyone will be affected in some way by its knock-on effects in society. However, it is *not* true that everyone has an addiction of some kind. When this ingratiating assumption is made, it is an insult to those of us who are addicts. We neither want nor appreciate "understanding" from those who do not understand.

Thirdly, I am concerned not to make the life of addicts even worse by being stigmatized even more than they are already. There is no need to call for their extermination when perfectly good treatment methods (the Twelve-Step programme of the various Anonymous Fellowships) already exist. My great fear of the actual proof that addictive disease is genetically inherited (as the human genome project is completed in the next few years) is that people will insist on abortions rather than let more addicts into the world. Lawyers may then stick their oar in and, at some point in the future, I fear that they will encourage addicts to sue their parents for allowing them to be born. Be that as it may, the primary need, as I see it, is for the general population to be educated in the effective method of treatment for addiction: the Twelve-Step Programme of Alcoholics Anonymous.

Fourthly, the most exciting recent work on genetics comes from functional MRI scans of the brain and from anatomical and physiological studies of the sea slug (which has particularly large neurons). These show that changes in the environment can influence the structure and function of the brain. Genes are not absolute determinants; their expression can be modified through environmental change. The implication for addicts is profound: we can change the way we are made by changing our behaviour - provided we maintain that change,

Matching study

When it is complete the massive Project MATCH study will have been carried out for over eight years in thirty treatment programmes and financed at a cost of $27 million by the US National Institute for Alcohol Abuse and Alcoholism. It revealed that Minnesota Method treatment programmes, based on the principles of Alcoholics Anonymous, have at least as good an outcome for alcoholism as the standard cognitive behavioural approaches (teaching people skills to resist situations that increase the chance of drinking, i.e. educating people in the hope of changing their behaviour) and motivational enhancement (helping people through looking at their emotional stresses and promoting individual responsibility and enhancing inner resources to overcome drinking). Further, the study showed that it is not a matter of horses for courses: alcoholics cannot be matched to the best treatment programmes, based on psychological factors presumed to have led them to drink - alcoholics do well in Alcoholics Anonymous.

This does not imply that other approaches have no value. In our treatment centre we use cognitive behavioural approaches and some forms of motivational enhancement as part of our therapeutic programme, but the concept of a primary spiritual disease requiring a primary spiritual therapeutic approach is fundamental to Minnesota Method treatment such as ours. The recommendation to give Alcoholics Anonymous a try, if the patient so wishes, is sometimes simply tacked on at the end of treatment (if at all) in traditional psychiatric centres. In Minnesota Method centres it is the basis of the whole treatment programme. It is this method that should be the first, if not the only, treatment approach.

I do not believe that we are currently seeing an increase in addiction in our society. All we are seeing is a change in the drugs most commonly used by people with addictive tendencies. Alcohol and nicotine are still by far the most popular addictive drugs in our society but I believe that pattern will change as a new generation grows up with greater availability of "recreational" (street) drugs.

If the principles of the Minnesota Method work for alcohol there is every reason to act on the assumption that they will work for drug addiction and for eating disorders. At the very least, the ideas of the Minnesota Method are worth looking at seriously, rather than being determinedly ignored.

If my personal feelings influence my argument it is perhaps not surprising. The best that traditional psychiatric approaches would have offered my son was (and still is) Methadone and "harm-minimization programmes" and the best they would have offered me is Prozac, Seroxat or some other chemical pathway to artificial suppression of feelings. Each of us has now been completely free from addictive substances and processes for many years and our thoughts, feelings and behaviour are very much our own and not by courtesy of legal or illegal pharmaceutical substances. To those who continue to resist looking at the ideas of the Minnesota Method I would ask, "What would you wish for your own family?"

As it happens it doesn't really make any difference whether or not one believes that addiction is genetically inherited (this is not a cardinal belief in Minnesota Method treatment centres), provided one does (or recommends) what works best: total abstinence and regular attendance at an appropriate Anonymous Fellowship. I believe that addictive disease is basically genetically inherited, but that this genetic predisposition then has to be stimulated by emotional trauma of one kind or another (abuse, abandonment, bereavement, failure, or acute distress of one kind or another). The final stimulus required for the development of full-blown addiction is the exposure to mood-altering substances or processes that "work" for that individual in producing a mood-altering effect that transiently fills the sense of inner emptiness. Environmental factors have significant influence on which particular addictive outlets are most likely to develop. Further, the problems that each addict gets from the use of addictive substances, behaviour or relationships will then cause further disturbance to the disordered mood, making him or her even more anxious and depressed. This, in turn, leads to increased use of addictive substances, behaviours or relationships in order to try to "treat" the mood disorder – and so the spiral goes on, round and round, down and down.

Minnesota Method

Minnesota Method treatment exactly reverses these contributory causes of addiction (in any form) as follows:

The first requirement is abstinence. There is no point in counselling someone who has had a drink or a drug that day. One can give information but that is all. The mood centres of the brain are inaccessible when already stimulated by a mood-altering substance. This further emphasizes the point that sufferers from addictive disease have no intellectual deficit: our problem lies in our mood centres, not in the thinking part of our brains. Granted, as Alcoholics Anonymous points out, that we suffer from "stinking thinking" but this is because we (along with those who observe us) try to rationalize our behaviour afterwards. Our behaviour is motivated by our feelings: our thoughts come later. "Normal" (non-addictive) people tend to do it the other way round.

The second part of treatment is to deal with the underlying emotional trauma. In our own treatment centre each counsellor has his or her own skills and approaches. My own limited experience is in gestalt therapy, transactional analysis, rational emotive behaviour therapy, reality therapy and choice theory, psychodrama, Eye Movement Desensitisation and Reprocessing (EMDR) and Neuro Linguistic Programming (NLP), and I have had some experience of traditional analytical approaches and, of course, cognitive behavioural therapy. My favoured approach is psychodrama because it is quick (a picture or image speaks a thousand words), patient-centred (psychodrama works with the perceptions of the patient, not those of the counsellor) and, when appropriate, it can be fun (why should therapy be so fearful and serious, even when dealing with fearful and serious issues?). Other members of my staff use Jungian methods, Rogerian person-centred counselling techniques and a host of other approaches. We prefer experiential to analytical approaches because, as emphasized previously, the problem in addiction is primarily with feelings rather than thoughts – but in practice we use both "thinking" and "feeling" approaches because ultimately addiction affects both thinking and feeling. Most importantly, however, one way or another, we try to help people to deal with their emotional trauma so that it loses its potential to trigger further addictive use.

The third part of treatment counters the genetic predisposition: being with other "recovering" addicts and reaching out to help (on an anonymous basis) those who are still active in their addiction. The mood-altering effect of reaching out to help others anonymously fills up the inner emptiness of addictive disease. This sense of well-being cannot be achieved simply through intellectual understanding, will-power, the support of friends and family, healthy exercise, hard work – or any of the other things that well-meaning people believe should be effective. They don't work. They are all very fine for the purposes for which they are primarily designed but they do not get through to the core of inner emptiness in addiction.

The central feelings of addiction are those of self-pity and blame. These are what need to be tackled. They cannot be reasoned, or encouraged or blown away. They have to be dug out from the inside by the addict, working the Twelve-Step programme of recovery and fundamentally transferring the focus of attention away from self and on to others.

What staggers me is the amount of resistance that this lovely philosophy engenders in those who have never seen it at work or used it themselves. It is for this very reason that addicts stick together in recovery, as well as in our days of active addiction: other people never will understand addiction as such, any more than I can understand my father's red/green colour-blindness. Even though I can understand colour blindness from a purely theoretical perspective, I shall never know what the world really looks like to my father. Nor will he (a non-addict) ever understand what the world feels like to me.

Addiction in its various forms is a huge problem that is not going to go away, it does not respond well to traditional approaches, and there are ways of looking at addiction, and hence of treating it, that are highly effective. The Minnesota Method approach is not generally understood by the medical profession, because it involves a conceptual jump as big as when Sigmund Freud set out to persuade his contemporaries that mental illness should be seen in its own right rather than simply as a consequence of physical illness. Indeed, there may well be a physical basis (at the molecular level) to mental illness and to addictive disease but it is helpful, both diagnostically and therapeutically, to see the problems of addictive disease in three separate entities: physical, mental and spiritual.

Other approaches

Again I need to be careful in what I say about other approaches towards the treatment of addiction so that I am not misunderstood. For my own supervision and continuing therapy (all counsellors need this because if we go crazy then the knock-on effects on our patients can be catastrophic), I now go to a clinical psychologist who has a broad range of clinical experience and skills. He now knows a lot about me but has no knowledge of addiction whatsoever. I don't need him to understand addiction: I go to Addictions Anonymous and Helpers Anonymous for the understanding and treatment of my addictions. I go to him in order to discuss the normal or crazy parts of me that I have in common with anyone else. He has a great deal to give me, using various approaches from his perspective as a clinical psychologist, and indeed he does give me a great deal of help.

In exactly this way other professionals have a great deal to offer to addicts, provided they steer clear of trying to understand or treat addiction as such. That is the specialist function of the Anonymous Fellowships. Even in our own treatment centre I make no claim to get patients better from addiction: we challenge, we support, we guide, we educate, we encourage, but ultimately we refer to the Anonymous Fellowships: that's where they get better. What we do is to help a greater number to be able to get better in the Anonymous Fellowships than would have done so in the absence of our preparation.

Peggy (45) was as comprehensively drunk as I have ever seen anyone. In that "blackout" state she was so aggressive and reckless that she damaged everything and everybody in her path, especially herself. On sobering up in our treatment centre she had no recollection of how she got there nor what she might have done while drunk. "I must have an AIDS test. I've no idea how many men I've slept with", she said in horror. The more she thought about it the more horrific the implication became – and she left treatment in order to console herself in the usual way.

A few days later she was admitted to another treatment centre and then to a psychiatric hospital and then back to us and then on again to yet another treatment centre, then back to us yet again and then off to yet another psychiatric hospital. On each occasion no sooner was she sober than she found a new compelling reason to leave.

It would be tempting to call this condition status alcoholicus or status addictus, along the lines of status asthmaticus or status epilepticus when patients get intractably stuck in these conditions. However, just as status asthmaticus and status epilepticus can be treated by emergency intervention, so can status alcoholicus. The difference in this case is that the emergency intervention should not be with drugs but has to come from the patient: all the professional can do is to provide an appropriate supportive environment and the clinical understanding of the condition. The Big Book *of Alcoholics Anonymous abounds with stories similar to Peggy's. In each of them the sufferer eventually got better on realizing the impossibility of self-control. Similar stories can be read in the corresponding* Big Books *of other Anonymous Fellowships dealing with other addictions. In each case the addicts describe how they eventually got better by abandoning any concept of self-control and getting out of their own way.*

Dennis (55), when he first left the treatment centre, after just one week spent mostly in the nursing station detoxification unit, did so because he had made a decision never to drink again. He had previously read a book by a well-known, "television personality" counsellor in which he encouraged people with addiction problems to "make a decision". Dennis now realized the importance of doing just that. I cannot think where this TV personality counsellor gets the idea that all addicts need to do is to "make a decision". My clinical experience is that addicts "make a decision" to give up almost every day of the year – and it doesn't work. Dennis shared his new insight, and his resolute decisions, with us in a deep and meaningful way and went home – and got drunk out of his skull. "Home" by this time was any hotel that would have him – and there are an increasing number that will not.
He was back with us, considerably the worse for wear, two weeks later and we tidied him up again. Before we could get him fully involved in the therapeutic programme he was off again. This time he had found religion. I don't know where he found it: certainly not from me.

Higher power

Despite the mention of God in the Anonymous Fellowships I myself am an atheist in so far as I have no religious God. My God (or "Higher Power than self") is other people. I know from my experience of three days as a patient in a blank room in a mental nursing home that, of myself and by myself, I am nothing: I only come alive when I interrelate with other people. Other people know me better than I know myself and other people (other addicts) have the capacity to help me in my addiction more than I can help myself, if I remember to ask them and allow them to do so. I know a lot about addiction but I still need the God of my own understanding (the precise phrase used in the literature of the Anonymous Fellowships) to help me with my own addictive disease, so that I never again return to active addiction. I cannot battle against it on my own. It defeats me, as ultimately it defeats all addicts, every time.

Dennis found religion and off he went – straight into bed with a lady who said she knew how to help him. I'm pretty sure he didn't meet her in church. "I needed sex", he said defiantly from yet another hotel room when he telephoned us to ask for further help.

"I'm probably the most important person you've ever met", he told me confidently on his next appearance at the treatment centre.

"That may well be so", I replied, with no intention of arguing the point, "but I can do something that you haven't yet learnt how to do: I know how to stay away from mood-altering substances and processes one day at a time."

The emphasis on "one day at a time" is important, because no addict can contemplate the prospect of giving up his or her closest friends ("sweethearts" would be a more accurate term) for life. People are friendly (sometimes) but no relationship with a human being gets close to the overwhelming sense of oneness that an addict gets from his or her preferred mood-altering substances or processes – and, what's more, they're reliable, initially at least. This indeed is madness – but to those who have this madness it all appears perfectly rational, whereas what other people would consider entirely rational appears to the addict to be completely insane: why would addicts want to give up the only things that make life bearable and which lead to a sense of well-being?

Yet the cumulative problems from the progressive use of mood-altering substances and processes eventually become unbearable. Something has to go. At this point the suggestion to give up for just one day is as much as can be contemplated: one can reconsider the situation tomorrow.

Neuro-transmission

How is it that genes have this devastating effect (if indeed they do: the actual genetic proof is yet to come)? I believe what happens is that they influence the neuro-transmission systems in the mood centres of the brain: something goes wrong in the way one cell transmits a sense of mood to another. The on/off switch in the electrical transmission of nerve impulses from one cell to another is a chemical switch. The electric impulse down a branch from one nerve cell causes chemicals (called neuro-transmitters) to be released at the tips of the nerve endings. These chemicals then produce a further electrical impulse in the tips of a nearby branch leading to another nerve cell – and so the impulse is transmitted from one nerve cell to another.

But supposing something isn't quite right in the way that this system works in some people? (There is nothing extraordinary in that supposition: every part of the human body has the potential for disordered function as a result of structural defects, and there are a whole host of clinical syndromes that result from those defects.) Supposing the chemicals don't get released properly, or supposing there aren't sufficient receptor sites for them on the receiving end, or supposing the chemicals don't get reabsorbed properly or supposing all sorts of things…

There are so many possibilities for error, it is amazing that the system ever works correctly. When one considers the full complexity of the human body, it is quite staggering that the developmental process results in our having as much in common with each other as we do. It would indeed be surprising if there were not variations and defects in the neuro-transmission systems.

The effect of these defects in the mood centres of the brain would be that some people would be able to think and act perfectly well but their moods would be disturbed. As a result, their motivation and subsequent behaviour would be disturbed and they would then try to rationalize their behaviour by applying their undamaged (and highly imaginative) thought processes. Indeed, they would become so good at reasoning and rationalizing that they would become highly creative, as well as developing a highly skilled capacity for argument. This is, of course, exactly the clinical picture that we see in addiction. Any addict worth his or her salt ought to be able to change sides in the middle of any discussion or argument and express complete surprise if anyone notices.

It is often supposed that highly creative people have a high risk of addiction in one form or another. I believe the true situation to be the other way round: people born with a defect in their mood centres will have a tendency towards addiction (when they discover the transient mood-altering properties of some substances and processes), but they will also tend to be highly imaginative and creative (because they are expert at thinking on their feet to explain their behaviour and are always searching for new ways to influence their mood).

Environmental influences

The implication of all this would be that addicts are primarily born and only later made. Again, I believe that this is exactly the picture that we see. Addiction (of one kind or another) does run in families, yet it does not necessarily affect all members of the family even though all the children in a family may have had very similar environmental upbringings. Environmental factors play a part in stimulating the heightened perceived need for mood-alteration in potential addicts but the exact same environmental factors (abuse, abandonment, bereavement, failure or acute distress of one kind or another) do not have the same effects on the non-addictive children. Those children may well be damaged, to be sure, and they may well benefit from (or, more likely, be further damaged by) therapy at a later date – but they do not become addicts.

There has been considerable controversy, for example, in a supposed link between early childhood sexual abuse and the subsequent development of bulimia. Reports of this supposed link have been hotly disputed: there is probably no higher incidence of sexual abuse in people suffering from bulimia than there is in other people with significant emotional disturbances. Thus, the facile "psychological explanations" of bulimia (that the sufferer is trying to vomit out the inner violation) are fanciful. What I think is a more probable explanation of the development of bulimia, or other forms of eating disorder, is that the genetic predisposition towards an addictive tendency is stimulated by some (any) form of emotional trauma and then the child turns to the mood-altering substance that is readily available: sugar – and off goes the eating disorder.

Mimi's father is a distinguished journalist. Nonetheless (so she says) he repeatedly sexually abused both her and her sister throughout their childhood. In adult life Mimi reminded her father of the sexual abuse but he totally denied it. (One would be tempted to say "well he would, wouldn't he?" but this would not be unique in my experience of "False Memory syndrome" – where the "memory" has been created by a distressed patient or even implanted by an over-zealous, or strangely motivated, therapist.) Mimi's father's response was simply to point to her behaviour – by this time she was both bulimic and drug-addicted – and to the normality of her sister. Further, Mimi's political leanings (socialist) and her choice of occupation (social worker of a sort) did not please her father. He repeatedly pointed out the disgrace that she brought to the family. His own robust frame, ruddy countenance and notorious short temper had, in his view, no relation to his alcohol consumption. When Mimi said that he too was an addict, he went apoplectic.

"At least my drug is legal!" he said, vehemently.

Childhood influences

Personally, I do not set great value in trying to find out all the details of childhood experience. Patients often want to talk about it in depth, partly from self-pity and blame (as previously mentioned, these are the prime emotional characteristics of addictive disease) and partly from a determination to find the *cause* of their addiction. Telling them "It's just the way you are" does not please them at all. They want to rake through all the garbage because they feel they ought to. I suppose they have an image of what "therapy" should be and that's that. Also, the last thing they want to acknowledge is that they are stuck with being addictive, let alone that they might hand it on to their children. They want treatment so that they can get rid of a problem for good – like having an appendectomy – or they want to learn how to use something sensibly and appropriately – like learning how to change grips between backhand and forehand at tennis. The very last thing they want to be told is that the addictive tendency will go with them wherever they go – like short sight or allergy to penicillin – and that it is not caused by people, places or things in their general environment.

It is not the job of family or friends or acquaintances to know about professional options for treatment of addictive disease. (The term "addictive disease" does not give permission for the sufferer to behave exactly as he or she wants and avoid all personal responsibility. In fact it formalizes the exact opposite by saying, "This is what you have got and this is what you need to do about it".) However, it is the job of professionals to know about therapeutic options. It is disturbing when doctors say that the Minnesota Method does not work, simply because some patients have difficulty in following its recommendations. They would not say the same when patients find it difficult to follow the dietary or medicinal recommendations for the treatment of diabetes. The treatment is correct irrespective of whether or not patients have problems with compliance. Perhaps the fact that Minnesota Method treatment centres use counsellors rather than doctors as their prime therapeutic agents and perhaps, even more, the fact that those counsellors are usually "recovering" addicts with no formal clinical training whatever, has something to do with medical professional apathy or hostility.

Lizzie (13) was a truant. Lizzie and I got on fine but there was always a question mark over my credentials in the eyes of her family – and those of her stepmother in particular. I have never made out that I am anything other than a general medical practitioner with a special interest in addiction. Sometimes the press label me as an addiction specialist, which I suppose I am by now, but I have no specialist qualifications, nor hospital experience in psychology or psychiatry. I refer patients for consultant specialist opinion when I feel that it is appropriate to do so, just as I follow exactly that principle in any other aspect of my general medical practice. But this wasn't good enough for Lizzie's stepmother (whose adamant belief was that "obviously" Lizzie's natural mother hadn't bonded with her properly in infancy) and eventually the family insisted on referral to a consultant specialist in family therapy. I sent him a letter of referral and a copy of all my detailed notes. I received no acknowledgment nor reply.

In due course, Lizzie was transferred to a "secure" (locked) unit after she had cut her wrists in a "suicide" attempt. I telephoned the unit and learned from the specialist looking after Lizzie that he had received none of my records. I sent him a copy but again got no acknowledgement nor reply. I can't do more than that. I am fond of her and concerned for her and, to be frank, I think that she is getting entirely the wrong treatment – but that's just my opinion and I may be wrong.

My own sense is that Lizzie is an addict who has not yet found a mood-altering substance or process. She runs away from the inner emptiness inside herself. My reasons for this thought (I wouldn't call it a diagnosis because there is no way of being certain) are that her father appears to me, from his manner as well as his size, to be a compulsive over-eater and that Lizzie herself has thought patterns and mood disturbances that are very similar to those of addicts – although similarity can be a dangerous clinical diagnostic trap in any aspect of medical practice. Lizzie is utterly pre-occupied by the prospect of having sex with a married farmer who lives nearby and she is close friends with a girl who "can't wait" to use the drugs that her elder sister uses. Already Lizzie (it appears to me) is making friends with people who have similar compulsive behaviour and she is becoming focused on alternative ways of changing her mood. Interestingly, it was her headmistress (whom I met on just one occasion) who said to me, unprompted, "I think Lizzie will be an addict one day". The only slight difference between the headmistress's view and mine is that I think Lizzie was born an addict, or at least born with the genetic tendency to addictive disease.

The tragedy of Lizzie's story is that I believe her present suffering could have been avoided. If I could have got across the concepts of addictive disease and recovery to her family then Lizzie just might have been forced to stop playing what Eric Berne, the creator of transactional analysis, calls "games" (psychological pursuits that don't really mean what, on the surface, they appear to mean). But this would have involved getting her father to look at his own behaviour and getting her stepmother to reconsider her own perception of appropriate diagnosis and treatment.

As for the farmer, did he lead Lizzie on? Well, maybe. I met him: I drove out one evening specifically to meet him in order to pick up whatever hunch I could. I have to say I wasn't totally comfortable with what I sensed – but how could I possibly make a rational judgement on that?

In any case, how rational was my own judgement as far as Lizzie was concerned? Did I get too close? Was I compulsively helping, rather than helping professionally and impartially?

What Lizzie illustrates for me is not just that I believe that addictive disease can be seen in distorted mood and behaviour before the development of any obvious addiction (although it is exceedingly difficult to differentiate addictive behaviour from normal adolescence) but also that counsellors run the risk of getting too close to their "subjects": both their professional discipline (seeing only what they see and having no wider concepts) and their patients. I was fond of Lizzie. Did that colour my clinical judgment? Did I so much want her to get better that I wanted to hang on to her and even try to make her fit my own field of clinical interest? Was I trying to say something about my own childhood when trying to guide hers?

Monitoring counsellors

It is exactly for reasons such as these that counsellors need continuing supervision for themselves. I have to say that my principal function over the years of running the treatment centre has been monitoring the behaviour of the counselling staff. Right at the start I asked the treatment director of Hazelden (along with St Mary's Hospital, Minneapolis, the original Minnesota Method treatment centre) what he anticipated would be my major problems. I thought he would say cocaine or sex or violence. Instead he said, "In the short term your problems will be staff, and in the long term your problems will be… staff". He was right.

But of course he was right. Human beings are difficult to manage. Counselling is tough. Being a recovering addict is a daily challenge, not so much to overcome temptation as to beware of complacency. Put all three factors together (managing recovering addicts as counsellors) and there is a recipe for gunpowder, treason and plot and we have had plenty of that, as in all treatment centres anywhere in the world. Coupled with that, an inevitable problem with pioneering is that one has a very small pool, if any, from which to choose one's initial staff and, as ideas and experience progress, one may out-grow one's own staff unless they themselves are keen to grow in their professional understanding and skill.

The director of another Minnesota Method treatment centre once told me that I have a reputation for losing my counselling staff. I am happy for that to be so. I am determined to provide the best team of professional counselling staff that I possibly can. If this means losing some of them along the way then so be it. I do not lose the "hotel" staff of the treatment centre any more frequently than in any other establishment of any kind but, as ideas develop, some counsellors get left behind. When they close their minds, dig their heels in, and then undermine everything they can, it is time to part company. I don't mind people disagreeing with me: that is precisely the route by which I myself progress. Being deliberately deceitful and disruptive, however, is another matter. If counselling staff have ideas of their own that are totally incompatible with ours, they should try them out in practice at their own expense and good luck to them. If the ideas are good they will deserve to succeed. If not, and they are simply motivated by jealously or vindictiveness, they will pay a fearful spiritual price, whatever their material success. Interestingly, when counselling staff do leave in anger they, like addicted patients, usually try to take others with them. The need to justify their own behaviour is overwhelming. Correspondingly, when former patients or counselling staff subsequently ask for help, they seem to find it necessary to repeat their previous criticisms and even try to dictate the terms on which they should be helped!

The principle of keeping a careful watch over the behaviour of our counselling staff has therefore stood us in extremely good stead. In place of some self-interested drama queens and incompetent dilettantes, whose only concept of professionalism was the possession of a certificate, we now have a superb team of equally dedicated professionals who work happily together in mutual respect. The treatment centre is a flourishing hive of new ideas. As a result, our time and energy is now focused upon our patients rather than upon the Machiavellian antics of spiritually diseased counselling staff.

I take a risk in telling tales out of school. The Minnesota Method has many enemies and providing ammunition for them may be considered imprudent. However, I believe that all human beings are fallible and that acknowledging our fallibility makes us stronger rather than weaker. For addicts, the acknowledgement of fallibility is the essential starting point of recovery.

Paradoxes

The first of the Twelve Steps of the Anonymous Fellowships is the acknowledgement of powerlessness over one's addiction and the acceptance that one's life has become unmanageable. At the very moment of that profound acknowledgement one finds that the world does not cave in but that there are other people (or some other concept of a God or

Higher Power than self) available at hand to help and guide. From the very acknowledgement of weakness comes strength. This is the great paradox of early recovery and it is followed by many others. My own favourite paradox is "I could not help myself until I realized that I could not help myself" (I need others to help me). And I love "We keep what we give away" (in continually reaching out to help other addicts on an anonymous basis – not at work – we ourselves feel good, and that process acts as a substitute for the mood-altering substances or behaviours of addiction).

Terminology

Much misconception comes from terminology. "Alcoholism" is totally the wrong term to use for the inner emptiness that drives some people towards solace in alcohol. It is like calling a sore throat "penicillinism". Penicillin is the treatment for a sore throat, not its cause. Alcohol is one of a number of unwise "treatments" for the inner emptiness of addictive disease – not its cause. Granted that excessive use of alcohol causes a great many problems and that these problems mostly resolve on stopping drinking – but the inner emptiness and its behavioural consequences remain in what is called the "dry drunk syndrome". When we observe the dry drunk syndrome we see alcoholism (or any form of addiction) in its purest form: we see the disease uncluttered by any of its "treatments".

Dry drunk

Families often find the dry drunk state very confusing. The sufferer has stopped getting appropriate "treatment" in Alcoholics Anonymous but has not yet returned to drinking. His or her moods and behaviour are abominable, grumpy, critical, depressed, volatile – the whole dreadful repertoire of "alcoholism" – but in the absence of alcohol. It is at this time that doctors provide a confident diagnosis of depression, anxiety/depression, clinical depression or even manic depression and reel off a prescription for pharmaceutical mood-altering drugs. Of course they work – they are designed to do so: they influence the actions of dopamine, serotonin and other neuro-transmitters in the mood centres of the brain. But at a fearful price: the dry drunk becomes a prescription drug addict. Any semblance of normal feeling is suppressed: O brave new world!

Depression or addiction?

I do not argue that depressive illness does not exist but I do believe that it is exceedingly rare. I see perhaps three or four cases a year whereas, by contrast, addictive disease is common and I see it once or twice a day in my general medical practice. On the basis of the recorded prescribing habits of doctors, I believe that the frequency of diagnosis of depressive and addictive illness is generally the wrong way round.

Dr Jack is a good friend of mine and the head of a medical group practice looking after nine thousand patients. I asked him how many alcoholics and addicts they had in their practice. He said "three or four".

I would predict from morbidity and mortality figures that he has almost a thousand but that he genuinely doesn't know what he is seeing. Jack is a delightful man and a concerned and committed doctor: but he can only see what he has been taught to see. He sees only the terminal state: the alcoholic on the park bench or the addict who has taken an overdose – because that is what he has been taught to see.

Behind every major morbidity and mortality statistic lies addictive disease, not necessarily as the sole cause but as a major contributor as follows: lung cancer (nicotine), heart disease (nicotine, alcohol, sugar), obesity (alcohol, sugar), chronic bronchitis and emphysema (nicotine), liver disease (alcohol), ulcers (alcohol and nicotine), accidents (alcohol and drugs). Incidentally, we eat the same amount of animal fat that was eaten a century ago whereas we eat one hundred times the amount of refined sugar and hence less fibre. The current epidemic of arterial disease leading to heart attacks and other significant medical problems is therefore primarily due to this particular dietary change in sugar consumption leading to increased cholesterol in the blood rather than anything to do with dietary animal fat. Sugar is insufficiently seen as the damaging substance that it is.

Behind every major social problem in our society lie alcohol and drugs as highly significant factors. Behind absenteeism, poor quality work and impaired professional relationships, very commonly lie alcohol, drugs or eating disorders. Employers do not need to learn how to identify alcoholism, drug addiction or eating disorders: all they have to do is to consult their own personnel department records. They will see the addicts staring them in the face, once they strip away the disguises of repeated minor illnesses or accidents and recurring domestic and financial problems. Again, addictive disease is not the only cause of these problems – but it is by far the major factor.

Damage from addiction

The Project MATCH study, funded by the US National Institute of Alcohol Abuse and Alcoholism, estimates that 100,000 Americans die each year of alcoholism and that alcoholism costs America $150 billion (no less) in lost work and medical expenses. Imagine what the figures would be when cigarettes, drugs and sugar are added in!

These are unquestionably the greatest scourges of our time, yet the medical profession commonly pays mere lip service, tut-tutting, frowning, raising the eyebrows, upbraiding the Government – and so on – and then returns to tidying up the end results rather than trying to understand the underlying cause: addictive disease. At best this is ignorance. At worst it is… heaven knows what.

I believe the principal reasons why doctors do not get interested in early diagnosis and treatment of addictive disease are, firstly, that they don't believe that it exists (that is certainly a very effective way of avoiding clinical responsibility: it reminds me that at the turn of the last century prostitutes were said not to exist in Vienna and therefore no provision needed to be made for their medical care) and, secondly, that they simply don't know how to treat it. The problem begins with the selection of medical students: they are chosen on scientific merit, yet the job that most of them will eventually do involves (or should involve) as much art and philosophy as science. The skills and understandings of art and science should not be mutually exclusive – but student selection and subsequent training does its very best to make them so.

Doctors prescribe medications and, for many substances, are the only people allowed to do so. However, the practice of clinical medicine should involve wider concepts than mere prescription. Some doctors have told me that addiction problems are "not medical". These doctors see me almost as a traitor to the profession. That statement would be fine if there was any substantial alternative channel for diagnosis and treatment. The population look to the medical profession to do their part in dealing with the problem, just as they look to the politicians and police and other professionals to do their parts. Doctors cannot afford to abdicate this area of medical practice. It is too big – and the clinical and social problems are getting progressively worse as drugs take over from alcohol in popularity as a new generation grows up.

Cynics often imagine that the label "addictive disease" and the working of a Twelve-Step programme lets addicts "off the hook". Part IV of this book gives a full account of working the Twelve Steps but the cynics might like to try looking at just two of the steps to consider what it would be like working them for themselves:

Step IV: Made a full and fearless moral inventory of myself.
Step IX: Made direct amends to those I had harmed except when to
           do so would injure them or others.

Disease of the human spirit

The whole purpose of a Twelve-Step programme is to get back to core values of honesty, trust, love, hope, honour, innocence and all the other beautiful abstracts that are laid waste by addictive disease. I call it a disease of the human spirit because that is exactly what it is. As previously mentioned, I believe that it is probably mediated through disordered neuro-transmission systems in the mood centres of the brain but what it actually does is to damage or destroy all the beautiful spiritual values that are the essence of life. Hope and trust are not mental skills; they cannot be achieved through mental or physical effort: they are spiritual values. When hope and trust are damaged in the mood centres of the brain, the end result is a spiritual disease. Inevitably there will be consequences in every other aspect of life: physical, mental, marital, social, professional, financial and so on. Treating any of these as a problem in its own right is a complete waste of time and effort, kind and compassionate though the intention may be. When the spiritual disease is given a spiritual treatment, however, then the secondary consequences in other areas of life resolve on their own.

This general principle of treating causes rather than consequences is the same in many areas of clinical practice: we treat the infections and the swelling resolves, we lower the blood sugar in diabetes and its consequences become less damaging, we lower the fever and the confused thoughts return to normal. Yet the mention of the word "spiritual" frightens people in general and doctors in particular. How extraordinary! Isn't it strange that the most sensitive and beautiful of all life's attributes should instil fear? I don't think this is simply a result of enforced religious teaching or practice at school or that it comes from fear of Bible salesmen or ayatollahs. It seems to me to stem from a more fundamental awareness that most of what many people think and do in life is mundane or even shoddy. To be reminded that life has value – every minute of it – is often something that is acknowledged only when losing it.

Religion

I am no priest. I preach no sermons. I believe that religious viewpoints restrict rather than enhance man's potential. Further, I believe that it is appropriate to encourage people to progress from narrow religious beliefs towards a broader spiritual awareness, rather than the other way round. Rather than being a convergent thinker (looking for successive answers to progressively fewer questions) I rejoice in being a divergent thinker (looking for what further questions each answer reveals). We already know from Douglas Adams' four-part trilogy, beginning with *The Hitchhiker's Guide to the Galaxy*, that the answer to the ultimate (unspecified) question in the universe is 42. With that problem out of the way, we can now get back to living the life we've got, each of us to the best of our ability. Living is a spiritual value. Conversely, having a sense of spirituality does not imply the possession of a specific religious tenet or doctrine. The development of spiritual values, and a positive, thrilling, sense of life, is the purpose of recovery from addictive disease through working a Twelve-Step programme of recovery.

One of my very special friends is Father Joseph Martin, a Catholic priest, an amazingly inspirational – and humorous – speaker, a truly lovely man, and the co-founder of Father Martin's Ashley, a treatment centre for alcoholics and addicts in Baltimore, Maryland, USA. He is also a recovering alcoholic, working the Twelve-Step programme one day at a time, as I and countless others do. Father Martin was a Catholic priest before he acknowledged his alcoholism (his priesthood didn't prevent him from becoming overtly alcoholic) and he is still a Catholic priest (but still works the Twelve-Step programme).

Religion and Spirituality are two distinct concepts and are not necessarily either in harmony with each other or at discord. It is time that the word "spiritual" came back into our general (and medical) vocabulary untainted or unenhanced (whichever way one likes to see it) by religion.

Michael (35) is an Anglican priest who was a patient of ours in the treatment centre. He came up for trial for embezzling church funds.

Altogether he misapplied a vast amount of money. (I didn't know the Church could possibly have so much money for one priest to be able to "lay his hands" on – and this gave a whole new meaning to that ecclesiastical expression.) He says he gave the money away to the deserving poor: all very Christian in intent – but still very illegal in law.

His alcoholism had got him into trouble before but his compulsive helping (revealed in questionnaires and not simply by his actions), has certainly walloped him this time. Rather than being sanctified, he went to prison.

Rational approaches

"Rational Recovery" is a movement set up as a "non-religious" alternative to Alcoholics Anonymous. It has a *Little Book* as a parody on the *Big Book* of Alcoholics Anonymous, which gives the stories of various members and the general statements of how the Twelve-Step recovery programme works. Rational Recovery is based on the work of the American psychiatrist Albert Ellis, who created rational emotive behaviour therapy, which we ourselves use in the later stages of treatment, helping our patients to get back into the "real" world. "Rational" approaches are everyone's dream and Albert Ellis has done recovering people a great service by reminding us of precisely what does *not* work for us. In my office I am as rational as I can be: I have to be – I have patients to look after and a business to run. In my inner life, however, I am spiritual: I live a life of hope and trust, of music and poetry, not simply of pounds and pence, lungs and livers. I have to be both spiritual and rational. The Twelve-Step programme is a guide to normal living – not a substitute for it. It enables me to start equal with other people each day, just as my spectacles do the same for my impaired eyesight.

Anthony Hopkins, the actor who won an Oscar for his performance as Hannibal Lector in *The Silence of the Lambs* is himself a recovering alcoholic (and happy for this to be known if it helps other people to be encouraged to get into recovery). He has done a vast amount to help other alcoholics and addicts but perhaps his greatest moment of help was when he said "If recovery is gloom, doom, ginger ale and Jesus, I don't want it". I totally agree: recovery should be fun, with or without ginger ale and Jesus.

Addictive nature

I remember fearing that life would be dreadfully boring if I were to give up all addictive substances and processes. I also feared that I would lose all my creativity. In retrospect I'm not sure what creativity I previously had or thought I had. Most of what I had created I subsequently lost, the rise and fall of my fortunes depending upon whether my luck was in or out in my crazy risk-taking schemes. Yes, I had talent – but I wasted it. I had moments of brilliance but followed them with great chunks of utter stupidity. The characteristic patterns of addictive disease were as manifest in me as they are in any addict. This sometimes leads people to talk of an "addictive personality". There is no such thing: we all have a common addictive nature but we each have our own personality. I have my own personality and this is what I have been able to reclaim in recovery, whereas my addictive nature will be with me for ever, even though the Twelve-Step programme keeps it in remission.

The origin of the thought that there is an addictive personality is that addicts behave in a boringly predictable manner when we are under the influence of mood-altering substances or behaviours.

Mary has food on her mind the whole time. She is always planning to diet even when she is actually bingeing.

John prefers to drink alone. He goes to the bar but reads by himself. He pretends to himself that he is in company but he would drink just as happily at home by himself.

Paul works excessively hard in order to feel better about himself. It's as if work is an antidepressant.

Joan took a double dose of her medicine because it gave her a sense of being in control.

Fred spent two hours a day on exercise of one kind or another, irrespective of whatever other things needed doing.

Alice found that if she had one line of cocaine she almost invariably went on to finish all she had. It was impossible to save any of it for later.

Daren said that he needed sex five times a day.

Judy was most embarrassed to find out from a friend how badly she had behaved at the party the night before.

Andrew wouldn't normally get out of bed before midday but he would cross town and wait for ages for his drug dealer.

Stewart couldn't remember a thing about his studies unless he chain-smoked and had a regular supply of coffee.

Barbara stopped her bulimia on will-power but became a shopaholic and got a buzz just from spending money, even though she didn't need or want what she bought.

Harry's friends kept telling him he was losing too much money but he kept on and on gambling.

This may look like a list of twelve different people involved in various ways with a range of addictive substances and behaviours. In fact the list is of the twelve basic characteristics of any addictive behaviour:

Addictive characteristics

1. Pre-occupation with use or non-use.
2. Preference for, or contentment with, use alone.
3. Use as a medicine, to help relax or sedate or to stimulate.
4. Use primarily for mood-altering effect.
5. Protection of supply, preferring to spend time, energy or money in this way.
6. Repeatedly using more than planned. The first use tends to trigger the next.
7. Having a higher capacity than other people for using the substance or process without obvious initial damaging effects, although in time this tolerance is lost.
8. Continuing to use despite progressively damaging consequences.
9. Drug-seeking behaviour, looking for opportunities to use, and progressively rejecting activities that preclude use.
10. Drug-dependent behaviour, "needing" the addictive substances or behaviour in order to function effectively.
11. The tendency to cross-addict into other addictive substances or processes when attempting to control use.
12. Continuing to use despite the repeated serious concern of other people.

Thus, the list could be re-written for each patient and each addictive substance in turn. i.e. Mary would have each of those addictive characteristics (or most of them) in her relationship with food, John would have each or most of them in his relationship with alcohol, Paul with work, Joan with prescription medicines, Fred with exercise, Alice with drugs and so on.

This is how we identify addictive behaviour and distinguish it from other aberrant behaviour: we look for these specific addictive characteristics. For example, we wouldn't ask John how much he drinks. His consumption might vary enormously: he might be a binge drinker rather than a continuous drinker but he would be alcoholic just the same if he comes up with four or more of these addictive characteristics.

The sad social fact of addiction is that each addict believes fervently that in his chosen behaviour he or she is establishing his or her individual right to behave independently exactly as he or she wishes, whereas independence is exactly what is being progressively lost. The truth is that each addict is absolutely in the grip of addictive disease and behaves in exactly the same way (or near enough) as any other addict.

In order to help newcomers identify the true nature of their illness and give them - through identification with the stories of other patients and counselling staff - the insight and inspiration that they really can change and get better, we look after just one clinical condition (addictive disease) and I employ as counsellors primarily those people who have had addictive problems themselves or in their families. I myself work in the treatment centre as head of the counselling team, not as a doctor: medical problems are delegated to the doctors and nurses I employ. My reason for separating medical work from counselling work is that we cannot get inside the madness unless we are allowed – and even invited – in: doctors and nurses usually are not. They are more commonly feared – and for very good reason.

Risks to treatment centres

Minnesota Method treatment centres such as ours are fragile. They are prone to rebellion from within when counselling staff take their eyes off their own need for continuing recovery – and hence become grandiose, believing in their own personal power to heal. They are also prone to destruction from the outside: they have few friends among psychologists and psychiatrists because the ideas are so different from theirs and the open–mindedness of those specialists is sometimes less than total. As psychiatrists tend to act as advisers to both the State and the private sector, influencing the money that is spent either through State provision or through private insurance company policies, it is miraculous that Minnesota Method treatment centres survive at all. Yet this warfare is exactly what the Minnesota Method was designed to avoid. The Minnesota Method is not simply the residential wing of the Anonymous Fellowships: it is intended as an alliance between medical and counselling staff. In the treatment centre we employ medical, psychological and psychiatric staff for their specific insights to go alongside our own as counsellors.

A more invidious risk comes from either the medical or counselling staff developing enthusiasms for particular therapeutic approaches. Thus, a psychiatrist might want to use an antidepressant where the counselling staff believe none is needed. Or a counsellor might develop a particular therapeutic interest – such as transactional analysis – and forget the fundamental reliance upon the Twelve-Step programme. When social workers come in with political or sociological perspectives of their own, everything else can easily be lost. There is nothing intrinsically wrong with antidepressants, transactional analysis or political or sociological insights when applied appropriately but in each case they can only too easily dislodge the central focus on the Twelve-Step programme, which is the clinical and philosophical cornerstone of treatment. If that goes out of place the whole house falls down. It is for this reason that Minnesota Method treatment centres tend to be so self-protective. We don't mind working alongside other people but we are frightened of being submerged.

On the other hand, Minnesota Method treatment centres can easily damage themselves through paranoia or through proselytizing zeal. I certainly damaged my own general medical practice by telling all and sundry about my work in addiction. I am fascinated and excited by it, but why should my general patients want to know about it if it doesn't particularly concern them and, most particularly, if they felt that I was not giving my full attention to their own concerns? Equally, I know that at times I have thought I had enemies where none exist. This level of paranoia is a normal human experience and is not confined to those who are frankly mad. In my experience it tends to rear its ugly head when one is struggling desperately for financial survival.

Nonetheless, there are occasions when the disease really does fight back as hard and as dirty as it can. I hear periodically that I am having an affair on the side (my wife works with me full-time so it would be difficult to manage) or, more commonly, that I am making vast sums of money. The most bizarre occasion was when a Health Authority senior official told someone (who happened to be a personal friend of mine) that I channel funds to support the provision of arms to Iraq! I speak a smattering of Arabic (it was useful in London in the Middle Eastern invasion a decade ago) but I never sold out that far. The point is that in Minnesota Method work, as in politics, one simply has to develop a thick skin and get on with the work. My true friends know me well enough and other people can check me out in person by coming to see me in the treatment centre if they so wish: so that's that as far as I'm concerned.

Nonetheless, this does again illustrate how careful any counsellor has to be in monitoring himself or herself. If I get carried away with my own importance, or see enemies around every corner, I could cause a lot of damage, just as sick doctors can cause damage in any branch of medical practice, whatever their sickness.

Dispelling shame

In order to dispel the sense of disgrace there is, I believe, a responsibility on those of us who are addicts to declare ourselves (if we so wish and if our families agree). Inevitably we get accused of self-indulgence. Certainly the television programmes on members of the Royal Family baring their souls in public have been, in my opinion, self-pitying and self-indulgent in the extreme. The true purpose of "coming out" in this respect is not to harp on about how dreadful life has been but to emphasize how good it is now. I know nothing of the story of Anthony Hopkins' alcoholism – but I can see in his films how professional he is now and I am inspired to follow his example.

Early diagnosis is tricky, however, for several very good reasons. Firstly, addicts can stop: they do so all the time – but then later they relapse. This clinical misconception (that one cannot be addicted if one can stop) causes terrible delay in appropriate diagnosis. Secondly, addicts commonly switch to another addictive substance or process when the damaging consequences of the original addiction begin to mount up. All an addict wants is to feel better "somehow": it doesn't really matter how, although each addict will have preferred addictive outlets. Thirdly, the progression of the disease is not a straight line downwards but a wavy path, with plateaus at some times and definite times of improvement at others. These plateaus and times of temporary improvement cause havoc with early diagnosis. The addict may convince himself or herself (determinedly) that all is well, the family members may believe that their prayers have been answered, and the employers may believe that their lectures have been heard. What false security!

Accurate diagnosis is made in simple technical stages: Firstly, look for a family history of any form of addictive disease. This is not an absolute indicator, because most people would not know how to diagnose their own families, let alone anyone else's.

Secondly, look for addictive characteristics, as outlined in our own questionnaires in Part II of this book. These do not look for childhood disturbances or for quantities consumed, but do look for the special emotional relationship between addicts and their mood-altering substances or behaviours.

Thirdly, look for the consequences of addictive behaviour: you may not see the elephant but you should certainly be able to see where it has been – in every aspect of the patient's life. The difficulty comes in persuading oneself that this is what one really is seeing. For example, when a man has lost his wife, lost his driving licence, has complaints from his professional colleagues and clients, is unpunctual and is for ever having minor illnesses and accidents, it is surely superfluous to ask about his alcohol consumption: no disease other than addiction would cut such a broad swathe through all aspects of his life.

David (42) came to my medical practice with a cut on his nose. He had fallen flat on his face in a drunken stupor. He was dragged in to see me by a dear friend of his whom we had treated for alcoholism a couple of years previously. (Sadly, she subsequently relapsed and died.) David was an actor and singer and a very good one: he appeared in many West End shows. As his drinking progressed, his professional status declined. There were times when he was too drunk to go on stage. He knew the famous drunks in the world of the theatre because he was one of them.

"You're an alcoholic", I said to him, using the full frontal technique that I have since generally abandoned.

"OK. then, I'll stop", said David – and he did.

Four whole years later he reappeared in my consulting room.

"I need help", he said. "I haven't drunk at all since I last saw you – but my life isn't any better. I'm working but I don't feel any better. Life isn't any fun any more. I feel as if I could do with a drink – or a couple of hundred to make up for lost time – but I don't want to go back to all that."

He went to the treatment centre, four years after his last drink but he was only just beginning to learn about true recovery from addictive disease.

Two years later he came back to me, asking for a job as a trainee counsellor. I refused, saying that it was too early. I recommended him to go to one of the training courses run by a central London teaching hospital. He would learn about epidemiology and AIDS and needle-exchange systems and all sorts of other things that he would never again need to know anything about (we treat addiction, irrespective of whether a patient has AIDS or not: other people can treat the AIDS itself) but at least he would get a formal certificate and that might eventually be useful if regulations change on counselling qualifications.

A year later he came back with his certificate and we took him on as a trainee. He had a hard time, to put it mildly. The treatment centre was going through one of its periodic bouts of madness (all institutions have them, just as all schools have drug problems, but some are more honest about them than others) but he survived.

For the next two years he was the director of our out-patient treatment programme in London. When he took it over it was a mess. Now it thrives – and so does he. David sang a song for us at our Christmas party. He's the same David he always was – but better.

Intervention wasn't really necessary in David's case: he intervened in his own life. He simply got progressively fed-up with life as it was and he wanted to change. He was shown how to change and he did it.

Intervention

In other people it isn't so straightforward and sometimes an intervention has to be done formally. There is a standard process for this, first developed by the Johnson Institute in the USA. First the family members, friends and employers have to meet to agree on their concerns and their strategy. If they don't plan things in advance the addict will simply divide and rule. On a later occasion, with the addict present and with a specialist counsellor to guide things, each person in turn says the following:

"I love you, or I am fond of you
AND (not but) I'm concerned for you.
These are the things I observe… (facts, not opinions).
This is what I want you to do…
This is what I shall do if you don't…"

Intervening on my elder son, Robin, was incredibly hard. I wouldn't want other parents to go through what Meg and I went through – but it worked so it was worth it.

Certainly nothing else had worked. We had loved him, as we loved our other children. We had tried also to set an example of love. That may well have influenced him in his own considerable capacity for love but I suspect it is simply part of his nature. We educated him. I remember him telling me that he had consumed sixteen pints of beer and eight measures of spirits in one day and was still not drunk, thus proving to himself that he wasn't an alcoholic. I told him that one of the cardinal features of alcoholics is that initially they have a higher capacity for alcohol than other people. But this insight did not change Robin's behaviour. I punished him at times: perhaps too much, as with our other children; certainly at times too severely. But that didn't change Robin's behaviour either.

Leaving him with the consequences of his own behaviour was among the hardest things I have ever done. But that's what worked. I knew precisely what the risks might be but I also knew that without a dramatic change in my behaviour towards him, by learning to love and let be, the risks would get progressively worse, just as they had before.

Learning that Robin was not only heavily into alcohol but was also heavily into cocaine was very painful. Interestingly (for me as a non-drug-user: I got my education the hard way, through my family), Robin tells me that, for him, getting off cannabis was much harder than getting off cocaine: he preferred it and therefore missed it more, whatever other people might say about "hard" or "soft" drugs and all that claptrap. Cannabis is addictive in exactly the same way that alcohol and any other mood-altering drug is addictive: it is addictive to some people – those with the genetic predisposition – but not to others.

In Robin's case, Meg and I knew that we couldn't force him to stop using drugs. All we could do was to make it uncomfortable for him to continue. This general principle holds good for any intervention: we do not need to do anything to the addicts – we simply give them the choice of action and then leave them with the consequences of their own behaviour – and do not bail them out.

We gave Robin the choice of a drug-free home with us or to find a home somewhere else if he wanted to continue to use drugs.

"I am an orphan," he replied magisterially – and left... at one o'clock in the morning in a cold winter night.

We didn't see him or hear from him for six months. We knew that he would probably be living rough – he had lost his job by this time. We knew the sort of things he would have to do in order to get drugs. We knew what his risks were likely to be. Yet still we made no attempt to find him. We waited... and it was a long wait.

Finally he came back, asking for help and we gave it to him. He went through treatment – twice – but is now many years completely clean from alcohol and drugs. He got himself into university to read psychology. Universities are not the cleanest of environments as far as drugs are concerned but he not only survived that but had a lot of fun – on orange juice and diet coke. He is now the director of our in-patient treatment centre. His knowledge of psychology, combined with his personal experience as an addict, give him superb qualifications for the post. When Meg and I took the risk to "love and let be" it stopped his addiction and revealed the potential within him.

I remember a meeting entitled "Students against drugs", held at King's College, London. I believe it was after the brother of one of the students had died of a drug overdose. I was one of six speakers. Five hundred chairs were put out. There was simply vast publicity, including a short piece on the front page of *The Times* on the day of the conference... Nobody came: not a soul... Students are not against drugs.

Family intervention

These experiences remind me what a lonely business it is trying to get addiction issues treated seriously and straightforwardly, rather than patronisingly or melodramatically, as they often are in the press. The difficulties confronting families afflicted by addiction are horrendous. They deserve more understanding.

Jane (35) was loved by her father from the day she was born. When she came home from the hospital he showed her the rockery that he had built in the garden. Jane was so small he could sit her in one of his hands as he showed her the miniature irises, gentians and other alpine plants that he had bought. In due course, as she grew up, he got her a baby bouncer and, later, he made her a climbing frame, the only thing he ever made with his own hands in his whole life.

At the age of fourteen she went on the pill. Any father would be saddened by that - and irritated that the prescribing doctor would consider her old enough. But, in due course, Jane's father calmed down, realising that the pill was better than a pregnancy. In Jane's case she decided (a couple of years later) that it wasn't: she got pregnant rather than stay on the pill. Then she had an abortion. Then she got pregnant again. Then she had another abortion. Her schooling was a mess and she was asked to leave. Then she took an overdose. Then she had another pregnancy and kept the child and then took another overdose. With each pregnancy she tried to prove to herself and everybody else that she was an adult (on the simple basis that adults have children) but then the dreaded reality of human existence (adulthood is a maturity of behaviour, not of years nor of social position) forced itself upon her.

It was, of course, all her father's fault - or so she said. He had never abused her in any way - but he was so dominating; yes, that was it. And so on and so on and so on through the years.

A clear pattern became established: Jane would want the world to work her way and when it didn't she would get angry. She would then express her anger either by damaging herself or by damaging something or somebody else in some way. Her father would then tidy up the resulting mess and give her presents as a form of encouragement for the future. His intention was to help Jane to find new ways of dealing with the world. In fact all that happened was that Jane went on believing that the world should work the way she wanted it to work and she never learnt from her own experience - and she knew that her father could always be relied upon to pick up the pieces even when (perhaps especially when) she blamed him for all her problems.

One would imagine this was yet another story of drug addiction - but it isn't. It's the story of a compulsive over-eater. Who would imagine that an eating disorder, of all things, could cause so much carnage? The answer to that is the family of any other compulsive over-eater. As things went from bad to worse it became clear, particularly with the successive overdoses, that the relationship between father and daughter would not change until one or the other was dead.

When Eric Berne talks of psychological "games" that people play, he includes suicide attempts and even suicide itself as psychological games, actions that have an ulterior motive. The purpose of a suicide attempt is to say "There now: look what you made me do". The purpose of suicide is to leave behind a morass of guilt, with people saying "We should have done more" or, better still, to have other people say to one particular person (such as Jane's father) "You should have done more."

In order to avert the inevitable progression towards this crazy end-game, Jane's father decided that he himself had to die, not in reality but in his relationship with her. He said that, at the age of 35, she could not go on blaming him for all her problems in the past, present and future; now she has to build her own life - without him. It remains to be seen whether she will do so.

I've known this type of dilemma - and solution - before but I usually hear it from the other side: from the addict rather than from the family member. Quite often I hear from recovering addicts of one kind or another that they didn't begin to get better until they were finally cut off from everyone else. Of course there's a risk in applying this policy (as Meg and I did with Robin) but there's an even greater risk in going on doing what one did before.

The major difficulties when trying to intervene in the addictive behaviour of a friend, employee or relative are, firstly, that one may not be convinced that he or she really is an addict and, secondly, one may try to use approaches that would probably influence other rational people but which would have little or no chance with addicts.

Love, education and punishment

Accepting that someone, particularly someone close, is an addict is an incredibly difficult process because it appears to be so final. The general perception is that there is nothing that can be done for anyone who really is an addict. One therefore clings to the hope that that person is simply going through a bad time, or has got in with a bad group of friends or is under some other cultural influence. The transient moments of improvement are clung to with desperate fervour. The disasters are blamed on something "outside his or her control".

Accepting that one's own chosen method of hoped-for influence simply doesn't work is even more difficult. Love should work: surely he or she would respond to that. Surely love will turn things round. Surely love will prevent him or her from becoming really addicted. For the friend, concerned employer or family member to believe that love, lenience or friendship will get through is hardly surprising: our whole culture is based, among other things, on the power of love, tolerance and understanding –

and so it should be. It is perhaps for this reason that people imagine that those of us who have addicts close to us simply didn't love them enough. Nothing could be further from the truth. Our experience in the treatment centre is that the addicts are desperately loved, sometimes to the detriment of other relationships. It is deeply hurtful to be told by a doctor or therapist – or, for that matter, a teacher, clergyman or anybody – that one "obviously" didn't provide enough love.

Education should work. Teaching people about the dangers of various addictive substances and processes is common sense. It is indeed a necessary part of general education – but it doesn't work with addicts. An addict craves mood-alteration and that craving overrides any awareness of risk. Furthermore, the addict is the very last person to believe that he or she may actually be an addict. There are always a host of reasons (rationalizations, intellectualizations) why he or she could not possibly be an addict. For example, he or she may believe that alcoholics drink in the mornings and have to drink every day, drug addicts use hard drugs or inject and could never stop for a time, people with eating disorders are obviously too thin or too fat, compulsive gamblers lose money at the races or at the casino, not on property deals or the stock market… and so on.

When alcoholics live on their own they may still hide the bottles. Similarly, compulsive overeaters will often have a stash of food "just in case of national disaster". In each case the worst possible event would be to run out of an immediately available supply of their principal source of mood-alteration. There is nothing rational about addictive behaviour. There is therefore no point in trying to understand it rationally or to explain it psychologically. Educational progammes don't get through to addicts. Correspondingly, addicts find identical difficulty in explaining their behaviour to non-addicts. When they say "I have to have a drink", they find it very odd that doctors and other people don't understand them.

The pull towards mood-altering substances and processes is central to any addictive behaviour, even in those in whom one can see no reason why they would want to alter their mood in the first place. Talented, rich or otherwise privileged alcoholics will still hide their bottles and still use alcohol primarily to change the way they feel about themselves. Explaining to them that they do so because they are too talented or rich misses the point yet again. They drink, or hide bottles, because they are alcoholics, just as other sufferers from addictive disease do what they do because they are addicts. Education can't get through to that. But even the addicts themselves, *especially* the addicts themselves, can't grasp that. Each addict always has a clear picture of what an addict really is – and he or she *isn't* (even though the dividing line has to be adjusted periodically).

Punishment should work but it doesn't. Prisons are crammed full of people who got there as a result of behaviour associated with one addiction or another. Furthermore, prison warders have been known to turn a blind eye to the use of drugs in prisons (leave aside any possibility of actually being involved in corruption) on the basis that addicts are difficult to manage at the best of times and allowing them to use drugs may keep them quiet for a time. The understanding of, and opportunities to use, the Twelve-Step programme are minimal in prisons, the very place where it is most needed. Outside prison, in a family or social organization of some kind, punishment is no more effective. I'm not saying that people should not be punished for what they do wrong, but I am saying that it won't by itself change addictive behaviour. More specific help is needed.

Sarah (44) loves her son Richard (16) to bits. Since divorcing her husband (because of his unreasonable behaviour) and since her daughters got married and moved away, Richard was all she had. She was only too well aware of the dangers of smothering him and she was also aware of the dangers of reversing roles with him and coming to rely upon him as the man of the house. He didn't drink much so that was one good thing but it became progressively more clear that his use of drugs, particularly cannabis, ecstasy and amphetamines, was getting out of control. She went on loving him and providing all the things any mother would provide but Richard went his own way, saying that he had a right to live his own life. Sarah asked her ex-husband to help Richard but, unbelievably, what he did was to give Richard some of his own supply of cannabis, saying that Sarah had a "thing" about alcohol and drugs. In his own way, Richard's father loved him, as did Sarah, but the end result, five years later, is that Richard has left home, finished school with poor examination results, is unemployed, and still takes drugs.

Sam (48) had done a total of seventeen years in prison before he came to us. All his offences had been drug-related. "They told me it was to teach me a lesson", he said, ruefully. I was not at all sure that he was in the slightest bit rueful – an old lag of his experience knows all the tricks and I suspected that he was simply trying to get something out of me, by playing for sympathy or trying to divide and rule between the legal authorities and the staff of the treatment centre. Either way, seventeen years of punishment hadn't taught him a thing and he came to us, I believe, only because he wanted us to write a supportive report for his forthcoming court appearance for yet another drug-related crime.

I sometimes meet a wall of resistance and resentment when I say that love, education and punishment do not work in preventing or treating addictive disease. However small some people's personal or professional experience in this particular subject may be in comparison with mine, there are always some who get very angry on this issue. Yet again the appropriate assessment and treatment of addiction falls down on the principle that one cannot have discussions with, let alone teach, those who "know" already.

As it happens, the correct, effective, way of treating addictive disease is through love, education and punishment – but of a different nature. What my wife and I discovered for ourselves, and many other addictive families also discover, is that we can provide an environment of love and an example of love, but that we cannot do our son's loving for him. The love that heals is not ours (commendable though that may be in its own right) but his. When he loves other addicts, taking his mind off himself, he himself gets better. To try to do his loving for him would be impossible but, even it if were possible, it would be counter-productive, just as doing a child's homework would not in fact help the child at all.

The education that works is the education on addictive disease and recovery. The isolation of addictive disease is dispelled by the discovery that there are other people who have the same bizarre sense of inner loneliness that has no rational basis. A major effect of the Anonymous Fellowships is implicit in that term: the value of anonymity is that one puts down all the trappings and assumptions of social life and is accepted, as one accepts others, with no preconceptions. The resulting sense of fellowship is healing in itself. The danger is of a Fellowship becoming a cult, with its adherents believing that they are God's gift to the world instead of merely a group of men and women using a specific corporate treatment for their particular disease. Knowing the danger is the best way of avoiding it.

As previously emphasized, the Anonymous Fellowships, like any other treatment for any other disease, are simply a bridge to normal living. People who become obsessed with the Anonymous Fellowships, so that they have no other interest in life, have simply developed another addiction. It could be argued that this is a healthier addiction than any other but it can nonetheless be very destructive of family life if taken to extremes.

Most people maintain long-term recovery on two meetings a week, although initially it is recommended that one goes to ninety meetings in ninety days and one should probably not do less than three or four meetings a week in the first two years, the time of maximum change in mood and hence in thoughts and behaviour. The temptation to drop meetings altogether after a few years can spell disaster either through relapse back to the original addiction or to another addiction or, alternatively, through leading to the miserable dry-drunk state in which the mood disturbance reasserts itself but has no appropriate or even inappropriate outlet. This is the education that is necessary.

The punishment that works is the misery that the addict gives to himself or herself. Behind the occasional determinedly happy exterior is an inner wretchedness. This is what leads to such a devastatingly high rate of suicide. There is no need to add further humiliation. Addicts, like everyone else, should be given the consequences of their behaviour and should not be bailed out from those consequences. Paying off debts, finding the best lawyer, taking the blame one's self, tidying up messes caused by the addict, telling lies on his or her behalf, all this merely perpetuates or enables the addiction. The addict has no need to change if he or she feels no pain from his or her destructive actions. In any other illness a kind person would do everything possible to get rid of the pain. To do so in addiction risks making the problem worse. This is what is difficult for friends, family members and employers to understand and accept: kindness prolongs this particular illness and is therefore not kindness at all.

Lucy (25) stole money on her mother's credit card in order to buy presents for friends. Then she did so again. And again. Her mother found out and told Lucy to stop it, but secretly wondered whether divorcing Lucy's father might have caused Lucy's recurrent stealing. Lucy apologized, said that she would never do it again – and promptly did. On our assessments Lucy had an addictive nature, with a specific tendency towards shopping, spending and stealing. I told her mother that Lucy was likely to get into big trouble if she began to steal from other people. Her mother was sure she would never do that and she went off to find a psychologist to help Lucy with her behavioural problem. Lucy is now in big trouble, very big trouble with the law. So, in emotional terms, is her mother with what I suspect is untreated compulsive helping.

Compulsive helper counsellors

The time when untreated compulsive helping causes most damage is when it occurs in counselling staff. They do everything they possibly can for their patients, helping them through every crisis, supporting them in every difficulty, understanding them in all their pain – and then they burn out (and often blame the institution for which they work). Compulsive helping sounds nice, or pathetic, one or the other. In fact it is neither: it is progressive and destructive like any other addiction. Counselling staff need to be particularly aware of this addictive tendency in themselves if they are to avoid causing great damage to their patients (by doing too much for them and thereby hindering their capacity to learn) and also to themselves.

George (42) is a kind and able man – or at least he used to be. However, he met the spoilt brat from hell. He got her to work with him in the treatment centre. I felt uncomfortable about it at the time but I said nothing, for fear that I would lose George from my staff. In time, George came to spend almost as much time and effort on her tantrums and fancies as he did on looking after the patients. Then he began to question why the treatment centre is run in the way that it is and he blamed me for his tiredness and irritability. Eventually I lost both of them from my staff. They're still fighting. We're doing fine.

That story illustrates not only George's compulsive helping but also my own. Time and time again I have tried to be a sympathetic employer but have finished up shooting myself in the foot. I have had to learn to follow my hunches and draw the line at an earlier, appropriate, time.

Addictive relationships

Any relationship formed by an addict has the potential for trouble. The type of trouble will depend on the type of relationship. An addict rarely survives for very long in a relationship with someone who is neither an addict nor a compulsive helper.

Mary (45) had been a member of Alcoholics Anonymous for three years before she decided that her husband ought to do something about his workaholism. She dragged him in to see me but, for the life of me, I could detect no sign whatever of workaholism. To be sure, he works hard but don't we all? I had the impression that love had died in his feelings for Mary long before she gave up drinking. He stayed with her for the sake of the children but, as they grew up and left home, he could see little point in staying on in the relationship with their mother. Because Mary had an addiction she decided that he must have one too. How else could anyone explain his behaviour in leaving the woman he loves? When I failed to endorse her diagnosis she dropped me, saying that my own workaholism prevents me from seeing anyone else's.

Relationships between addicts and compulsive helpers are the classic co-dependent relationship, with each playing into the other's sickness.

Daniel (35) met Juliette (30) while they were both in treatment with us. We always advise people to beware of making new relationships (or ending old ones) in the first two years of recovery. We find that if the relationship goes wrong, first one partner and then the other relapses on the pain. In the case of Daniel and Juliette, they fell in love with each other and they certainly had their difficult moments – but they survived and are now into their third year together. They came to my aftercare evening sessions in London together for over a year and fought through all the problems of his continuing unemployment and her problems of doing a job that didn't stimulate her. They persevered and they won through. They are now engaged to be married. Nobody could be happier than I that our general advice didn't apply to them.

Gerry (45) and Anne (40) became enmeshed in a macabre way with Albert (42) and Georgina (38). The two women were both in treatment with us for alcoholism and other addictions and became good friends. They supported each other in their recovery, encouraging each other when things were going well, but they also supported each other in their madness, with each one feeling it almost obligatory to follow the other off the rails if one slipped. The two men were even stranger. Neither seemed to like his wife and we had our suspicion that in each case they stayed only for the money, each wife being independently wealthy, or at least reasonably well off. Both women used to get beaten up – but nonetheless stayed in their relationships. Thus far we understood what was going on: it was addictive madness, with four addicts playing their various addictions off each other, the two men with dominant relationship addictions (and probably a lot else besides, but we never got close enough to them to be certain) and the two women with their alcoholism (and drug addiction and nicotine addiction and eating disorders all at once) and with an apparent willingness or, dare I say it, even a desire to be beaten up. After Anne died in a drunken stupor, Georgina got drunk and went to Gerry's home and, as she told us later, asked him to beat her up. In that one sentence is the full madness of the self-loathing and self-destruction of her addictive disease.

Psychopathology

Psychological tests on our in-patients show that they have a higher average index of psychopathology than the average score for in-patients in mental hospitals. Obviously we refer for in-patient treatment only those patients whom we feel need it (the others are treated in our out-patient centre in London or are referred directly to the Anonymous Fellowships), but it is startling to discover just how ill they are. No wonder our work is difficult. No wonder the staff find it hard. No wonder we find it hard looking after the staff. Yet the outcome studies performed independently by the local university, show that 65 per cent of our patients are significantly improved (only 35 per cent in the case of anorexia) one year after completing treatment. I believe that other Minnesota Method treatment centres have very similar outcome studies. These figures are stupendously good when it is considered that we are doing work that other people very often don't want to do at all. What I believe this shows is precisely what the US matching study showed: that addicts (or certainly alcoholics) do well in Minnesota Method treatment centres, following the Twelve-Step treatment programme of Alcoholics Anonymous. We know how to get inside the madness and we know how to do something about it.

Most importantly of all, we have something of value to offer in the terrifying battle against the spread of drug use, particularly in young people. In the UK it is now estimated that the illegal drug market is worth £3,000 million pounds a year. In the USA it is estimated to have a value greater than the top ten companies put together. The sales of Microsoft, General Motors, Ford, Exxon and the other giants are nothing financially compared to the market for illegal drugs. When massive quantities of drugs are seized, all that happens is that the street price goes up for a few days until an alternative supply gets through. There is no more chance of getting drugs out of our society than there is of getting rid of television – and for the same reason: people like mood-altering substances and processes, just as they like watching television, however much either activity may be bad for them.

We cannot begin to tackle the problems associated with alcohol, drugs and nicotine until we recognize that addictive disease often drives these various forms of drug use. Most people who use addictive substances do so casually: addicts use them professionally and are responsible for the greater part of the consumption and the greater part of the associated damage. Identify the addicts and the problem becomes more manageable. But identifying addicts is easier said than done before the final phase of degradation when the problems are obvious to everybody. Nonetheless, early diagnosis and treatment is certainly possible.

The first step must be to recognize addictive disease for what it is: a progressive and utterly destructive illness that is not the fault of the sufferer and which can be helped with appropriate treatment. When addictive disease is seen in the same light as myxoedema (thyroid deficiency) or epilepsy, both of which had historic struggles for recognition as illnesses rather than as insanity or demonic possession, then the stigma will be removed and doctors, teachers, families and others will be more prepared to make the crucial early diagnosis.

The second step is to use the most obvious, widespread, clear-sighted and motivated of all resources: schoolchildren. They know perfectly well who are the potential addicts in their midst, but they are not going to ask for help for them while the response of adults is shock and horror, leading to disgrace for the child, expulsion from school, and even summoning the police. If a schoolchild has an asthma attack or breaks a leg, his or her friends would immediately summon help. They dare not do so if the child has problems with drugs or other addictive substances or processes. Thus, the attitude of adult society perpetuates the problem in the children and so the drugs disaster grows and grows.

We adults need first of all to look at our own use of addictive substances and processes before we start preaching or lecturing to children. Then we need to help to create a concerned and compassionate society by recognizing, and doing whatever we can to help the most devastating scourge of our time: addictive disease.

Part II

Specific Addictions

Alcohol; Nicotine; "Recreational" (street) drugs; Eating disorders; Exercise; Caffeine; Shopping, spending and stealing; Gambling and risk-taking; Workaholism; Prescription drug addiction; Sex and love addiction; Relationship addictions; Compulsive helping; Other addictions.

Alcohol

There is a belief that one becomes alcoholic simply through drinking too much alcohol for too long. I do not believe that to be true: alcoholics are primarily born, not made.

There is another belief that one can protect oneself from becoming alcoholic by drinking sensibly, within a specific number of units (1 unit = 1 glass of wine, half a pint of beer or 1 measure of spirits) per week. The "safe" level is said to be 21 to 28 units for men and 14 to 21 units for women, although these recommended figures vary from time to time according to government rethink and they also vary from one government to another. I do not believe the principle of sensible drinking is valid. The confusion comes about because alcoholics can go completely dry at times whereas people whom I term "cultural" drinkers (those whose heavy drinking may be part of the culture in which they live or work) may not be alcoholic but may still cause a lot of damage to themselves and to others through their alcohol consumption.

There is a third belief that people who have been alcoholic at some time can still be taught to drink sensibly. I don't believe that. Once an alcoholic, always an alcoholic.

The scientific reason for these incorrect beliefs originated when S. Ledermann, a French statistician, showed that the problems relating to alcohol in any society were directly related to the amount of alcohol consumed in it - i.e. more drink leads to more problems and less drink leads to fewer problems. This statement seems obvious and the conclusions drawn from it (the three beliefs outlined above) therefore seem equally obvious. Nonetheless, while I am sure that Ledermann's observation is correct for a whole population, I believe it is wrong to deduce conclusions applicable to individuals.

The basic flaw can be seen through a comparison with road accidents. Certainly one could reduce the total number of accidents by reducing the total number of vehicles. What really matters, however, is to be able to identify those drivers who are most likely to have accidents and then target them.

Ultimately the process of identifying and targeting alcoholics comes down to how one defines alcoholism. Mostly, people do indeed think of alcoholics as being those who drink more than a certain amount or who accumulate particular forms of damage. I believe one should look more at *why* a person drinks and at what emotional, mental and behavioural changes may happen in any day as a result of just one drink.

Thus, the traditional approach looks at the total number of units consumed and looks at liver function tests and other indices of damage. I would also look at liver function tests and at other indices of damage, but I would hope to be able to make a diagnosis of alcoholism a lot earlier than indicated in this way, just as I would hope to be able to diagnose arterial disease long before someone had a heart attack or stroke.

The social reasons for the three incorrect beliefs are more obvious and understandable but they are also more sinister. The reasons for the belief that people become alcoholic when they drink too much, that we can protect ourselves from becoming like them, and that we can return to sensible drinking if we do ever cross the dreaded line into alcoholism, is that we *want* to believe these things. Those of us who fear that we ourselves may have a problem with alcohol are the ones who are most passionate in these beliefs. The truth is that the issue is generally only of any importance to those of us who do have a problem.

Meg, my wife (age unspecified because I want my breakfast tomorrow), can leave half a glassful of wine. When I ask her how she does that, she replies that she doesn't want any more. I then point out to her that I didn't ask her why she did it but how. She looks at me blankly because she doesn't understand the question. I look at her blankly because I don't understand why or how she doesn't understand the question. If I left half a glassful of wine it would sing to me – so strongly that I would have to go back to it to finish it off.

This illustrates the essential difference between addicts and non-addicts and the fact that we shall never understand each other in this particular aspect of our lives.

Why should my wife care what sensible drinking limits are? She drinks alcohol for the taste, not the effect. Obviously she needs to know the figures for safe limits if she is going to drink regularly and she needs to know the legal limit if she is going to drive a car. But she doesn't want to drink regularly – it simply isn't important to her, nor is it part of her culture – and, if she is going to drive, it would be no big deal for her (and it would be sensible for her, as it would be for anyone else) not to drink at all.

At the opposite end of the scale, an alcoholic uses alcohol for its mood-altering effect. He or she might have pretensions to being a connoisseur of fine wine, real ales, or blends of malt. (Some alcoholics genuinely are connoisseurs.) However, the real purpose is to alter the mood, to use alcohol as a medicine.

Once an alcoholic takes the first drink in any day, something "magical" (as he or she would describe it) happens. It is as if a switch goes on and the light comes on. Life suddenly feels better. Very commonly alcoholics can remember the first drink they ever had – because they remember the first time they experienced the magic. Later, one can actually see the switch go on when an alcoholic takes the first drink in any day, or even has the first overwhelming thought of it: he or she becomes emotionally inaccessible after that dominating thought or first drink. In time this leads to a "Jekyll and Hyde" split in the personality before and after those thoughts or before and after drinking. As time goes on the mental switch changes its nature so that it determines not just whether life feels better but also whether one wants to feel better and better and better by drinking more and more and more alcohol. This activation of the switch is unreliable: Sometimes it clicks in and sometimes it doesn't. Consequently the alcoholic loses control of the predictability of what would happen after the first drink in any day.

This is in fact how I was taught (by Dr Richard Heilman of Hazelden, the renowned treatment centre in Minnesota, USA) to define alcoholism: the inability to predict what will happen in further alcohol consumption after the first drink in any day. This is a million miles away from any concept of safe units or sensible drinking. For the alcoholic it is the first unit, the first drink in any day, that does the damage – because of what it might lead to: a binge. An alcoholic can stay dry – and often does – but cannot predict further drinking or abstinence after the first drink in any day. Thus, the alcoholic can in fact, initially at least, stay within overall guidelines for sensible drinking and have no damaging consequences whatever – but he or she is still an alcoholic and always will be.

Alcohol becomes the central feature in the life of an alcoholic long before it ever causes any trouble. It is a magical drug. (Valium used to be described by alcoholics as "alcohol in tablet form". Nowadays Prozac or ecstasy, or any other mood-altering substance, might take the place of Valium, but the principle remains the same.) Alcohol becomes established in life as a true friend, reliable and trustworthy, uncritical, supportive, understanding and comforting. What else could one possibly want from a friend? Which human friend or family member could possibly compete with that?

Already, at this stage, alcoholism is diagnosable and the future is predictable. Yet still the alcohol consumption may be within "sensible" limits overall and there may be few, if any, damaging consequences. This is why the concepts of safe units and sensible drinking are dangerous: they miss out on early diagnosis and on the opportunity to pre-empt many years of suffering.

As far as the alcoholic himself or herself is concerned, it seems utterly crazy to diagnose such a friend as an enemy, and there are indeed many people in a far worse state and in much greater need of help.

Nigel (17) was always shy and retiring. He didn't make friends easily. He discovered that alcohol gave him a warm glow. He found friends in the bar and could talk to them. But in the absence of alcohol he was as tongue-tied as before. As he drank more, he withdrew more from other areas of life. He was brought to see me because he was depressed. It would have been easy to make the diagnosis of depression – and in a strict sense that would be true – but that diagnosis would give only half the picture: Nigel's depression is due to his alcoholism, not to the effects of drinking but to the underlying mood-disorder (confusingly called alcoholism) that led him to drink alcohol in the way he does.

Nigel came into our out-patient programme but he didn't stay: he couldn't see that he needed help like the other patients. He wasn't a real alcoholic like them. He will be – given time.

In The Twelve Steps and Twelve Traditions of Alcoholics Anonymous in the chapter on Step I, it says:

"In AA's pioneering time, none but the most desperate cases could swallow and digest this unpalatable truth (that they were powerless over alcohol). Even these "last-gaspers" often had difficulty in realizing how hopeless they actually were. But a few did, and when these laid hold of AA principles with all the fervour with which the drowning seize life preservers, they almost invariably got well. That is why the first edition of the book Alcoholics Anonymous, published when our membership was small, dealt with low-bottom cases only. Many less desperate alcoholics tried AA, but did not succeed because they could not make the admission of hopelessness.

"It is a tremendous satisfaction to record that in the following years this changed. Alcoholics who still had their health, their families, their jobs, and even two cars in the garage, began to recognize their alcoholism. As this trend grew, they were joined by young people who were scarcely more than potential alcoholics. They were spared that last ten or fifteen years of literal hell the rest of us had gone through."

It is remarkable how few old-timers in AA today appear to have read this. One often hears them say that one has to hit rock bottom before being prepared to give up alcohol. This simply isn't true – or, rather, a rock bottom can be at different levels in different people. Hopefully Nigel will be back with us before too long and particularly, I hope, before he has damaged himself.

When Nigel fails to see that he is an alcoholic, I believe there are several things going on in his mind. Firstly, he has an image of what an "alcoholic" is – and he himself does not conform to that image. For this reason we tend, when doing initial assessments with patients, to refer to "problems with alcohol" rather than use a specific term, such as "alcoholic" or "addict". These terms are seen as both inaccurate and insulting, whereas patients may be more likely to accept that they have "problems with alcohol". Secondly, as mentioned previously, Nigel sees alcohol as his closest friend and cannot contemplate the prospect of separation. Thirdly, he believes that if indeed he has got "problems with alcohol" they are because of problems with something else – and that is the area of his life in which he believes he needs help. Fourthly, most important (and bizarre) of all, he really doesn't see that he does have problems with alcohol. He thinks he is managing rather well.

This fourth disorder of thought process is known as "denial" and this is the basic psychopathology of any addictive process. This is precisely what other people (professionals as well as friends, employers and family members) find so difficult to understand and sometimes infuriating to observe. Furthermore, as the disease progresses in time, the denial gets worse. The alcoholic, face down in the rose bushes, really doesn't think that he or she has a problem.

Malcolm (42) was referred to me by a doctor who looks after a number of large companies in the city of London. The doctor was concerned, quite simply, that Malcolm was going to die. Remarkably, Malcolm is still in full-time work. His tolerance of alcohol used to be phenomenal, but it has declined: previously he could drink anyone under the table, but nowadays he can't handle his alcohol at all well. What this means is that his liver was initially stimulated to respond to his high alcohol intake (in the same way that the muscles of athletes respond to physical training), but eventually his liver couldn't cope and is now giving up. Examining Malcolm physically was startling. His liver was hard and was enlarged right down to his tummy button, whereas normally a liver is soft and cannot be felt below the rib cage. His lower legs were swollen with tissue fluid. (When the liver is diseased it fails to make sufficient albumin, a blood protein that draws in the tissue fluid through osmotic pressure.) He had numerous bruises that he could not remember being caused by any particular trauma (the blood clotting mechanisms, controlled by the liver, were seriously damaged so that he was indeed getting spontaneous bruising). I took a sample of blood and the results were faxed to me the same evening. There were numerous abnormalities but, in particular, the liver function tests were a disaster area. The gamma GTP, the liver enzyme that is particularly sensitive to alcohol, should be less than sixty units. Anything over sixty spells trouble. Patients in the treatment centre often have results of three or four hundred. Occasionally we get patients whose results are over one thousand. Malcolm's gamma GTP result was five thousand three hundred and twenty-eight, the highest I have ever known.

"My doctor told me I might die", he said. " I told him that, if I do die young, it's been a good life."

Telling Malcolm his test results has no effect whatever on his understanding of the true nature of his problem. He can understand that his liver is damaged (there is nothing wrong with his intellect) but he does not perceive that he has a problem with alcohol. This is what other people find so difficult to understand: surely he can see it – it's only rational. But that's just it – Malcolm's capacity for thought is still intact but he has severely damaged his capacity to perceive or interpret. (The same process happens in other addictions – which is why educational programmes do not work for those who most need them.) It is as if he knows perfectly well how a gun works but cannot grasp that he will blow his head off if he points it at himself and pulls the trigger.

Any doctor would diagnose Malcolm as being alcoholic. Having said that, however, I fear that some would diagnose him as a "heavy drinker", purely on the basis that he is still in full-time work and earning his living. This is what is so bizarre in the concept (or hope) that one could teach Malcolm to drink "sensibly". Why would one want him to drink at all when alcohol has very nearly killed him and probably will before long? Why take the risk? What is so important in being able to drink alcohol? It is only when spelt out like this that one can see that the people who believe that it is important for Malcolm to be able to drink alcohol (and therefore be "normal") may be those for whom alcohol has a similar central importance in their own personal lives.

There is nothing normal about drinking alcohol or abnormal about not doing so (or vice versa), any more than there is anything normal or abnormal about being a vegetarian or playing cricket or voting socialist or being a Christian. However, if any of these things have become such a fanatical preoccupation that they are causing significant damage in other aspects of someone's life, then one might venture to suggest that he or she has gone too far. That person may listen to reason then and may change the behaviour if it is thought worthwhile to do so. In these issues (other than addiction), however, it comes down to a matter of personal choice. The crucial factor in alcoholism, or any form of addictive behaviour, however, is that this is not a matter of personal choice: it is the product of an inner compulsion that sees suicide or living death as the only alternatives. Addiction cannot be understood in rational terms: if it could it wouldn't be addiction.

Maud (65) lived in one of the flats above my office. She was bed-bound from severe rheumatoid arthritis and she was cared for by a companion. Her abnormal liver function tests were a mystery: her companion never bought her any alcohol on her shopping trips and therefore she couldn't possibly be alcoholic. She wasn't on any medication that might damage her liver and she did not appear to have any other possible cause of liver disease. It was a mystery how she was drinking – but I was sure she was.

One day the porter of the block came to ask me to try to persuade my patient not to throw empty vodka bottles out of the window into the next door garden. Evidently what happened was that Maud used to telephone the local shop as soon as her companion left the flat. They delivered the vodka, letting themselves in with the keys she provided for them. She paid monthly by cheque – but had a problem disposing of the empties.

This story would be funny, if it were not also tragic. One could say that she has few pleasures in life and might therefore be left alone with her alcohol, which I myself might say – although I'm not sure even then – if she were fifteen years older. But the whole subterfuge gives the true insight into her loneliness and sense of shame. Vast numbers of elderly or disabled people live highly productive and imaginative lives. Nobody should be written off and left to soak himself or herself to death.

I can't stop people doing what they want to do (I have no right to do so and would not wish to have that right), but there are two reasonable limits to freedom of choice in human behaviour. The first is obvious: one should not do things that restrict other people's freedom of choice. The second is more problematical: how does one help people who have a disorder of perception and on what basis does one say that a disorder of perception (rather than an idiosyncrasy) exists? The first limit is simply social and political but the second is clinical and philosophical. It isn't easy. Nothing in addiction is easy – which is precisely why it is so exasperating when people suggest "obvious" solutions such as "tell him not to drink" or "show her the damage that she is doing to herself". If that kind of approach would work on Malcolm or Maud, or others like them, it would have done so years ago and would do now – but it doesn't. The madness doesn't respond to reason: that's the nature of the madness, that's why it is madness and that is why cognitive behavioural therapy is largely ineffective.

When an alcoholic accumulates progressively more damage in every aspect of his or her life, and then goes back to alcohol for comfort, *this* is alcoholism: not the drinking itself, nor the damaging consequences of it, but the sheer madness of going straight back to the source of all the trouble in the crazy belief that it will make life better or more acceptable. Alcoholics drink alcohol primarily in order to feel better rather than to enjoy it. This is the aspect of alcoholism that no one other than another addict could ever understand except in purely intellectual terms.

Prof Basil is an addiction specialist. He sees everything to do with addictions as a result of defects in brain biochemistry. I agree with him. He prescribes medicines – one after another (Valium, Prozac, Antabuse, Heminevrin, Naltrexone) – in order to counteract the defects and render the patients functional. I believe this chemical approach makes the problems worse: the human mind can be drugged into submission but not into health. Far from being functional in emotional terms (although they may be more functional in other ways) the end result in these patients, in my view, is a row of robots or zombies. They become dry drunks and sometimes prescription drug addicts.

There are many other addiction specialists who do excellent work. I simply highlight this example in order to illustrate that, in this particular speciality, one can know a great deal about the subject without understanding it at all. I remember, from my days as a professional musician, a particular conductor being described as someone who knew the notes but not the music. The same principle applies here. The most popular idea in clinical practice is that people become dependent upon alcohol. This does not even put the cart before the horse: it sees the cart but doesn't see the horse at all. It sees the end result but not the cause.

The best insight I know comes not from medicine, but from literature, from Terry Pratchett's *Guards, Guards*:

"'You're right,' said Colon. 'The thing about the captain, see, I read this book once... you know we've all got alcohol in our bodies... sort of natural alcohol? Even if you never touch a drop in your life, your body sort of makes it anyway... but Captain Vimes, see, he's one of those people whose body doesn't do it naturally. Like, he was born two drinks below normal.'

'Gosh,' said Carrot.

'Yes... so, when he's sober, he's really sober. Knurd, they call it. You know how you feel when you wake up if you've been on the piss all night, Nobby? Well, he feels like that all the time.'

'Poor bugger,' said Nobby. 'I never realized. No wonder he's always gloomy.'

'So he's always trying to catch up, see. It's just that he doesn't always get the dose right.'"

As far as I am aware, Terry Pratchett has no knowledge of alcoholism: he is simply exceedingly observant. (We doctors could benefit from his example.)

The image of being born "two drinks below normal" and "always trying to catch up but not getting the dose right" is absolutely correct. This is a true insight into the madness. This explains why the rent and the food and the holiday money and the school fees are all negotiable whereas the alcohol money is sacrosanct. It explains why second wives are found in the bar: they don't criticize in the way the first wives did. It explains why everything goes before the job goes: without the job there is less purchasing capacity for alcohol. It explains why so many of the remaining friends are also "heavy drinkers": the rest had other interests.

Being "two drinks short" also explains the most bizarre behaviour of all: what I term the "safety curtain". In a theatre the safety curtain comes down to separate the audience from the stage. In alcoholism – or any addiction – the "safety curtain" does exactly that: it separates the sufferer from those around him or her. Furthermore, as in the theatre, one can see the safety curtain come down and, once on its way, there is nothing whatever that can be done to stop its inevitable progress.

Duncan (62) told me in the middle of a group therapy session on a Sunday morning that he would make an appointment to see me in my London office on Monday.

"I either need to give up my long term relationship of thirty years or I need to give up alcohol. Of course, I shall have to have a drink before I see you."

"You don't have to leave here," I replied. "I shall not say anything tomorrow that I don't say now. You may have some difficult choices to make in your life but you describe what may be a false one. You need to look at giving up alcohol because it has caused you so much damage, time and time again. However, all relationships inevitably change in recovery so you and your partner have an opportunity to create something new, if you wish to do so."

I didn't get through. Nor did any of the group when they tried. There was nothing any of us could do. The safety curtain had come down and his addictive disease was impregnable behind it. I can only guess at what was going on in his thought processes but I suspect it was something like this:

"I am in pain. Alcohol helps my pain. I need alcohol. What reason can I find for drinking?"

This final question is not to convince other people but to convince himself. Once he has done that, however illogical the process may appear to anyone else, there is nothing anyone can do to shift him. It is at this moment one wishes one had the power to confine him against his will, but I fear that the abuses of that power by well-meaning doctors could cause even greater damage.

Marilyn (42) suddenly declared undying love for one of the other patients, thereby making it "impossible" for her to stay in treatment. Last time round her son needed her (like a hole in the head in the condition she would be in by the time she got home). On each occasion she convinced herself of her absolute need to leave treatment and she presented reasons that she felt couldn't possibly be challenged.

Judy (50) was altogether more direct.

"I'm leaving now. I'm going to have a drink."

What on earth could I say to that?

Last time Marilyn was thrashing around on the nursing room floor in self-pity and agony after realizing that she had "done it" yet again, we took a video of her. The purpose was not subsequently to shame her or frighten her but simply to inform her. The memory circuits in her brain will not function when she is paralytically drunk and she will therefore genuinely have no knowledge of how she behaved. The video might have given her an insight that could possibly protect her next time round – but it didn't. Once her safety curtain came down she was totally inaccessible.

In Judy's case she found a new meaning for the Anonymous Fellowship recommendation to take life "one day at a time". She takes recovery one day at a time. She begged us to take her into treatment and then she left again the next day. We have tried prolonging her detoxification regime. We have even used minature bottles of alcohol in place of the tablets that we normally use for detoxification. Yet the *Big Book* of Alcoholics Anonymous was written by people exactly like Duncan, Marilyn and Judy and their stories are recorded in that book. They can get better, and we ourselves have seen many similar patients get better, when they finally give up the battle with their inner alien addictive disease and simply recognize it as a fact. All they have to do is to acknowledge that they are alcoholics and know that that is true down to the very last fibre of their being. Then they can begin to get better.

Duncan asked me to give a lecture on "How do you help someone who wants to get better but can't". I acknowledged his use of the word "can't" in place of "won't". I am sure that he genuinely wants to get better. His problem, as I see it, is that he hasn't yet established giving up alcohol as his absolute priority. He and Marilyn and Judy still have other preoccupations and they are not going to get better from their alcoholism until it becomes the one and only focus of their attention.

Therefore, it might be thought that they should deal firstly with these outside preoccupations, from problems in their childhood, upbringing onwards. That would be entirely the wrong way round. Popular though it would be (addicts always like to believe that their problems are caused by somebody or something "out there" rather than by something "in here" inside themselves), it would be disastrous, simply fuelling more blame and self-pity rather than encouraging them towards self-honesty. Alcoholics and addicts of any kind love to search their childhood, their social life, their family life, their professional life, anything at all, for the reasons why they became as they are. It is a fruitless and damaging quest. Their real need is to focus solely upon their own addictive disease and learn how to deal with that before they look at anything else.

Doctors often believe (or at least they try to sell this idea to patients) that a course of antidepressants would help patients to solve their outside problems so that they could then begin work on their inside problems in a better frame of mind. Again this underestimates the infinite capacity for outside problems that any addict can generate in his or her mind. The focus has to be on the inside problem: all the outside problems can wait until body, mind and spirit are in better shape to be able to deal with them.

A further mistake that is often made (I have learnt this from my own repeated mistakes), is the belief that alcoholics or addicts of any kind will respond favourably to encouragement.

"I think you're doing wonderfully" is a death sentence if it isn't true. It can even be a death sentence if it is true. From the moment that the alcoholic or addict of any kind takes his or her mind off the primary issue of the absolute totality of addiction, the curtain comes down. The only way to give appropriate encouragement (or, for that matter, criticism) is to tie it into a specific event. If someone has done a particular thing well or badly it is appropriate to say so – but not to generalize from it to that person's entire behaviour. Alcoholics and addicts of any kind learn from the consequences of their behaviour. If we want to be truly helpful, we should do nothing that might get in the way of that process.

The worst mistake of all is to believe that a time of abstinence leads to addictive disease becoming less powerful. The opposite is the case. It progresses relentlessly, no matter how long the period of abstinence might be. "Surely I can have just one" or "Surely you can have just one" is the way to begin the nightmare all over again. The universal experience of relapse is that it is faster and more terrible each time. Whether or not addictive disease is genetic in its origin, it is irreversible once it is established and this is the only fact that matters. Once abstinent, the sufferer should stay abstinent for life. It might be thought that I have such a preoccupation with alcohol that I believe that everyone should give it up. I believe no such thing. My wife drinks alcohol. Why shouldn't she? She gets no problems from it. I don't drink because I would get problems from it. My nephew Michael owns and runs a hotel: it's superb and I warmly recommend his real ales to those who have the capacity to enjoy such things without damage. All that I say is that alcohol isn't good for alcoholics, any more than sugar is for diabetics.

To begin to get inside the madness so that we can begin to treat it, we need to be able to identify it accurately. In particular, we need to be able to distinguish alcoholics from cultural drinkers, those who for some reason feel that it is a necessary part of their culture to drink. If we were to sweep the streets for drunks in the early hours of the morning, a fair number would be medical students or journalists. That has nothing to do with alcoholism and a lot to do with going with the crowd. Some of them may be alcoholics and for these people we need to have accurate measures of assessment in order to be able to distinguish them from the rest and help them towards early treatment.

The questionnaires that we use were developed from the twelve characteristics of any addiction (see page 58). Initially they were shaped into thirty questions that looked specifically for addictive behaviour (rather than for quantity or type of alcohol consumed). The ten questions that most frequently received positive answers were then selected for the definitive questionnaire. Patients were then given this questionnaire and a whole range of other questionnaires commonly used by other organizations and in this way we validated our own. (The same addictive characteristics – and the same pathway of derivation for the definitive questionnaire – were used for all other addictive tendencies in order to get the best possible tool for assessment of specifically addictive behaviour. This was particularly valuable for those addictions where there are few or even no other questionnaires or where the ones that do exist are confused because they are not looking specifically at addiction.)

The following ten questions give an assessment of the tendency towards developing the problems with alcohol that are customarily called alcoholism. Two or more positive answers indicate the need for further assessment. Four or more spell trouble – and the opportunity to get help before further damage is done.

1. Do I find that feeling light-headed is often irrelevant in deciding when to stop drinking alcohol?
2. Do I find that having one drink tends not to satisfy me but makes me want more?
3. Have I had a complete blank of ten minutes or more in my memory when trying to recall what I was doing after drinking alcohol on the previous day or night?
4. Do I use alcohol as both a comfort and strength?
5. Do I tend to gulp down the first alcoholic drink fairly fast?
6. Do I have a good head for alcohol so that others appear to get drunk more readily than I do?
7. Do I find it strange to leave half a glass of alcoholic drink?
8. Do I get irritable and impatient if there is more than ten minutes conversation at a meal or social function before my host offers me an alcoholic drink?
9. Have I deliberately had an alcoholic drink before going out to a place where alcohol may not be available?
10. Do I often drink significantly more alcohol than I intend?

Nicotine

Meredith is a Cambridge University contemporary of mine. In his professional life he has become an expert in diseases related to cigarette smoking.

"You will agree", he wrote to me, following a meeting in which we had disagreed,"that cigarette smoking is different from all other addictions: that everybody who smokes is addicted".

In fact I disagree again. The subject of our earlier disagreement was when I pointed out that I was sitting between two doctors, both of whom were at that moment using an addictive substance – a glass of wine. My point was that alcohol is addictive to some people but not to others.

"Controversial", interjected Meredith.

Well, if that is controversial, he must have found my return letter even more so. Perhaps that is why he never responded. I'm sure that there are many people who smoke cigarettes who are not addicted to nicotine (or to any of the other addictive substances in cigarette smoke). They can give up when they want to. The medical profession, for example, has dramatically reduced its own cigarette consumption. Far fewer doctors smoke nowadays than used to before smoking became linked epidemiologically to lung cancer, chronic bronchitis and emphysema, heart attacks and a whole series of other significant illnesses. But what of the doctors who still smoke? Are they less intelligent, less informed, more stressed or what? In fact there are famous cardiologists and lung specialists who are notorious smokers. I myself once worked for one – which was a strange experience, considering what we saw on the hospital wards each day.

What Meredith may be confusing is physiological addiction and psychological addiction. The first group may need some help (nicotine patches or chewing gum, acupuncture or hypnotherapy or some other methods of detoxification) in getting off cigarettes comfortably but they will have no great craving to return to smoking. The second group may get off (even by going "cold-turkey", which is as good a method as any: the major withdrawal effects are usually gone in under a week, however long and however much may have been smoked), but their cravings to go back to smoking may last for months.

Annabel (indeterminate age because she looks a wreck after years of smoking) works as a journalist and came to us as part of her research into different methods of giving up smoking. She stopped smoking and sat in group in our out-patient centre for two days but couldn't take more than that. It wasn't simply the withdrawal from nicotine that distressed her, it was also the waves of emotion that threatened to come to the surface after many years of suppression.

I must say that I have considerable sympathy with the message I once saw on a T-shirt: "Thank you for not sharing your feelings". In day-to-day life one does not necessarily want to be flooded with someone else's emotional outpourings. On the other hand, a life of suppressed feelings has no colour. One needs to be able to feel one's feelings and then decide upon the appropriateness of sharing them with anyone else at any particular time.

Annabel said to the group "You're wonderful people, all of you" – and ran like a scared rabbit back to the emotional security (and relative

*emptiness) that cigarettes help her to maintain."I don't want to get fat",
she said as an afterthought, as if trying to convince herself that there
was a good reason for ducking out.*

In fact it was Annabel's own decision, not my suggestion, to go cold-
turkey. I leave patients to decide for themselves how they will get off
cigarettes. Getting off is the easy bit and any method will do. Staying off is
difficult. For what it's worth, my own suggestion for getting off cigarettes
follows the principles in Terence Rustin's excellent book *Quit and Stay
Quit.* Patients should first cut out all the "unnecessary" cigarettes that they
don't absolutely need, then cut out the "automatic" cigarettes, that go with
a cup of coffee, or a telephone call or some such everyday behaviour, and
then finally – when they are ready to do so – they just stop. Some people
like to use nicotine substitutes but my fear is that they can become a
substitute addiction, leaving the door more than half way open for a return
to the real thing.

It is for exactly this reason that I suggest to people addicted to other
mood-altering substances and processes to take the opportunity to give
up smoking while they are with us in the treatment centre. There is no
point in hanging on to one addictive behaviour while giving up others.
The whole point of giving up addictive substances or behaviours is to be
able to feel one's feelings (as well as to avoid the long-term risks of those
particular addictions).

The capacity to suppress feelings is what nicotine addiction has in
common with other addictions. The differences are, first, that unlike some
but certainly not all addictions, nicotine is legal and, secondly, that nicotine
causes more physical damage than all the other addictions put together.
By contrast, heroin is a relatively safe drug, its risks coming more from its
route of administration than from the medical consequences of using the
substance itself.

To get straight to the heart of the matter (leaving aside the issue of
legality, which can blind people when looking at the possibility of genetic
inheritance of all addictive disease) a nicotine addict is the same as any
other. The plain fact is that all addictions follow the same general pattern
of progressive destruction and serve the same general purpose: to suppress
feelings.

The same general characteristics of addiction (see page 58) can be
applied to nicotine as to any other addictive substance or process and a
similar questionnaire for nicotine addiction has been derived, as follows.

1. Do I prefer to use nicotine throughout the day rather than only at
    specific times?
2. Do I tend to use nicotine as both a comfort and strength even when
    I feel that I do not want any?
3. Am I afraid that I will put on excessive amounts of weight, or
    become particularly irritable or depressed, if I give up using
    nicotine altogether?

4. Do I often find that having my first use of nicotine in any day tends not to satisfy me but makes me want more?
5. Do I continue to use nicotine even when I have a bad cold or a more serious respiratory problem?
6. Do I find that my nicotine consumption goes up or down when I am off alcohol or drugs or when I am on a diet?
7. Do I deliberately use nicotine before going out to a place where I may not be able to use it?
8. When I run out of my favourite form of nicotine, do I accept the offer of an alternative that I do not particularly like?
9. Do I often use nicotine to calm my nerves?
10. Do I often use nicotine significantly more than I intend?

As with alcohol, any two positive answers indicate the need for further assessment. Any four positive answers spell addiction – and it's going to take a lot more than common sense or will-power to give up nicotine and stay off it indefinitely without blowing an emotional fuse or taking up another addiction. Interestingly, these two prospects, blowing an emotional fuse or taking up another addiction, such as food, are precisely the reasons (they think they are being rational!) that people give for continuing smoking. Wouldn't it be better to follow a Twelve-Step programme and get the best of all worlds: a drug-free, healthy, long-lived and emotionally appropriate life?

My uncle, Lord Stewart of Fulham, a brilliant and kind man, said to me once, "There is no music in my life". I believe that he meant rather more than the fact that he was tone-deaf. He died a terrible death from cancer of the oesophagus, pleading to my son that he should give up smoking. At the time Robin paid no attention: he was too young to care about health issues and had plenty of reasons for wanting to suppress his feelings. Now that Robin has given up alcohol and drugs – and he works a Twelve-Step programme because he finds it works for him, not because I told him to – he has given up smoking as well. Why on earth would he ever want to go back to the emotional and physical madness of cigarette smoking? He doesn't.

"Recreational" (street) drugs
Drugs of choice – heroin, cocaine, LSD, ecstasy, magic mushrooms, "designer" drugs, amphetamines, cannabis, solvents.

Why would anybody ever want to know what various drugs look like, how they are used, and what their slang names are? The only people to whom these issues are important (extremely and boringly) are the addicts themselves. I suppose the police and customs and excise people need to have some idea of what they are looking for, but I can think of no good reason why the rest of us (teachers and parents in particular) should have any healthy interest in the subject.

There are, of course, various unhealthy reasons why we tend to be fascinated by drugs. The first and foremost reason is fear. The drug problem is huge and it is getting worse. We have every reason to fear it. But that means that we need to know how to identify addictive disease, not necessarily know about the drugs themselves. What good would it do us if we knew the ins and outs of the ways that drugs are marketed and used? Incidentally, those people who believe that cigarette advertising should be banned might ponder the widespread use of cannabis and cocaine, substances that have no legitimate advertising whatever.

The appropriate way for parents and teachers or, for that matter, friends or anyone else who is concerned that someone might be on drugs is to look for changes in behaviour. The *Sunday Times* (2nd Feb 1997) got it right when they listed the following ten warning signs, although, in my view, even these characteristics are difficult at times to distinguish from normal adolescence:

- Sudden and irregular mood swings.
- A gradual loss of interest in hobbies and sport.
- Staying out more, possibly with a new circle of friends.
- Reduced interest in personal grooming and hygiene.
- Use of colognes or deodorants to hide smell of drugs.
- Sores or rashes, especially around the mouth.
- Excessive spending or borrowing money.
- Decline in performance at school.
- Excessive tiredness.
- Loss of appetite.

My own belief is that we should focus our attention on young children by trying to identify potential addicts even before they have discovered any mood-altering substances or processes. We should look for the following identifying characteristics of an addictive nature:

- Having an addictive family background in which a parent, grandparent or other close relative has a significant addiction of some kind.
- Having frequent mood swings for no good reason.
- Being a loner, even in a crowd.
- Being excessively manipulative
- Being easily frustrated and rarely satisfied.
- Being easily hurt and over-sensitive.

Again, these characteristics are individually difficult to distinguish from normal childhood behaviour, but taken all together they would certainly add up to concern for the possibility of an addictive nature. This concern is important not only in its own right in trying to protect the child from developing overt addictions, but also in preventing misdiagnosis of hyperactivity, attention deficit disorder, seasonal affective disorder, depressive illness, metabolic deficiencies, allergies and heaven knows what else.

But suppose subsequently we do find a drug of some kind in a child's room. What would we do as a result? Love? Educate? Punish? Yes, all three, if you like, and these are all effective in discouraging further drug use by children who have no potential for addictive disease. However, none of these things makes any difference whatever to the progression of addiction disease, once it is established, unless they are coupled with a Twelve-Step programme of recovery.

When tragedies occur and a young person dies from drug use – particularly after just one episode – the press jump on it, publicizing the grief of the family and doing everything they can to "educate" (frighten) other children. As an educational programme, this doesn't get through to the population most at risk: the addicts believe themselves to be immortal. They have vastly more experience of drugs than the people who customarily write the press stories, or who give lectures in schools or who participate in parliamentary debates, and they know that the scare stories are exceptional. The risks of being killed or maimed in a road accident, or in a motor-cycle accident in particular, are very high; the risks of death from something to do with drugs certainly exist but they are very low by comparison.

By all means let us educate our children on the dangers of even one experiment with drugs – but are we giving them equal education on other risks and are we spotless in our own behaviour? If not, our strictures are a sham – and the children know it.

Suppose, as a teacher, we expel a child from school as a result of drug use of some kind: the damage to the child's education is obvious but the benefit to the school is questionable. There will be plenty more drug users – and suppliers – in the school: no school will ever be free from drugs, any more than any company will ever be totally free of alcohol or nicotine.

Of course there has to be discipline. Of course there have to be consequences from breaking rules. What I am challenging is the belief that rules can in themselves prevent or suppress the problem.

Sandy is the deputy headmaster of a leading private school. I gave two talks there recently, one to the pupils in the afternoon and one to their families in the evening.

"We've just caught a thirteen year old with some cannabis", he said, proudly. "Of course we had to expel him – otherwise parents would be worried about us being lax on the drugs issue – and I expect he'll have real difficulty in getting a good school to take him."

"How about offering him assessment and treatment, the same as you would for diabetes, asthma or epilepsy?", I asked.

"We don't need to", he replied. "We have more applicants than places."

So there it is: *floreat antiqua domus* and damn the boy. What kind of preparation for a compassionate society is that?

At the end of my talk they distributed a pamphlet supplied by the police. It listed various drugs, including anabolic steroids, which may be abused by athletes and body builders, in the same way that laxatives and diuretics (fluid-reducing tablets) may be abused by jockeys, but are certainly not addictive, because they are not mood-altering.

The pamphlet contained pictures of the various drugs and details of how they are used. As mentioned previously, the addicts in the school will have known all that – and a lot more – already and the rest of the pupils don't need that information as much as they need to understand that addiction is an illness that can be helped. They also need to know that people who are addicts do not believe they are. The non-addictive pupils need to be encouraged to bring addicts to the attention of the school medical people, in the same way that they would report someone who had an epileptic fit or a fractured arm. For the school then to expel the addict (rather than saying perfectly appropriately that expulsion will inevitably follow if the pupil does not go for help to a specialist addiction unit) would defeat the entire exercise of trying to clean up the school and keep it clean. The children would clam up.

Addicts are ill, not bad. They do bad things in the course of their addiction and they have to be punished for that behaviour – but, at the same time, they need to be helped towards getting well. Punishment, as such, does nothing to help the addict. The idea that it will discourage the addict from doing the same thing again simply misses the point: if addicts could change their behaviour on their own, they would do so.

Billy (18) is a market trader from the East End of London. He began to use cannabis at the age of eleven. By thirteen he was using amphetamines and a year later he was using LSD and ecstasy. By fifteen he was using cocaine on occasions and by sixteen he was using it regularly as well as getting any pill he could: "uppers", "downers", "poppers", anything. He didn't need to know the name of the things he tried, all he wanted to know was whether they worked. By seventeen he was heavily into heroin, injecting it daily. He remained doing his job but augmented his income (in order to get his own drugs) by dealing in drugs for other people. Every addict's dream is to buy some, use some, and then sell on for the original price or more. It may start that way but it doesn't continue that way: too much gets used in the middle part of the plan.

"Well, Billy," I said "What trouble are you in now?"

"Well …, the police caught me with a kilogram of cocaine but it wasn't mine, see."

"Are you telling me that someone trusted you with a kilogram of cocaine?", I asked incredulously.

"Well, not exactly," said Billy, squirming in his seat and wondering how to present the situation in the best light. "When the police car overtook us and stopped our car, the other two fellas dumped the cocaine on me and ran away."

"And you never knew it was there in the first place? I have just a slight hunch that the judge isn't going to believe you, Billy, and I don't believe you either. You're a villain and you know it. If you want to get better, you're going to have to give up all that crap – not just the drugs but the cheating and stealing and dealing and lying and all that stuff as well. What does your mother want you to be? A convict? A shithead? Is that the best you can be?"

Appealing to Billy's better nature would never work on the outside. He needed to be in a treatment centre (on probation and with the prospect of a heavy prison sentence hanging over him) to be able to be sufficiently clean from all drugs to feel anything at all, other than the pseudo-feelings of self-pity and blame that form the melodramatic focus of all addicts' lives.

Not everyone who uses cannabis progresses to using heroin. Billy did, but he is the exception rather than the rule. A great many people use cannabis without being addicted to it, just as a great many people use alcohol without being addicted to it. For this reason, among others, there are clamours for the legalization of cannabis. I have to say that I would not support that, even though it is illogical for the most dangerous drugs of all in our society (alcohol and nicotine) to be legal while cannabis remains illegal.

The idea of some liberals is that making drugs (not just cannabis) legal would take out the corruption and crime. Ha! Would it? I very much doubt it. Already people taking regular prescriptions for Methadone will often use other drugs on top or may even sell it to people whose principal addictive drug is Methadone.

Consider this: supposing we gave four cans of free beer to all adults in the country. Would that cut down the incidence of alcoholism? Would it prevent alcohol getting into the hands of children? Would it reduce the incidence of domestic violence, drunk driving, accidents at home and at work, domestic fires and all the other damage that is alcohol-related? Would it put the brewers and the bars out of business? I'm sure it wouldn't: it would simply increase the general amount of alcohol consumed and, as Ledermann said, that would lead to an increase in the alcohol-related problems.

We need to treat all addictive substances (including alcohol, nicotine and sugar, as well as cannabis, cocaine, LSD, ecstasy, amphetamines, heroin and other drugs) in the same consistent manner. Firstly, their personal use should be legal but there should be legal constraints where there is risk or damage to other people. That legal situation already exists for alcohol. Secondly, the Mental Health Act should apply to the disorders of perception seen in addictive disease, as it does already to schizophrenia and other psychoses. In this specific instance people should be protected from themselves by the law of the country: there is no liberty in compulsion.

Firms that do pre-employment urinary drug screening find that they can never get a full set of clean samples. Addicts cannot stay clean even when their possibility of employment depends upon it. Drugs are in our society not because they are being pushed upon us (at the school gates or anywhere else), but because we want them: we draw them in. There is never such a thing as enough drugs. Addiction knows no boundaries – geographical, social or clinical. Love may be as strong as death: addiction is stronger. Again, the need is not for us to try to put up impregnable boundaries but to understand, identify and treat addictive disease.

So, would the answer be to develop pre-natal genetic screening and abort all those who were found to have the potential for addiction? What else would we abort? What would we be left with? My own family would be pretty well wiped out on that principle and I believe that would be a shame, not simply because it is my family, but because we tend to be highly imaginative and creative, as all addicts are. This is often presented the wrong way round: that addiction is a consequence of creativity. In fact both go hand in hand. The child born with the inner emptiness of addictive disease is also born sensitive and curious, searching to understand and modify the world. In due course, addiction dominates the creativity but, in recovery, the creativity can blossom again. Society has a great deal to gain from keeping its addicts alive, helping them to get into recovery, and then reaping the benefits of their sensitivity and creativity.

Margaret (35) once earned in one night what I earn in a month. She is married, beautiful, intelligent, all sorts of things that belie the standard image of prostitutes. Margaret is an addict and she uses prostitution to finance her addiction. (I loathe the word "habit" because it so underestimates the nature of the problem of addictive disease.) She came to us when she couldn't go on: her addiction got the better of her, as it always does. (There is absolutely no such thing as a "stable" addict: the dose of one particular substance may be stable but that is the best that one can say for a miserable existence.) She came to us and, on the second time round, got better. Then, when she was settled and with good social support (and, incredibly, with a progressively improving relationship with her husband) she asked for an AIDS test. It was negative, but the test for Hepatitis C came back positive. She did not go straight back on to drugs or back on the game: she has more to live for now, whatever the duration and quality of her life might be.

The population at large is advised to practice "safe sex". Indeed we should. I fear, however, that the origin of this sensible recommendation has a murky history. The accepted belief is often that drug addicts are impossible to treat: they always relapse. I have even been told that taking addicts off all drugs, as we do, is dangerous, partly because of their risk of suicide (which is true if one has no recovery programme to put in place of the addiction) and partly because they will inevitably go back to drugs. Instead of staying "safely" on Methadone (on the hallowed principle of "harm minimization"), they will go back to crime and prostitution. The essence of this clinical philosophy is "damn the addicts, they're not worth helping anyway – but we must reduce crime and keep AIDS out of the nice, normal, population". If the pundits want to keep AIDS out of the nice, normal, population, they should tell nice normal people not to screw hookers. If they want to reduce crime, they should understand and treat addictive disease – not perpetuate it with Methadone maintenance, needle exchange schemes and even Social Security payments. The one thing missing from the highly realistic film *Trainspotting* was the sardonic joke:

Question – What's green and gets you high?
Answer – A Social Security cheque.

Am I saying that addicts should be denied Social Security support? Actually, I'm saying rather more than that: the dependency culture has a great deal to answer for and the perpetuation of addiction (through addicts not having to face the full consequences of their addiction) is only one of its consequences. Society itself is indeed sick when it helps to maintain people in their addictive disease, yet does virtually nothing to help them to get into full and lasting recovery.

For a start we need to be able to identify addictive behaviours as such, rather than waste more time and effort on identifying and talking about the drugs themselves. Our own questionnaires identify addictive behaviour with respect to any "recreational" (street) drug. As before, two positive answers require further assessment and four positive answers (on any drug whatever: cannabis, LSD, amphetamines, ecstasy, cocaine, heroin, "designer drugs", and any drug that is bought in order to produce a mood-altering effect) spell trouble and the need for specialist help from those who know something, not necessarily about drugs as such, but certainly about addictive disease and recovery.

1. Do I particularly enjoy getting a really strong effect from recreational drugs?
2. Do I have a sense of increased tension and excitement when I know that I have the opportunity to get some drugs?
3. Have others expressed repeated serious concern about aspects of my drug use?
4. Do I find that getting high tends to result in my going on to take more drugs?
5. Do I tend to use drugs as both a comfort and strength?
6. Do I often find that I use all the drugs in my possession even though I intended to spread them out over several occasions?
7. Do I tend to make sure that I have drugs, or the money for drugs, before concentrating on other things?
8. Do I get irritable and impatient if my supply of drugs is delayed for ten minutes for no good reason?
9. Do I tend to use more drugs if I have got more?
10. Do I use drugs before going out if I feel there might not be the opportunity to use them later?

Eating disorders

More rubbish is written and spoken about eating disorders than about any other addictive or compulsive behaviour.

The first point of contention is the adamant – and often aggressive – statement that eating disorders have nothing to do with addiction. Our rebuttal of that is based on our questionnaires. Using exactly the same method of derivation from the characteristics of addictive behaviour (page 58) we formulated the following two questionnaires:

FOOD BINGEING

1. Do I tend to think of food not so much as a satisfier of hunger but as a reward for the stress I endure?
2. Do I tend to use food as both a comfort and strength even when I am not hungry?
3. Do I find that being full is often irrelevant in deciding when to stop eating?
4. Do I find that I sometimes put on weight even when I am trying to diet?
5. Do others express repeated serious concern about my excessive eating?
6. Do I prefer to eat alone rather than in company?
7. When I have eaten too much do I tend to feel defiant as well as disappointed in myself?
8. Do I prefer to graze like a cow throughout the day rather than ever allow myself to get hungry?
9. Do I have three or more different sizes of clothes in my adult (non-pregnant if female) wardrobe?
10. Am I aware that once I have consumed certain foods I find it difficult to control further eating?

FOOD STARVING

1. In a restaurant or even at home do I often try to persuade others to choose dishes that I know I would like, even though I would probably refuse to eat them?
2. When I eat in company do I like to be with special friends or family members whom I can rely upon to finish off some foods for me?
3. Do I have a list of so many things that I dare not eat, that there is very little left that I can eat?
4. Do I often chew something and then take it out of my mouth and throw it away?
5. Do I particularly enjoy eating raw vegetables and also salty or sour things?
6. When I eat in company do I tend to time my eating as a form of strategy so that others are not really aware of just how little I am eating?

7. When I have eaten something reasonably substantial do I tend to feel disappointed or even angry with myself as well as slightly relieved?
8. Do I get irritable and impatient at meal times if someone tries to persuade me to eat something?
9. Do I often avoid meal times by claiming that I have already eaten when it is not true?
10. Do some foods make me wish I could eat them like other people, but nonetheless I find that I cannot bring myself to do so?

Positive answers to any two questions in either of these questionnaires indicate the need for further assessment and four positive answers in either questionnaire indicate an addictive relationship with food, which is what I would call an eating disorder.

We find that people with eating disorders commonly have other addictive tendencies. In fact, only very rarely do they not. Eating disorders are very definitely part of the spectrum of addictive and compulsive behaviour and they have to be diagnosed and treated in exactly the same way as any other addictive or compulsive behaviour. Eating disorder questionnaires used elsewhere often seem to me to be very wide of the mark: they look for all sorts of things that can also be found in a normal population and they do not concentrate sufficiently on those behavioural characteristics that are found only in people who suffer from eating disorders.

The second point of contention is that the treatment of eating disorders should be primarily concerned with food and body weight. In fact this approach misses the principal point altogether: eating disorders are primarily disorders of feeling, in exactly the same way as any other addictive or compulsive behaviour is primarily a disorder of feeling. In alcoholism the disorder shows itself in alcohol-related behaviour but mere abstinence does nothing more than convert a wet drunk into a dry drunk; it does nothing to correct the underlying disorder of mood and sense of inner emptiness. Correspondingly, changing the shape of someone with an eating disorder, simply by altering the calorie content of food intake or altering the exercise output, does nothing more than alter the body shape. It does nothing for the eating disorder, the mood disturbance and sense of inner emptiness, as such.

Obviously, except in the case of bulimia, in which the body weight may be an artificially controlled normal, the body weight of someone with an eating disorder will usually be outside the normal healthy range and this is one of the things that needs to be helped. It is, after all, the aspect of the problem that may be most obvious and distressing to the patient and to others. However, the central principle with eating disorders is the same as for any other addictive or compulsive behaviour: first become abstinent from all mood-altering substances or behaviours and then deal with the mood disorder. Then the various consequences of previous addictive behaviour (in this case abnormal body weight, among other things) will correct themselves.

The third point of contention is that the various eating disorders are said to be distinct conditions. Anorexia is commonly seen as a completely different condition from bulimia, with each condition having more in common with other forms of psychopathology than with each other. More is written on the differences between anorexia and bulimia than on their similarities. Compulsive over-eating is generally not identified as a distinct condition at all but is only seen in its consequence in massive obesity. This tends to be thought of as a product of weak will, greed or gluttony, personality inadequacy, poor childhood nurturing, cries for help and heaven knows what else. Again I profoundly disagree and see all eating disorders as no more than different manifestations of the same underlying mood disorder.

The fourth contentious point is that there are sub-classes of eating disorders, just as researchers try erroneously to establish sub-classes of alcoholism. Further sub-dividing eating disorders, for example, into giving a particular name to the common anorexic process of chewing something once or twice and then taking it out of the mouth and throwing it away or Pica (eating strange substances such as coal or foam rubber, as in a ten-year-old patient of ours who systematically destroyed his parents' furniture), Tanorexia (the quest for the body beautiful through repeated sun tans, irrespective of the attendant risk of skin cancer), Bulimorexia (whatever that may be: probably something that gained a researcher a higher degree), are all unhelpful. They take something away from the general understanding of eating disorders by looking at a particular behaviour, rather than at the sense of emotional compulsion that lies behind it and any other form of addictive behaviour.

Furthermore, these sub-divisions cause further confusion by detracting from the awareness that any specific eating behaviour, or concern for body shape or appearance, may simply be a temporary stress-release, rather than evidence of an underlying eating disorder. These temporary stress-releases are often culturally induced, in exactly the same way that in some people repeated high alcohol consumption is culturally related to, but not necessarily indicative of, alcoholism. Schoolgirls have a high incidence of self-induced vomiting at the time of examinations, but this does not mean that they all necessarily have eating disorders. Our specific questionnaires, looking for addictive characteristics, will diagnose those patients who do have eating disorders. The universal treatment for them, whatever their individual eating behaviour or distortion of body image, is the Twelve-Step programme.

The fifth contentious point is that there are no mood-altering substances or processes in eating disorders – because one has to eat to stay alive. This completely misses the point: alcoholics have to drink to stay alive but they don't have to drink anything that is mood-altering, i.e. anything containing alcohol. Correspondingly, people with eating disorders have to eat but they do not have to eat substances that cause them to crave. Most sufferers from eating disorders find that the refined carbohydrates (sugar and white flour) have this effect. Some people find that wheat flour or fats can also trigger a binge – or even fruit or, for that matter, almost anything. This may be true, but I myself believe that abstinence from sugar (including honey but not fruit) and white flour is essential but that is all. These specific mood-altering substances are the equivalents of the first drink in any day for the alcoholic: this is what sets up the craving. After that the eating disorder sufferer will indeed binge on anything. Initially it is sensible to avoid previous binge foods but these (other than those containing sugar and white flour) can be safely reintroduced later.

I am often challenged on our recommendation that people with anorexia should abstain from sugar and white flour, food substances that would help them to put on weight. Anorexic patients themselves will often say that they haven't eaten sugar or white flour for ages so they see no point in this particular recommendation for the future. The point is this: it was the craving that caused the fear of putting a weight in the first place. Showing the patients that they need never experience that craving again (by avoiding sugar and white flour), is an extremely important part of re-establishing a healthy relationship with food.

Eating disorders are complicated by associated behavioural addictive tendencies (as all substance addictions are to some extent). Bingeing, starving and vomiting are mood-altering processes in their own right, however strange this may appear to other people. Not that all addictive behaviour doesn't seem strange to other people, but the behaviour associated with eating disorders sometimes seems strange even to other addicts – which is actually helpful because they then come to realize that their own behaviour also looks strange to other addicts of one kind or another, including eating disorder sufferers, even though they all share the same common basic disease. Behavioural abstinence therefore has to be implemented alongside abstinence from specific mood-altering substances.

Getting rid of all sorts of misconceptions and preoccupations over so-called food allergies, and the supposed need for vitamins and trace elements, is another important path towards healthy eating. Food obsession has become an industry built on this disease. Healthy eating involves a normal mixed diet with proteins, fats, wholewheat flour, plenty of fresh fruit and vegetables, three regular meals a day and nothing in between, normal portion sizes that anyone else would be happy to eat, and abstinence from sugar and white flour and that's that. Weighing and measuring food – and even weighing and measuring oneself – can become another obsession. The human body puts itself right when one stops abusing it and when one learns to use food for fuel and for simple culinary pleasure rather than for mood-alteration or as a substitute for appropriate human relationships.

And finally the sixth contentious point is that eating disorders come from distortions of body image and that these come from something in the sufferer's background. The most common culprits are thought to be abuse or abandonment in childhood, a dieting regime taken to excess, or the undue influence of the fashion industry. I don't believe any of that. Certainly, people with eating disorders have distorted body image: thin people think they are fatter than they are and vice versa, but this distortion of body image is part of the disordered perception that is a characteristic of any addiction. Distortion of body image is part of the eating disorder itself, not a cause or consequence of it.

As for dieting regimes and the fashion industry, these have an effect on everyone, and can indeed cause a lot of stupidity (the inaccurate saying that it is impossible to be too rich or too thin was attributed to the Duchess of Windsor, who gave all the appearance of nicotine addiction and an eating disorder), but they don't *cause* eating disorders. The cause of eating disorders, along with other forms of addictive disease is, in my view, probably genetic. Abuse and abandonment, or any other emotional trauma may trigger the genetic predisposition and set up the craving for mood-alteration but they are not the cause of the subsequent eating disorder or, for that matter, any other addiction. If they were the cause then many more people would have eating disorders and other addictions than actually do.

Life is hard and childhood is frequently painful. Addicts of one kind or another have no monopoly of suffering but they certainly know how to pump self-pity and blame for all they are worth.

Gillian (40) used to be a member of my counselling staff. She came to me when there were very few counsellors who knew anything about addictive disease, let alone the Twelve-Step residential treatment of eating disorders. In fact we ourselves were the first to introduce the Twelve-Step treatment of eating disorders to the UK and we put up with a lot of mockery for doing so. Gillian came to us as a trained alcohol and drug counsellor. I had no idea that she also had an eating disorder. (It might even have been against employment legislation to ask.) Nonetheless, it was my fault: I should have found out somehow.

Gillian looked normal and gave no sign of being bulimic: her teeth were fine and there was no tell-tale smell of mouthwash or peppermint. I discovered eventually that she used to weigh almost a hundred pounds more than her current weight and that she kept it off by running five miles to work in the morning, ten miles at lunchtime, and five miles back home in the evening.

I like all my counselling staff to develop wider skills and familiarity than simply skills with Twelve-Step counselling and I sent Gillian on an introductory course for gestalt therapy that I myself had attended. She fell in love with it (as I did myself but, I believe, at a more appropriate level) and she thought that she had discovered the true cause of all her addictions: an uncompleted gestalt – childhood experiences that she had not fully processed. In due course she left my staff to become a full-time gestalt therapist. She now believes that the Twelve-Step programme is "superficial". She has gone back to drinking alcohol and I fear that it will not be long before she is back on drugs.

I myself have learned to be more careful in the selection and supervision of my counselling staff and I have also learned to take good care of myself. I don't want my own eating disorder and other addictions waking up again. I've had enough of that trouble for one lifetime.

Exercise

Where are all the other men with eating disorders? The answer to that is that a few of them are in treatment (we have two anorexic men in treatment with us right now and we have had several previously, including a hospital doctor who was bulimic), but most of the men with eating disorders are pumping iron in the gymnasium or out pounding the pavements.

Graham (39) runs six kilometres every morning before he goes to work. In the evening and at weekends he often plays squash in the winter and tennis in the summer. These have taken over from horse riding and rugby football that he used to do when he was younger. He proposed to his wife after scoring a try at rugby: it was the greatest achievement that he could lay at her feet. He has many other talents but exercise is in many ways the centre of his life. He has run six marathons in various countries. What would happen if he couldn't exercise any more? Would life lose its point? Is he merely fit and healthy – or is he an addict?

We can help him to answer that question (if he so wishes, which he almost certainly does not: when someone is so perfect, the need for change is not obvious) through our questionnaires. As before, two positive answers indicate the need for further assessment, four positive answers spell trouble.

1. Do I often get so tired with exercise that I find it difficult to walk or to climb up stairs?
2. Do I prefer to exercise alone rather than in company?
3. Do I often try to take exercise several times a day?
4. Do I particularly enjoy getting wringing wet with sweat when I exercise?
5. Do I often feel a sense of tension and excitement when about to take exercise?
6. Do I respond positively to an unexpected invitation to exercise despite having just finished my regular exercise?
7. Do I feel that I become a real person only when I am exercising?
8. Do I tend to use exercise as both a comfort and strength even when I am perfectly fit and do not need any more?
9. Do I often take exercise just to tire myself sufficiently for sleep?
10. When I go out do I often take sports clothes and equipment with me "just in case" the opportunity to exercise arises?

But does being an exercise addict spell trouble? Surely exercise is a healthy addiction and one that we should actively encourage patients towards? The answer to these questions is that exercise addiction is just like any other addiction: progressive and destructive. It will take over Graham's life, if indeed he is an addict. It will push other activities out of his life. His perfectionism and self-centredness will get worse so that his relationship with his wife and children are bound to suffer. He may be fit – but fit for what?

Naomi (22) has a rather different complication from her exercise addiction: she is a professional dancer. She is anorexic as well but our questionnaire revealed that her exercise addiction is the more intense of the two. But does this mean that she has to change her profession?

"I don't want to do anything else", she says. "Dancing is my life."

In Naomi's case her addictive behaviour has parasitized a perfectly normal wish to be a dancer. Perhaps she was "guided" towards her particular profession by her addiction but, either way, I do not believe that she necessarily has to give up dancing. As with other behavioural addictions, she needs to be able to distinguish between, on the one hand, when she is using the behaviour addictively (when she gets an addictive "high" from it and when it displaces other normal, healthy, activities and relationships) and, on the other hand, when she is using it for its primary purpose of earning her living and giving simple pleasure to herself and others. This distinction is difficult. Behavioural addictions are difficult. But it is comforting – and this solves half the battle – to be able to understand precisely what one is up against.

Caffeine

Drugs of choice – ProPlus, chocolate, cocoa, coffee, lemonade, coke, pepsi, etc.. Substitute your own caffeine drug of choice for "caffeine" in each question.

Who cares about caffeine addiction? Well… caffeine addicts do, particularly when they go into withdrawal and get fearful headaches. Tea, coffee, chocolate, cola, lemonade and various other drinks as well as ProPlus and various pharmaceutical preparations, contain caffeine and the drinks, at least, are used as part of normal social life. Long may that continue. But for caffeine addicts the pleasure has long since gone.

Rosemary (25) caught me out. I thought I should have to go back to the drawing board and start formulating the addiction questionnaires all over again. She weighed over two hundred and fifty pounds yet had given only one positive answer on the eating disorder questionnaires. I then asked her what it was that she thought had made her so fat.

"Chocolate", she said.

Idiot that I was, I might have had the sense – and good manners, let alone clinical care – to spend more time listening to her before bundling her off to do my blessed questionnaires. She got fat on the sugar that came along with the caffeine in chocolate, yet was not addicted to sugar itself. However, having survived that error, I then – after an appropriate pause – gave her the caffeine questionnaire and she came up with a full set of positive answers. The questionnaires lived to fight another day and so did Rosemary.

Two positive answers indicate the need for further assessment; four spell trouble:

1. Do I have an intimate relationship with caffeine so that in a strange way I feel real only when I use it?
2. Do I prefer to take caffeine on my own rather than in company?
3. Would it be more painful for me to give up caffeine than to give up a close friendship?
4. Have I regularly stolen or helped myself to other people's caffeine even though I had enough money to buy my own?
5. Do I tend to time my intake of caffeine so that others are not really aware of my total intake?
6. Do I have a sense of increased tension and excitement when I buy caffeine substances or when I see advertisements for them?
7. Do I find that my intake of another form of caffeine tends to increase when I am off my own favourite?
8. When I have used too much caffeine do I tend to feel defiant as well as disappointed in myself?
9. Do I sometimes rush through a meal or skip it altogether so that I can have some caffeine?
10. Am I often capable of drinking twenty cups of tea or coffee or cola or lemonade or eating twenty chocolates in a day?

The only other patient I have ever come across whose primary (and in fact only) addiction was caffeine was a church organist. He used to have to take a flask of black coffee with him to the church service. Otherwise he went into withdrawal during the long prayers and sermon so that his hands shook so much that he couldn't play the final hymn without smudging the notes. In his case, unlike that of many church organists I have known, one could tell the difference.

More commonly in the treatment centre we see caffeine addictions alongside an eating disorder (as an appetite suppressant) or alongside nicotine as a stimulant.

Carol (36) was in treatment with us for multiple addictions. It was predictable, from the moment that we saw her answers to the full set of questionnaires, that she was going to need extended care in a halfway house. (The questionnaires are very valuable in this respect because they give us an indication of the spread and the overall intensity of a patient's addictive disease – and hence a guide to treatment plans.) Carol gave up alcohol and drugs because she recognized how much trouble they had caused her. She didn't want to look at her relationship addiction (using people as if they were drugs) because she couldn't see how she could do without them (an issue that we tried to explain, but on which we couldn't get near her: she just didn't want to know and she thought we were just being silly). She had the same attitude to caffeine. Her regular intake was twenty cans of cola a day (the company must love her) and, come hell or high water, she was not going to give that up. She relapsed back onto alcohol and drugs shortly after leaving us, having refused to go to a halfway house.

I can't force Carol, or anyone else, to give up caffeine, even though we supply only decaffeinated drinks in the treatment centre. Five cups or cans a day is the recommended medical maximum if one is to avoid damage to the cardiovascular system. I would give addicts a recommended level of zero.

Shopping, spending and stealing

Shopping and spending fit closely together and stealing (shoplifting) is commonly what happens when the money runs out. This is not the same as stealing in order to buy drugs or stealing as a hedonistic criminal activity. Under those circumstances, compulsive stealing comes more appropriately under gambling and risk-taking and may be picked up on that questionnaire. In this case, shopping and spending (and stealing when the money runs out) are more closely associated with the eating disorder processes of self-nurturance.

Everybody likes to buy things, although perhaps few husbands acknowledge that they like to go shopping except for computers or tool kits or sports equipment or anything in garden centres. Mostly people buy what they want, sometimes purely for necessity but at other times for pleasure. This latter process is referred to in my family as "retail therapy".

The compulsive shopper, or shopaholic if you like, gets no lasting pleasure. The buzz is in the anticipation. By the time the purchase has been made, remorse is beginning to set in. Then, afterwards, the shopaholic may be stuck with yet another bundle of things not needed or wanted.

Angela (35) is a sucker for bargains, usually food or clothing but sometimes books and occasionally household appliances. Some of her purchases are still wrapped; most of them are unused. The food "bargains" often have to be thrown away when they go off before they can be eaten. She buys on credit – and is getting herself into a lot of trouble.

Robert (eternally young) has a wonderful model train set. It covers twenty square metres of roof space above the garage. He says he bought it for his sons. They never played with it. Nor did Robert. I know he didn't: I'm Robert.

Robin (a mere boy) has computers and computer bits and pieces in every room in his house. The spare bedroom is inaccessible. His own bedroom needs a pole vault to get into it. Please, Robin, would you like to do the questionnaires before the sitting room disappears altogether? You, of all people, should know the form: two positive answers mean further assessment by your father and four mean big trouble from your staff and patients.

I may make fun of my son Robin in this way, although he is now the managing director of the treatment centre. We would go even more mad than we already are if we didn't laugh at ourselves occasionally. However, I have to stress that this addiction can be just as destructive as any other. I've known it destroy marriages. I've known it lead to suicide. That isn't funny.

1. Do I feel uncomfortable when shopping with other people because it restricts my freedom?
2. Do I particularly enjoy buying bargains so that I often finish up with more than I need?
3. Do I tend to use shopping as a comfort and strength even when I do not need anything?
4. Do I tend to go shopping just in case I might see something I want?
5. When I shop with family members, friends or other people, do I tend to disguise the full extent of my purchases?
6. Do I often buy so many goods (groceries, sweets, household goods, books etc.) that it would take a month to get through them?
7. Do I prefer to keep my shopping supplies topped up in case of war or natural disaster, rather than let them run low?
8. Do I buy things not so much as a means of providing necessities but more as a reward that I deserve for the stress that I endure?
9. Do I feel that I become a real person only when shopping or spending?
10. Do I often go shopping to calm my nerves?

Gambling and risk-taking

We all take risks every day of our lives. We take risks in the house, in the garden, on the roads, at work, on holiday, everywhere. Every action involves some element of risk and some measure of judgement. How on earth are we to distinguish between a normal, necessary, sensible, reasonable risk and a compulsive gamble? The answer, as before for any behavioural addiction, depends on whether we get an addictive buzz from the activity and on whether the overall process of risk-taking of one kind or another is progressive and destructive.

Roland (42) is, or was and maybe will be again in the future, a business tycoon. He built up a chain of thirty shops before he was thirty. He has real talent and he got all the "toys" (as he describes them) - the Rolls-Royce, the mews house in town and the cottage in the country, the wife and two point four children - and then lost the lot before he was thirty-five. Guess how...

The guess may be wrong: Roland did not play cards or go to the races or the casino or take bets on a white Christmas or on which raindrop would reach the bottom of the window pane first. He lost his money in what he might previously have called the normal ups and downs of business life. Now he knows he is a compulsive gambler: no one other than a compulsive gambler would take the crazy risks that he did, always believing that the next deal would be the lucky one, careless of the security of his family, taking on more than he could possibly supervise appropriately. When he crashed he crashed big time – and is only now coming to the end of paying off his creditors.

Barry (65) is Roland's friend and it was he who referred Roland to us after he himself had been through treatment with us. He always brings a smile to our faces when he describes himself as "a recovering alcoholic, addict, compulsive gambler, nicotine addict and addict and addict and addict…" He does it to remind himself of the sheer extent of his addictive disease. He's been free of it now for two years, despite some dreadful domestic difficulties that were not primarily due to him at all, although he has been more than ready to look at his own contribution to the mess. He takes some time on the telephone every day to keep in touch with other addicts and to share his addictive experience, strength of recovery, and hope for the future in encouraging them.

This description of Barry will immediately identify him to his many friends in Gamblers Anonymous. What a wonderful reputation to have: to be known (anonymously) for what he does to help others. He used to be a millionaire many times over. He says he feels richer now – and that he is happier. He has more fun and he lives contentedly within his means. Another close friend of his is still "out there", as recovering addicts say of those who are still dominated by their addictive disease. Barry tried to help him but got nowhere. One doesn't always win.

"Gambling and risk-taking" includes property ventures, speculating on stocks, shares and commodities and other business risks. Two positive answers indicate the need for further assessment, four spell trouble.

1. Do I find that the amount that I have won or lost is often irrelevant in deciding when to stop gambling or risk-taking?
2. Do I steal or embezzle to cover gambling losses or to cover my losses in risky ventures?
3. Do I find it more painful to give up gambling and risk taking than give up a close friendship?
4. Have others expressed repeated serious concern over my gambling or risk-taking?
5. Do I tend to accept opportunities for further gambling or risk-taking despite having just completed a session or project?
6. Do I prefer to gamble or to take risks in one way or another throughout the day rather than at particular times?
7. Do I tend to use gambling or risk-taking as a form of comfort and strength even when I do not feel that I particularly want to gamble or to take further risks?
8. Have I gambled or taken risks at the first opportunity to do so in case I did not get the chance later on?
9. When my favourite form of gambling or risk-taking is unavailable do I gamble on something else I normally dislike?

10. **Do I get irritable and impatient if there is a complete break of ten minutes in a gambling session?**

Workaholism
Behaviour of choice – professional work, hobbies, particular interests, cults, internet activites and computer games. Substitute your own behaviour of choice for "work" in each question.

I work hard. I have done a seven-day week (running my medical practice and the treatment centre) for the last fourteen years. The work I do in the treatment centre and counselling centre is very different from my medical work, from which I earn my living. I have a lot of energy, I believe mostly as a result of using no mood-altering substances. There are a lot of "masculine" things I don't do: I don't drink, I don't understand cars and don't want to, I have no girlfriends (I'm happy with the wife I've got and I hope she is with me) and I have little interest in sport except for my daily morning run. I very rarely watch television except for the news. My total travelling time each day is ten minutes. This leaves an enormous amount of time to do the things I enjoy: theatre, opera, ballet, film, reading and writing, and my work in the medical practice, the treatment centre and the counselling centre.

Does that sound like workaholism? Maybe it does – but I no longer score as high as I used to on the questionnaires: Nowadays I score positive only on questions 2 and 9 and that may say more about other people than about me. (Interestingly, people who try to persuade me to cut down on my work always want me to cut down on what I do in other aspects of my life rather than in what I do that affects them.) Yet, I still need to be careful to remember that I am an addict by nature and that any addiction can drag me down again. Maybe I defend myself too hard: maybe these are the rationalisations of a using addict. I need to beware.

As before, two positive answers require further assessment, and four spell trouble.

1. Do I take on work that I actively dislike, not out of necessity but simply to keep myself occupied?
2. Do I tend to work faster and for longer hours than other people of my own ability, so that they find it difficult to keep up with me?
3. When I have definitely overworked and got myself irritable and over-tired, do I tend to feel defiant as well as slightly ashamed?
4. Do I tend to tidy up the mess that someone else has got into at work, even when I have not been asked to do so?
5. Do I find that finishing a specific project is often irrelevant in deciding when to stop working?
6. When working with others do I tend to disguise the full amount of time and effort that I put into my work?
7. Do I tend to keep reserve projects up my sleeve just in case I find some time, even a few minutes, to spare?

8. Do I regularly cover other people's work and responsibilities even when there is no need for me to do so?
9. Have others expressed serious concern over the amount of time I spend working?
10. Once I start work in any day do I find it difficult to get out of the swing of it and relax?

Previously I used to work for the sake of working, believing that it made me something special. "Mankind lives through his productive work", I pontificated, quoting Ayn Rand, my favourite author. But my work at that time certainly wasn't productive: it was excessive and unproductive because I couldn't keep track of it, and it was destructive of myself and of my family. I was involved professionally or semi-professionally in medicine, music, politics and farming. I used to imagine I was a "complete" man from the age of enlightenment. I wasn't: I was merely a workaholic and it all fell apart.

Archie (45) is a lawyer and he is also a Christian. I've nothing against lawyers: my brother is a lawyer. I've nothing against Christians: both my parents were Christian missionaries. One might imagine that Archie had everything going for him. In fact he has nothing. His Christianity has become such an obsession that he pesters his legal partners, who are fed-up with it, his friends, who are friends no longer, and his wife and children, who say prayers of their own that he could be restored to some level of sanity.

Archie's story could just as easily have been that of a financial trader, a political activist, a birdwatcher, a stamp collector or anyone with an obsession that goes so far that it destroys normal life and relationships. There is nothing wrong with any of these activities in their own right as professions or as hobbies and interests, and I've nothing against people wanting to join religious or political organizations (I would fight for their right to do so, as most of us would). But that's not what we see in Archie. He's a workaholic, although it isn't his primary work that has fallen prey to his addictive disease.

Prescription drug addiction
Drugs of choice – tranquillizers, antidepressants, painkillers, cough mixtures and cold cures, sleeping tablets, slimming pills, antihistamines.

WARNING: Do not suddenly stop taking any medication that you have used regularly – withdrawal symptoms may be very severe.

DISCUSS YOUR CONCERNS WITH YOUR DOCTOR.

Now here's a conundrum: who creates the prescription drug addiction: the doctor or the patient? I believe the answer is both – inadvertently.

Some non-addictive patients become physiologically addicted when mood-altering prescription drugs such as painkillers, tranquillizers, antidepressants and sleeping tablets, are prescribed over a long period of time (against pharmaceutical company recommendations maybe). These patients may have severe withdrawal symptoms when the drugs are discontinued and my own recommendation is that withdrawal should therefore be gradual over a period of at least seven weeks.

The addictive patient, on the other hand, craves mood alteration and goes to the doctor with a whole list of physical and emotional symptoms. The doctor's heart sinks and he or she prescribes once – and then again and again and again. Eventually the doctor (or a partner or deputy) wonders whether it would be better for the prescription to be reduced. The doctor tries to do this but the patient goes into a spin, reproducing the original symptoms – and a few more for good measure – and thus demonstrating (to both doctor and patient) that the patient "needs" the drugs. Then there are reports in the press that that particular drug can cause dependency (people don't like to use a nasty word like addiction to apply to such a no-blame condition as dependency or habituation or continual use of prescription drugs) … and then the patient sues the doctor. Certainly, doctors have to take the blame for inappropriate prescribing, but it is easy to be wise after the event.

Six years ago or so the manufacturers of a brand of painkiller wrote round to doctors to say that "in order to reduce the risk of addiction" they were henceforth going to present that particular drug in a gelatin capsule rather than in an ampoule. I wrote to them from the treatment centre saying that addicts are interested in the drug, not necessarily in its route of administration, and that, in any case, if addicts want to find a way of converting a gelatin capsule into something injectable they would do so… In due course they did exactly that.

I do not make myself out to be a pharmacologist. I hate the subject, because of all the false claims and damaging side-effects that I have seen in my professional lifetime and so I have no interest in it whatever. I simply see a lot of addicts and I listen to them and therefore I know the subject from that perspective.

But now let's look to the future and see the horrors that are in store for us. Many doctors say that antidepressants are not addictive. They once said the same of cocaine because it had no withdrawal symptoms, required no detoxification, and wasn't necessarily taken regularly. What I hope these same doctors are now saying about cocaine will, I believe, be what they will say in the not too distant future about antidepressants.

Prozac, Seroxat and the other so-called new generation of antidepressant drugs act on the serotonin, dopamine and other neuro-transmitter systems that I believe are the exact site of the abnormalities that cause addictive disease. Of course they work as "antidepressants" – so do alcohol and heroin! The idea that something is fundamentally different in effect simply because it is made by a pharmaceutical company rather than in a back-street laboratory is spurious. The most tenacious addictive drugs of all, in my experience, are prescription medicines such as the benzodiazepines and Methadone. Ask any addict – and then ask about antidepressants, unless he or she is still taking them.

When patients start trying to come off Prozac, Seroxat and the other antidepressants, the sparks will fly. Just watch. Or should these drugs be prescribed for life? I would be very concerned, philosophically as well as clinically, at that prospect. The pharmaceutical companies (and many doctors) are for ever searching for a magic bullet to stun patients out of depression or addictive behaviour. This is completely inappropriate when the Twelve-Step programme already exists to help patients to get themselves right.

In many general conditions the pharmaceutical companies have been dramatically successful in changing the quality of people's lives. I can well understand their hope to be able to do the same for psychiatric illness and I believe that medicinal treatment for accurately diagnosed schizophrenia, for example, can at times be helpful, especially when given early in the development of the disease. In the spiritual illness of addiction (and in the underlying mood disorder commonly misdiagnosed as depressive illness), however, the last thing one wants is a medicinal approach. For one thing, the dosage could never be adjusted from day to day, and circumstance to circumstance, in the way that the body itself delicately adjusts the secretions of its own neuro-transmitters. Blunderbuss therapy (blasting the problem out of existence) may be acceptable in some areas of clinical practice but surely not when acting on the delicate tissues that determine calibre of mind, sensitivity, feeling and personality. For another thing, taking away the very essence of individuality in human existence is a crime, not an advance in clinical practice.

It simply isn't true that "a short course of medication helps people to sort out their problems and they can then come off those tablets at a later date and have a better life to go back to". This is bullshit of the lowest order. It isn't what happens: the patients get stuck on the tablets and are progressively less able to do without them, because they lose the belief in their own capacity to feel good or solve problems without medication. This may be good business for the pharmaceutical companies, and there may be some doctors who genuinely believe that they are doing good when they drug people's minds, but in my view it is the worst of all unethical practices. How is it that we are scandalized by assaults to the human body and yet we almost revere such assaults as these on the human mind and spirit, the most valuable possessions we have?

Penelope (52) is a pillar of her local church and social set. Her husband is a Member of Parliament. He drinks a bit – but that goes with the job, of course. Their son had a bit of bother, don't you know, but that's just young people these days, isn't it? It was upsetting, all that business with the courts and the publicity, and it was so kind of dear doctor Richard to be so understanding – and his tablets were wonderful: he's such a good diagnostician!

How on earth could we help Penelope when she had so much emotional investment in staying on prescription medicines? She didn't have to look at the sad wreckage of her life, devoid of anything resembling intimacy in her close relationships, while the tablets each day confirmed her "sick" status and therefore the indisputable fact that she was not responsible for the monotonous emptiness.

In fact, we weren't able to help Penelope. She would rather stay as she is, twittering and dithering, a travesty of the person she used to be and could be again.

Is she really an addict, only different in choice of drug from alcoholics or "street" addicts? Had the eating disorder of her earlier years come back to haunt her in a different guise? The questionnaires will show... using the same interpretation as before: two positive answers indicate the need for further assessment and four spell trouble – for her now and for her doctor later.

1. Do I feel an increased tension or awareness at the time when I normally take my prescription medication?
2. Have others expressed serious concern about my use of prescription medication?
3. Do I take more than the prescribed dose of my prescription medication whenever I feel it necessary?
4. If my prescription medication supply were being strictly controlled, would I hang on to some old prescription medicines even if they were definitely beyond their expiry date?
5. Have others (e.g. doctors) commented that they would be knocked out by a fraction of the prescription medication that I regularly take?
6. Do I find that my previous doses of prescription medicines are no longer successful in controlling my symptoms?
7. Do I continue to take prescription medication because I find that it helps me, even though the original stresses for which the medication was prescribed have been resolved?
8. If I had run out of my prescription medication would I take an alternative even if I was not sure of its effects?
9. Do I get irritable and impatient if my prescription medication is delayed for ten minutes?
10. Do I often find myself taking more prescription medication than I intend?

Sex and love addiction

Who's the lucky one, then? Way hey!... Certainly not the sex and love addict. It's a miserable existence, using sex rather than enjoying it, craving love rather than creating it.

It's not up to me to determine what other people choose to do or not do in their sex lives. It's up to them and, as far as I'm concerned, it's a private matter. If people choose to sleep around, or to get involved in various strange sexual practices or fetishes, that's their affair – provided they don't damage anyone else, physically or emotionally, in the process. However, I have to say that I find it difficult to imagine how a sex and love addict could be anything other than emotionally damaging to other people.

Sex and love addiction, however, is a part of my professional work. Adrian, our treatment director, once put the phone down in a live radio interview when the compère trivialized the subject. I fully supported Adrian on that issue. Even so, we are not without our sense of humour (I thought of illustrating this chapter with two patients called Dick and Fanny but my ever-proper wife overruled me) and we addicts are generally renowned for laughing at ourselves. When other people mock an addict, or even an entire addictive tendency, however, it isn't very funny for those on the receiving end, any more than it would be for people who have epilepsy or cancer.

In our patient population we have not yet made formal studies on whether sex and love addiction occurs as commonly in women as in men, although it appears to do so. Nor have we yet studied whether there is a difference in the incidence in heterosexuals and homosexuals. It is interesting to note that in the early days of Alcoholics Anonymous, and subsequently Narcotics Anonymous, the membership was largely male whereas nowadays there are as many women as men. My guess is that there always were the same number of male and female addicts in general. All that has changed over the years, under environmental influence, is the particular addictive outlets that women have increasingly discovered – the incidence of nicotine addiction is another example – and whether social attitudes enabled these addictive tendencies to develop.

Lilly (35) is strikingly good looking and highly intelligent. She is married with four young children and she has a high income from her work on the board of an investment bank. She can get anywhere she wants on talent: she doesn't need to sleep around in the way that she does. She's already had the managing director and finance director of her own company on the go at the same time, along with a theatre director. She's always ready to start a new relationship if she tires of an existing one, although she finds it difficult to manage more than three simultaneously.

Her previous husband didn't like it and moved out. Her present husband wanted children and he has them and they give him great pleasure, even though he knows perfectly well that the chances of him being their father are only one in however many consorts Lilly may have had at the time of conception. He doesn't seem to mind and I've never discussed it with him.

One of Lilly's previous conquests fell for her in a big way. He was devastated when told that he couldn't have her for himself. He had been with her to swinging parties, bought all sorts of rubber things and lace things and videos and I know not what else. He had even left his wife for Lilly (or, to be more accurate, he didn't put up a fight when his wife discovered the contents of their wall safe and threw him out), but Lilly wasn't having him. She wanted her "freedom".

Is that sex addiction? Or is it merely promiscuity or stupidity or simply an attractive emancipated woman behaving exactly as she chooses? I don't know – but the questionnaires will determine the answer on whether or not Lilly has a sex and love addiction:

1. Do I find it difficult to pass over opportunities for casual or illicit sex?
2. Have others expressed repeated serious concern over my sexual behaviour?
3. Do I pride myself on the speed with which I can get to have sex with someone and do I find sex with a complete stranger stimulating?
4. Do I take opportunities to have sex despite having just had it with somebody else?
5. Do I find that making a sexual conquest causes me to lose interest in that partner and begin looking for another?
6. Do I tend to ensure that I have sex of one kind or another rather than wait for my regular partner to be available after an illness or absence?
7. Have I had repeated affairs even though I had a regular relationship?
8. Have I had three or more regular sexual partners at the same time?
9. Have I had voluntary sex with someone I dislike?
10. Have I tended to change partners if sex becomes repetitive?

I never found out whether Lilly scored two positive answers, which would have indicated the need for further assessment, or four, which would have confirmed the sex and love addiction and spelled trouble of all kinds, because she never returned the answer sheet. I suspect that she is a sex and love addict (a close relation of hers is alcoholic) and that either she doesn't want to change or, perhaps more probably, fears that nothing would be left of her life (despite all her talents) if she were to lose this, to her, vital comfort and support.

Freddie (28) is altogether different. He's one of the lads. He puts it about because he's good-looking and the girls seem to want it and he gets lucky. That's fine isn't it? Well, his wife didn't think so and she left.

"You knew what I was like", he called after her as she was leaving … and he was surprised when she didn't turn back.

He reminds me of the beauty queens who say they want to travel and meet people. There are plenty of people right here: the purpose of travel, or of multiple relationships, is to avoid developing just one relationship to any significant depth.

Again, is Freddie a sex and love addict? Does it matter if he is (other than for the risk of broken hearts and sexually transmitted diseases)? Again, the answers will lie in the questionnaires and further action will depend on what Freddie himself wants. If he ever does want to get really close to another human being, he has no experience (other than possibly physical – and I wonder about that) to guide him.

Sally (28) told us in group that she opens the door of a bar and, at a glance, decides which man she is going to sleep with that night. She finds it difficult to get into lasting recovery from alcoholism, drug addiction and an eating disorder. I'm not surprised.

Relationship addictions

"But I love him, I need him, I want him"

"You've only just met him and, in any case, a treatment centre isn't the best place to make conquests because neither of you has any idea what the other is like in the real world outside."

"But I can't live without him."

Henrietta (35) and Adam (21) left the Treatment Centre together arm-in-arm. They were using drugs again before they even got to London. They had used each other as a substitute for drugs – but the pull of the real thing was stronger and, in due course, we got them back into treatment, one at a time.

Relationship addictions are difficult because of the continuing need to differentiate a normal (even loving) relationship from an addictive one. Doesn't it take all the fun out of life to have to check on relationships all the time? No, it doesn't. This is precisely how a relationship addict can make sure that a particular relationship is the real thing rather than just another fantasy, doomed to destruction.

Not all relationships that addicts make are necessarily addictive. Not all addicts are relationship addicts. But some are and their problem can be determined on either of these questionnaires, depending upon whether they tend to make "dominant" relationships, threatening to harm the other person in some way, or "submissive" relationships, threatening to harm themselves if the other person doesn't act in the way the addict wants.

As before, two positive answers indicate the need for further assessment, four spell trouble.

DOMINANT

1. Do I tend to look for, or take on, positions of power or influence so that I rise to a position of emotional or practical power over others as rapidly as possible?
2. Do I find it difficult not to take up a position of power or influence when it is available, even when I don't really need it and see no particular use for it?
3. Do I prefer to have power and influence in all my relationships rather than allow myself to be vulnerable?

4. Am I afraid that my life would fall apart and that others would take advantage of me if I were to give up the power and influence that I now hold?

5. Do I regularly undermine other people's positions of power or influence even though they may have significantly less than my own?

6. Do I find that having all the power and influence I need for my own personal and professional life is irrelevant in deciding when to stop seeking more?

7. Do I tend to use a position of power or influence as a comfort and strength, regardless of whether there are particular problems needing my attention in other aspects of my life?

8. Do I look for all opportunities for power and influence as and when they arise?

9. In a new relationship do I feel uncomfortable until I hold the most powerful position?

10. Do I tend to neglect other aspects of my life when I feel my position of power or influence is under threat?

SUBMISSIVE

1. Do I tend to be upset when someone close to me takes care of someone else?

2. Do I feel that I am a real person only when I am being totally looked after by someone else?

3. Do I find that other people tend to express progressively more concern about my dependent relationships?

4. Do I tend to find someone else to be close to me when my primary partner is away even briefly?

5. Do I tend to find a new close relationship within days or weeks of the failure of a previous one?

6. Will I venture into company only if I have someone to look after me?

7. Do I feel an overwhelming sense of excitement when I find a new person to look after my needs or a new way in which an existing partner could look after them better?

8. Do I tend to think that a close friendship is when someone else really looks after me?

9. Do I tend to get irritable and impatient when people look after themselves rather than me?

10. Do I feel most in control of my feelings when other people are performing services of one kind or another for me?

Lance (20) (a dominant relationship addict among other things) knew how to get anything he wanted from his mother. If he wanted money he wouldn't even bother to ask for it. If he got into trouble in any aspect of his life he could guarantee that his mother would do her best to tidy things up and smooth things over. He tried the same with us - and with other patients - in the centre but we've seen that game before.

***Denise (22)** (a submissive relationship addict, among other things) walked out of group. I let her go and made no attempt whatever to follow her or to send anyone to find her. We could hear her stomping around upstairs, packing her things, but I just carried on with the group. Denise may have hoped that the compulsive helpers in the group would be worried that we ought to do something: but that's their problem.*

Although patients need to focus their attention primarily upon their own behaviour rather than on their past and present relationships, they very much need, as a part of examining their own behaviour, to examine their own disastrous capacity to make addictive relationships. If they use other people as if they were drugs, then their relationships will inevitably fail. On the pain of those failed relationships they will tend to revert to their principal addictions, whatever they may be.

Compulsive helping

Addicts love compulsive helpers: they can pick them out at a hundred metres. They are the addict's potential passport to eternal supply.

***Serena (30)** sold her jewellery because her drug-addicted boyfriend told her that he needed it to pay for a specialist medical detoxification under general anaesthetic. (There's no end to the ridiculous - and even dangerous - ideas that people come up with over detoxification which, in practice, is the easiest, shortest and smoothest part of all recovery.) She was so proud of him - and gave him the money. He spent it on drugs. She apologized to him (it took her some time to work out precisely why it should be her fault but then she got it) for not taking the day off work to go with him.*

***Hazel (21)** was so thrilled to be in recovery and off all drugs for the first time since she was fifteen that she bounced out of treatment, clutching her graduation medallion, and did exactly what we had warned her not to do: she went to see her friend Ronnie, with whom she had used drugs for many years, because she wanted to show him the wonders of life without drugs. She hoped to get him to come to us for treatment. Instead he had her back on drugs within a week: the pain of her failure to help him was too much to bear.*

***Dick (45)** loved his wife even though he didn't like her drinking. "She isn't an alcoholic", he told me insistently. "It's because she has had a lot of stress. She... she... she...". His wife just sat there. There was no need for her to find any reasons for her behaviour: Dick found them all for her. She could go on drinking indefinitely while this wonderful, loyal husband of hers went on explaining things so well.*

Compulsive helping is probably the easiest of all addictions to mock. Certainly addicts themselves commonly laugh at it. The laugh while they are still in active addiction (seeing compulsive helpers as dupes) and quite often laugh at it in recovery (believing that only they themselves have ever suffered). This insensitivity should be infuriating – but the compulsive helpers take it all, believing that they themselves must have contributed to the problem by not doing enough or doing too much or doing things incorrectly or not finding the right specialist or not reading the right book or…

Getting compulsive helpers to look at their own behaviour and see it as progressive and destructive addictive behaviour in its own right – one that has significantly damaged their own lives without actually helping (and possibly even hindering) the lives of others – is exceptionally difficult.

"Oh yes, we're all addicted to something", said Serena brightly. Give me strength!

The questionnaires, as with those on relationship addictions for which these are the mirror image, separate the two types of emotional blackmail: dominant and submissive.

DOMINANT

1. Do I fear being thought of (and perhaps becoming) a callous person if I do not show my capacity for self-denial and caretaking on a daily basis?
2. Do the things I do for others result in there being not much left of my personal life?
3. Do I prefer to look after other people on my own rather than as part of a team?
4. When someone I was caring for recovers do I find life rather empty and sometimes resent no longer being needed?
5. Do I tend to use my self-denial and caring for others as a comfort and strength for myself?
6. Do I tend to adopt a self-denying and caretaking role in many of my relationships?
7. Do I regularly give unsolicited advice to others on how to solve their problems?
8. Do I find it difficult to leave any loose ends in a conversation in which I am trying to be helpful?
9. Do I often stay up half the night having "helpful" conversations?
10. Do I become a real person only when I am tidying up the physical, emotional and social messes made by those for whom I care?

SUBMISSIVE

1. Do I tend to pride myself on never being a burden to others?
2. Are others concerned that I am not doing enough for my own pleasure?
3. Do I try to avoid upsetting other people?
4. In serving other people, do I tend not to count the costs even though they mount progressively?

5. Do I tend to remain loyal and faithful regardless of what I may endure in a close relationship?
6. Do I like to make myself useful to other people even when they do not appreciate what I do?
7. Do I tend to take on more work for someone close to me even if I have not finished the previous batch?
8. Do I feel like a real person only when I am performing services for someone else?
9. Do I often help someone close to me more than I intend?
10. Do I feel most in control of my feelings when I am performing services of one kind or another for someone?

Two positive answers on either questionnaire indicate the need for further assessment, four spell trouble for all addicts everywhere – but most of all for compulsive helpers themselves (if they could ever bear to look at the concept of self).

Other addictions

One thing that really upsets an addict who has battled against compulsion and lost the battle time and time again is when some right twit says "I used to be addicted to collecting matchboxes" or "to scratching my nose" or "to looking at pretty girls ha ha ha". Habits and foibles aren't addictions. They give no insight whatever into a true addiction.

Our questionnaires are intended to cover the whole range of addictive behaviour. The workaholism questionnaire covers hobbies and interests, cults or sects, and the gambling and risk-taking questionnaire covers professional work as well as social activities. Yet there are two areas of human psychopathology which might also be part of the spectrum of addictive or compulsive behaviour: phobias of any kind and obsessive compulsive disorder. I mention these because we see them occasionally in our addictive patients in the treatment centre.

I remember *Shirley (26)* in my general practice, many years before we established the treatment centre. I wonder whether we could have helped her if we had known then what we know now. I remember her being so shy about telling me her problem that she wrote it all down. I still have the note:

"There is something strange about my skin because all the time I feel sensations everywhere on my body, like something wet landing on me. It's only a tiny prick and gone in an instant but I still feel there is something on me – like saliva. Sometimes now it's so bad that it's not even a wet feeling – just something touching me. I feel that something has landed on my clothes. And I have to clean them, have baths, wash my hair, clean tables, chairs, doors, anything that I may have touched. I take a wet soapy cloth and I wipe things.

"I do have the will to get rid of this and have done so in the past. But I feel that I've made the effort so many times I just can't do it any more.

I'm wasting my life away. I know that without this I can have a good life. It's a vicious circle because I find that if I get better and begin to see people again I can't communicate because I have nothing to talk about because all I've been doing is washing and cleaning and this is all I've been thinking about. Therefore I'm a boring person and this makes me depressed and I go right down again.

"Suicide has often occurred to me – but even that is not a way out for me because I care too much for the people who love me to do that. I'm afraid that even when I get better I'll never be rid of it completely because there are places everywhere that I won't be able to go into again.

"When I'm bad I won't leave the house – because the house is the only place that I can actually clean. I'm afraid to go on buses because I've been on them when things have happened – and sat on the seats, touched the railings and so on. When I feel all right and am clean, with clean clothes on, I don't want to go anywhere I've been when I've been 'dirty' because if the thing takes hold again it means going through the same old things again. It's so time-consuming and also money-consuming because I spend a fortune on laundry and cleaning bills. Sometimes it's so bad that I can even imagine things happening to clothes which are in locked cupboards which I don't even touch. I think in my brain that I have touched them and I just don't know whether I have or not."

It seems to me that there is much in common between Shirley's story and many that we hear in the treatment centre. The preoccupation is total and the course of the illness is certainly progressive and destructive. However, that could be said for many clinical conditions. There is no reason why one form of psychopathology should exclude the possibility of another, any more than having diabetes should prevent one from also having appendicitis. Nonetheless, we have seen phobias and obsessive compulsions resolve along with the primary addiction as treatment progressed and on working the Twelve-Step programme. It just makes me wonder.

Part III

Treatment

Quality of life; Brain-washing; Damaging treatments; Spirituality; Detoxification; Anonymity; Therapy; Passive or active therapy; Choice Theory; One-to-one or group therapy; Powerlessness; Intuitive counselling; Recovering addicts as counsellors; Fallibility; Trust, risk and share; Failure; Group power; Life story; Monitoring the patients; Rock bottom; Twelve Steps in group; Research; Counselling skills; Psychodrama; Eye Movement Desensitisation Reprocessing (EMDR); Neuro Linguistic Programming (NLP); Stages of Change and Motivational Interviewing; Expressing feelings; Collage; Writing; Mini groups; Family groups; Magic fixes; The Twelve-Step programme; Unsafe drugs; Love.

In my experience, helping people to rediscover the beauty of life is the most rewarding of all clinical endeavours. This is what I do in my general medical practice, helping people primarily with their physical ailments. That, I hope, influences the quantity of their lives by helping them to become healthier. How much my medical work influences the quality of their lives depends most of all on what that was like in the first place. I may tidy up someone's diabetes, psoriasis or blood pressure, diagnose hernias or cancers and refer on for hospital treatment, do the inoculations and all the other things general medical practitioners do (I enjoy them and I like the patients, otherwise I wouldn't do that work), but the actual quality of my patients' lives – whether they are happy in life and excited by it – depends mostly on issues outside my influence. In patients with addictive disease, however, there is no quality of life: addiction has taken it all and anything and everything I do is designed to help them to get it back.

Katherine (26) came to us from another planet, or so she said. She was one of twelve visitors from space charged with the responsibility of spreading evil in the world. While at university she had become a member of a cult that believed in devil worship and she took regular hallucinogens (mostly LSD but occasionally ecstasy or magic mushrooms) to "broaden her mind". They broadened her mind to the extent that it shattered.

Kay (23) was in treatment at the same time as Katherine, and they made an extraordinary pair. She was also from another planet. She was convinced that she herself was evil and that she should be done away with. Periodically she would slash herself with razor blades or bits of broken glass. She had previously been diagnosed as being depressed or, more specifically, as having "clinical depression", which simply makes it sound more medical and therefore justifying treatment with even more drugs. She was certainly a zombie by the time she came to us.

We gave her nothing more than we had given Katherine: time in a drug-free supportive environment alongside people who also had addictive disease.

It may seem strange that we know perfectly well that self-harming is an addictive behaviour but that we should simply tell Kay to stop doing it. However, we would make exactly the same point to a patient drinking alcohol or using drugs on the premises. The point is that we offer a specific constructive alternative to addiction: the Twelve-Step programme, worked on several times a day in group with similar patients, seven days a week, every day of the year, with no days off (addictive disease doesn't take days off either).

Brain-washing

That level of intensity might be described as brain-washing and of course it is: the brains of addicts need a wash. If the worst that we are trying to do is to put in the willingness to reach out to help other addicts, on an anonymous basis, there can't be too much amiss with that brain-washing, particularly as the Anonymous Fellowships themselves are entirely free and, quite specifically, have no allegiance to any organization of any kind.

One might go further and argue that the rest of the world might, with advantage, follow the example of recovering addicts by giving their brains a good wash and sorting out their real values. This is the ancient lever which anyone can use in improving the stability of his or her own life and thereby come to move the world.

Kay came back into group, sheepishly, and got on with the work... Then she told us that the (lady) consultant specialist in the psychiatric hospital in which she had been treated previously had said that she might have been sexually abused by her father.

If it wasn't one distraction it was another. If Kay had not been abused, then this was false memory syndrome or perhaps just another game to defocus from her primary responsibility of looking at her own behaviour and changing it. If, on the other hand, she had been abused then she deserved to be heard.

I therefore suggested a family conference with Kay and her mother and the three of us sat down on our own to go through it all for as long as it took. Kay's mother expressed total amazement at the suggestion of abuse. She had been very happily married for 25 years and, up to the time of her husband's death from a heart attack, there had never been even the slightest hint of his being anything other than a responsible and naturally loving husband and father. Kay acknowledged that she had no specific memory of any sexual contact whatever with her father. She had simply told the consultant psychiatrist that she couldn't remember much about her early childhood. Evidently the specialist had deduced from that memory blank-out the possibility of sexual abuse. I could not know one way or the other what the truth might be so I suggested that we look in turn at each possibility and see how each situation might influence our actions today.

Kay's mother immediately said that she was prepared to consider the possibility that her husband might have abused Kay if, by doing so, Kay could see how devoted she is to her and how much she would have wanted to protect her. Alternatively, Kay's mother said, if there had been no abuse, then she wouldn't think any the less of Kay simply for considering the issue in the course of a consultation at the psychiatric hospital. Kay then acknowledged that there had been no sexual or other abuse whatever.

Again, as in the case of Katherine but on a shorter time-scale, all we had provided for Kay and her mother was time. They did the work. I must say, however, that I thought Kay's mother was brilliant: I would use her as a psychiatrist any day! The families of people with addictive or compulsive behaviour tend to be much abused. Kay's mother illustrates just how kind and understanding the families can be, despite fearful trauma and even provocation.

Kay and her mother both said later that they felt closer to each other that afternoon than ever before. They both thanked me for giving them back their lives...

Well, did I? I don't see it that way. I'm a professional. I do my work. I do the same for all patients: I provide the environment, establish the clinical philosophy, select and train the staff… and then some of the patients get better and some don't. I'm delighted that Katherine and Kay got better (so far) and I'm sad that others didn't – but I have to be back at work the next day, so I'm not going to lose too much sleep praising or criticising myself. My one overriding responsibility is to see that we continually modify our treatment programme with one aim in view: to ensure the maximum recovery rate. If my ideas don't work in practice then I should change them or I should leave clinical practice: it's as simple as that in my mind.

What these two stories of Katherine and Kay illustrate most of all is the truth of the clinical maxim, "first do no harm". By taking people off inappropriate medications and simply giving their bodies and minds time to sort themselves out, we use their natural healing powers. By providing a supportive environment, with specialist counselling staff and patients selected from the same clinical background, there is no sense of us and them, no sense of overt authority, other than on a purely managerial basis. Even when, on our own insistence, we discharge patients from treatment, we try to ensure that they know what they need to do in order to get better or, alternatively, to find somewhere else to take over their care so that they can start again with a fresh peer group of fellow patients (the primary instrument of therapeutic change). By keeping medical people at a distance from the counselling work, while at the same time respecting their specific professional skills and working in cooperation with them in the overall management of patient care, we try to get the best of both worlds.

Damaging treatments

Mick (30) came to us from Brussels, where his parents work for the European Union. He had been actively addicted to drugs for half his life. Initially he followed the standard progression from cannabis to heroin. By the time we got him he was on 160 milligrams of Methadone a day (40 is a big dose) plus 300 milligrams of Diazepam a day (a colossal dose, 15 milligrams a day would be a typical dose). On top of this he was prescribed both Rohypnol and Temazepam for sleep and had been taking Dihydrocodeine for back pain for over a year. The consultant psychiatrist who was attending him had told him that it would be dangerous for him ever to consider coming off drugs. On top of all of this (and obviously without the specialist's awareness) he was buying other recreational drugs on the black market and funding his activities through drug deals.

His parents were distraught. They had asked and paid for what they thought was the best available advice and had watched their beloved son being prescribed more and more drugs rather than less and less. They too were unaware of his additional illegal supply, but knew about his drug dealing because they came across a police charge sheet for forging prescriptions. Mick himself wasn't aware that his parents knew about it. The situation was already a catastrophe, not simply an accident waiting to happen.

At his parents' request, we took him in for one weekend so that he could see what the place was like and consider coming for treatment. In retrospect I think I made a mistake there: addicts only get better when they are desperate to change, not when they think that treatment might be a nice idea. Yet some patients come in for the wrong reasons but stay for the right ones.

After a month of deliberation, Mick came back to us. Together with the nursing director, I worked out an appropriate detoxification schedule, taking the Methadone down over two weeks and the Diazepam down over four. (As a general principle, addicts who take fistfuls of drugs can be detoxified safely and comfortably much quicker than those who have taken a much smaller dose of tranquillizers, antidepressants or sleeping tablets over many years and are primarily prescription drug addicts rather than "street" addicts.) Mick went ape. He wasn't prepared to reduce Methadone at all. Anyway, he had a holiday booked with his parents in three weeks time and he wasn't prepared to do anything that might upset that: the holiday was important to him. I told him that I would personally drive him to the station.

Mick could have been helped years ago but it will be much more difficult to help him now. The standard clinical approach, using drugs of various kinds, does nothing towards preparing a patient for the philosophical as well as clinical prospect of being totally drug-free, and does a lot to damage it. He is now frightened for himself, but he is also totally in charge of his family emotionally and everyone else, including his doctor who appears to have no alternative strategy to prescribing more and more drugs. We ourselves can only help Mick when he is committed to coming off drugs altogether as an absolute priority. Without that commitment he will duck and dive, weave and wobble, and find one reason after another why it is we who should change our approach rather than he change his. I am not trying to dictate to him; if he wants to stay on drugs, and to continue living the sordid and miserable life that they have brought him, that's his choice. If he comes to us and asks for our help, however, he needs to work alongside other members of the group, supporting them rather than undermining them and expecting the same in return from them.

Anna (30) *was referred to us by a doctor in the Channel Islands. For her depression, for which she had treated herself with numerous illegal drugs and the doctors had treated her with numerous pharmacological drugs and also electro-convulsive therapy, she was now being prepared for the ultimate "treatment": a frontal lobotomy. In this surgical operation the front lobes of the brain, inside the forehead, are cut off from the rest of the brain, and the patient is said to lose the depression, but tends also to lose all inhibitions, with disastrous social consequences.*

Two weeks before the proposed operation, her family doctor, desperate to give her one last chance before the irreversible surgery, referred Anna to us. Both the doctor and the patient knew that our treatment was the end of the line. (It is extraordinary how such a benign approach as ours – not using drugs – should so often be considered only after virtually everything else.) Anna committed herself to the treatment programme and became totally drug-free for the first time since her early teens.

She then got God in a big way, went off to California for training of some kind and is now working with Jackie Pullinger, helping the destitute drug addicts in the walled city in Shanghai. (It is interesting to note that Miss Pullinger's Christian approach is based upon one addict being committed to helping another, as is the non-religious Twelve-Step programme.) If Anna chooses a religious path for her life that's up to her. Whatever else, it's surely a better choice than a frontal lobotomy.

Simply committing oneself to becoming drug-free, and free from all other addictions, is not sufficient in itself. Addicts get themselves off their addictive substances and processes time after time, either with or without help, and are repeatedly determined to stay off. They succeed for a variable time but then most commonly relapse. This is precisely why so many doctors despair of them. The doctors' intentions are good: they want to understand and they want to help. However, because of the way that doctors are trained to think solely in physical, mental and social terms, they tend to fail to understand or help a primarily spiritual condition.

Spirituality

A spiritual disease of hope, love, trust, honour, innocence and all the other beautiful abstract aspects of our lives needs to be treated primarily with those abstracts on a continuing daily basis. That, rather than simply getting off addictive substances and processes, is the real treatment of the madness. The common factor in long-term success (not only in coming off and staying off addictive substances and processes, but also in maintaining a happy, constructive life and developing mutually sustaining personal and professional relationships) is the practice of taking attention off oneself, putting down all self-pity and blame, and committing one's self to helping other addicts.

Then why should it be that we have doctors and nurses, teachers and clergy, and all manner of people from the caring professions coming to us as patients? Surely they already do focus their lives on helping others?

The answer to that appears to be in two parts: firstly, that they may not be as caring as they thought when they first chose those professions and, secondly, that there appears to be something specific in the process of helping other addicts. The madness of other addicts reminds one of one's own, and one's own recovery resonates with theirs.

Nonetheless, when patients first come to us with their addiction problems, it is reasonable for them to be focused on their immediate fears: the process of detoxification and the days of initial abstinence when their inner emotional and spiritual emptiness is laid open and raw. The process of detoxification is very much easier than patients and their families, and even other doctors, usually imagine.

Detoxification

In the treatment centre we have a set of standard protocols for each addiction and we very rarely need to go outside those guidelines. Cannabis, ecstasy, LSD, amphetamines and even cocaine (including its smokeable, and therefore faster-acting derivative, crack) require no medicinal detoxification. A gentle physical and emotional environment is all that is required. Occasionally some mild night sedation is helpful for the first week, but no more.

Alcohol is safely detoxified on Chlordiazepoxide (Librium), starting in doses that often frighten the chemists: 25 milligrams of Librium or 10 milligrams of Diazepam (Valium) three times daily and then reducing to zero over four days. Phenobarbitone will need to be added in a reducing regime over the first week if the patient has ever had epileptic fits, as severe alcoholics often do when trying to give up by themselves.

Heroin can be safely detoxified on Methadone or Lofexidine over four days but we sometimes extend that to eight. Methadone addiction itself takes longer because, in our experience, it is a more addictive drug than heroin and is harder to come off. Even so, two weeks detoxification on Methadone itself in reducing doses, should be enough. I have known treatment centres use Clonidine rather than Methadone because this enables them to avoid all the palaver of getting a licence to stock dangerous drugs but we find that addicts prefer the smoother detoxification that Methadone or Lofexidine provides.

I know of some treatment centres that simply use warm baths and massage for heroin withdrawal and there are many that use all sorts of physical and quasi-spiritual approaches to assist withdrawal. This leads to many spurious claims for methods of "treating" addiction. Simply getting off the drugs is not treatment: it is only the first and easiest part of it.

The really difficult physical detoxification is from benzodiazepine tranquillizers and sleeping tablets and from antidepressants. As previously emphasised, benzodiazepines have to be taken down very slowly to avoid severe emotional backlash and even the risk of suicide. By reducing the total quantity taken each week by one seventh, and spreading the remainder as evenly as possible throughout the week, the full detoxification programme takes seven weeks. Sometimes we take people down at half that rate, according to our clinical assessment. Antidepressants should also be tailed off slowly, usually over a period of three or four weeks.

The real problem with these prescription drugs lies not so much with the detoxification process itself but with other factors altogether. Firstly, the cost of in-patient treatment is prohibitively high for a long-term detoxification but the reliability of out-patient detoxification is highly suspect, particularly when patients find it so easy to persuade doctors to prescribe. Secondly, the benzodiazepines in particular, but other prescription medications as well, can have an enormously long-term effect on suppressing natural feelings. Patients who have come off benzodiazepines often say that it took up to eighteen months to feel their true emotions, whatever the pharmaceutical literature may say about various drugs being short or long acting. This has great significance in group therapy: the prescription drug addict is not fully sensitive to the feelings of the group and may see the process in merely intellectual terms. This helps neither the patient nor the overall function of the group.

There is no easy solution to the problem of managing prescription drug-addiction. The best approach is for doctors not to prescribe mood-altering drugs in the first place, other than in the very short term, but preferably not even then. There are better ways of dealing with emotional stress and there may be better people than doctors for dealing with anything short of major psychoses.

Phyllis (55) had been prescribed tranquillizers and sleeping tablets by her doctor when she got into an agitated state soon after the birth of her first child thirty years ago. She has gone on taking them ever since. She came to us because her husband had said that he was fed-up with living with a zombie. We gradually reduced her medication over a period of eight weeks. Other patients came and went and Phyllis said that she felt she was a failure. From our point of view she certainly wasn't one of our successes. She had attended all the groups but she never really became part of them. She was polite and respectful, of course, but never spontaneous or creative. It just wasn't in her to be so: such spontaneity and creativity as she may once have possessed had been systematically drugged out of her over the years.

She asked for a weekend at home, just to be normal with her family again. On the Saturday morning she went straight round to her doctor, complained that she felt stressed, and came away with a prescription for tranquillizers and sleeping tablets.

Dr John (50) was a benzodiazepine addict and was, and still is, a practising doctor. He told me that one of the happiest days in his life was when he found tears running down his cheek during a sad moment in a film. It had been eighteen months since his last use of any prescription drug. His feelings had returned. Nowadays he does what he can to help other benzodiazepine addicts. He has no interest (any more than I do) in helping people with court cases against the pharmaceutical companies (the proof of blame is too complex and time consuming) but he is devoted, as I am, to helping patients to get off inappropriate medication (not all medication is inappropriate) and to increasing the awareness in the medical profession of the dangers of prescribing any mood-altering drug at any time.

The most difficult of all detoxification, in my experience, is from anorexia. How do you get someone not to *not* do something? The double negative illustrates the problem. One can, of course, use intravenous or naso-gastric tubes and force-feed patients. When one sees the CT scan films and realizes how physically shrunken the brain of an anorexic patient can become, it is reasonable to wonder whether any counselling programme is appropriate at that stage. The first responsibility of care must be for the physical recovery of the brain, as much as for the rest of the body.

Shirley (35) has been a determined anorexic for years and has seen pretty well every doctor in London who has any interest in the subject. When we took her into treatment it caused a furore. I was told by the consultant psychiatrist who had seen her for the last year that it was irresponsible of me to take her into a non-hospital environment when her weight was only seventy pounds, which at a height of five feet four inches is very thin indeed. My response was that we had been asked to see her by her own family doctor and we were simply trying to help her in a way that had not been tried before in twenty years of treatment.

In the eight weeks she was with us she put on only four pounds. I did not consider that to be sufficient commitment on her part and, following my specific repeated warnings, I discharged her back to the care of the consultant psychiatrist. We hadn't done her any harm but I cannot say that we did her any good. Interestingly, both Shirley herself and her family doctor believe that we did help her and Shirley tells us that her hope is to put on another ten pounds in weight and then come back to us for further treatment. She understands our approach by now and says she wants to try it. In the meantime she has returned to her work as, would you believe, an alternative therapist.

I'll say she's alternative! I suppose the consultant psychiatrist would say that I am as well, but I certainly do not see myself that way. I am an orthodox practising doctor with no interest in what are generally called alternative therapies. In fact I am adamant in keeping acupuncture, homeopathy, osteopathy and chiropractice, Chinese herbal medicine, radionics, Reike, reflexology, irridology, neuro-linguistic programming, hypnotherapy, astrology (which has therapeutic pretensions), art therapy and flower arranging and even dietetics out of our treatment programme because I want nothing whatever to dilute the clear message of the Twelve-Step programme. For the same reason I keep all religious denominations outside the treatment centre; we have no chapel or even religious books of any kind. What people themselves choose to believe is up to them, but in the treatment centre and counselling centre we do Twelve-Step treatment, just as dentists do teeth, gums and jaws, and that's that. My concern is that the Twelve-Step programme in Minnesota Method treatment centres should be seen not as something alternative but as mainstream (exactly as confirmed by the USA matching study).

Spirit is as much part of human life as body and mind, and it is this concept that I want to be seen in its clear form, uncluttered by other therapeutic approaches, in the treatment centre and counselling centre. If at times I challenge my professional colleagues head on, it is only because I think it clinically inappropriate that Minnesota Method ideas should

117

continue to be peripheralized (particularly since the publication of the NIAAA matching study in the USA). Other people make similar points on the peripheralisation of different therapeutic approaches but, while respecting them, I leave them to fight their own battles.

The exciting advances in any branch of medical practice rarely come from looking at sensible ideas. Existing approaches come from what are considered sensible. Advances can only come from looking at ideas that initially appear crazy. One cannot make an exciting new omelette without breaking a few traditional eggs. This principle applies to heart surgery, immunology or any other branch of clinical practice: if we don't look outside our existing concepts we shall stay stuck. In the tragic and fearful case of our existing understanding of, and treatment for, addictive and compulsive disorders, we simply cannot afford to stay stuck: we are being overrun. I respect my professional colleagues for their specialist training and experience but I shall always challenge ideas and hope that they will challenge mine. In that way we shall progress in our understanding of addictive disease and modify our treatment so that more patients benefit.

Shirley made no spiritual movement at all, in my view, in the eight weeks that she was with us. I wouldn't expect any movement in the first four weeks in someone with anorexia because it takes at least that long for the patients to trust us not to bribe and punish them in the ways that they are traditionally bribed and punished. ("Eat up and you can have your visitors to see you; lose weight and we shall put the tube down again.") After that first four weeks we expect patients to show that they understand the nature of a spiritual disease and spiritual recovery programme and get on with it. We do not supervise meals any more, we simply expect the natural consequence of working the recovery programme: that the body weight will put itself right when the feeding regime puts itself right after the spiritual commitment is made. In this respect there is no difference in our treatment of anorexia and our treatment of any other addictive or compulsive behaviour.

We look at the underlying spiritual disease, not solely at the physical or mental ways that addictive disease affects each individual. Obviously the specifics of each patient's addiction are important (we are concerned for each patient as an individual, with a unique blend of addictive behaviour, background and consequences), but the similarities between all addicts and addictions are the solid foundation on which we base our understanding of addictive disease and our treatment for it.

Shirley was still playing food games, discussing the merits of this or that nutritional build-up programme and so on, whereas we had wanted to move her towards talking about Shirley.

Our clinical approach towards detoxification from anorexia (starving is a mood-altering process) is to use Naltrexone. This drug is used elsewhere as an anti-euphoriant "to maintain abstinence" in heroin addiction and, more recently, for the same purpose in alcoholism. We use it for neither and shall never do so because we have the opposite aim: we want people to express rather than suppress their feelings. We use the Anonymous Fellowships (with the alternative mood-altering process of reaching out to help other addicts anonymously) to maintain abstinence and maintain a drug-free life, so that the patient is free to experience all the joys and sorrows of daily life. In anorexia, however, we use Naltrexone for the first four weeks of treatment simply as a detoxification regime, countering the mood-altering effect of starvation and hence enabling the patients to take in sufficient nourishment to enable their brains as well as the rest of their bodies to be less starved. After that four weeks, the treatment proper can begin, by which time at least we have more of a human being – and less of an automaton, as we had in Shirley – with whom to work.

Clint (40) is a pop singer. We have had a number of well-known people through the treatment centre but the press cause us particular difficulties when we have pop singers in our care. They do their best to make the patients "special and different" at the very time that we are emphasizing to them that their recovery depends fundamentally upon seeing themselves, in this particular aspect of their lives, as just the same as any other addict. Doctors can fall into exactly the same trap when treating famous patients: by seeing them as "famous" we risk giving them bad clinical care because we take into account something that is clinically irrelevant. Exactly the same principle applies to famous (notorious) addicts. They should be respected as individuals, not worshipped as idols, when they are in treatment.

Clint had been given primary treatment for his eating disorder elsewhere but had been prescribed Prozac as an antidepressant "to help him through the particular stresses of his job". Like hell it did: it simply provided an alternative drug for his addictive disease to latch on to. I don't believe we have ever seen the real Clint. I don't believe he has either and I believe he deserves better than that.

Anonymity

As far as the Anonymous Fellowships are concerned, there is no big difficulty for famous people. Alcoholics Anonymous in London even pokes fun at itself by having a Sunday morning meeting entitled Stars on Sunday (after the name of an old television programme) which various well-known stars, and other hopefuls, regularly attend. They are no more conspicuous there than a boy with a title at Eton. However, the famous alcoholics soon get known in AA for who they really are, rather than for their professional persona, and they blend into the background with everyone else. They are no more special and different than any other addict turning up, say, at the Narcotics Anonymous "early risers" meeting at midday on Saturday. It is this general principle – that all addicts are the same in their addictive disease but different, once they have the capacity to be so, in their recovery – that we emphasize in treatment.

Evelyn (50) is a man. His parents thought it special to give him a name more commonly used by women. He has thought himself special ever since. He is special as an individual – but he's a very ordinary drunk.

"I need a private room and a television and my own telephone. I won't be attending group therapy: I need individual counselling, preferably with a consultant psychiatrist – but one of the junior doctors would do at times… Do you have access to the local golf courses?"

Therapy

I am often asked why we don't do much one-to-one counselling, except for initial assessments. The first reason is very simple: it doesn't work. At the very time that Evelyn is asking for help, his internal spiritual parasite – his addictive disease – does its best to push it away. In a one-to-one consultation the disease easily gets the upper hand. It will connive and manipulate every way it can. The counselling session becomes a tug of war or a stand-off, with a truce being the furthest that the disease is prepared to go in any negotiation. Addicts want one-to-one consultations precisely because they know they can control them. They want to talk about their childhood and their depression and all the unfair things that they want to believe caused them to behave as they do. They have years of experience of manipulating and controlling their families and many other people, including their employers (who often want to prove themselves to be good employers by being as helpful and understanding as they can be) and their doctors (who like to believe that they have counselling skills above all other). Tackling one counsellor is child's play.

The second reason is that it can be very damaging to the counsellor. Addicts know perfectly well that a bit of flattery will get them everywhere.

Evelyn knows exactly how to play it. "I must say you have extraordinary insight. Nobody before has ever asked me quite the questions you asked, nor paid such personal (if I may say so) attention to my answers."

In theory, any counsellor should see that blatant strategy and be aware that whatever follows it will be the true game-plan for which this was the set-up. In practice, the only counsellors fully immune from this will be the strictly analytical psychotherapists because they, quite deliberately, have no human interrelationship with their patients – which is precisely why they would not be able to help addicts in this aspect of their lives (the addiction itself) in the first place.

As counsellors we get carried away with our own importance only too readily. When patients say "Thank you so much – you were wonderful", we should wonder what we have done wrong. Our function must always be to help patients to use their own and each other's resources and to know that they are doing so. I knew that there would inevitably be trouble when I heard one of my former counselling staff being described as a "healer". I fear that he himself also thought that. It was only a matter of time before his personal grandiosity led him to cause more damage than good. It is because of this precise addictive characteristic of grandiosity that Alcoholics Anonymous warns that the focus should always be on principles rather than on personalities. It did not surprise me to learn that this counsellor had stopped going to meetings of Alcoholics Anonymous some months previously. (There is no way of knowing when a counsellor stops going to meetings unless he or she says so. One can only note changes in each counsellor's behaviour and be concerned over possible causes.)

Passive or active therapy

The tragedy is that patients themselves can collude with the problem of inappropriate counselling or, at least, help it to grow. By wanting passive therapy (anything that is done to them or for them such as prescriptions, homeopathic medicines, Chinese herbal medicines, acupuncture, massage and manipulations of various kinds, radionics, reflexology and a whole range of cosmetic or emotionally interventionist surgical procedures such as liposuction and stomach stapling), patients become their own worst enemies. By devolving responsibility for themselves on to a medical or non-medical therapist of some kind, they lay themselves open to much damage. Patients, by abdicating responsibility for how they feel, create their own feeling of vulnerability. They need to be actively involved in their own care.

Choice theory

The alternative to active therapy, in which the patient has responsibility and the counsellor merely reflects, informs, offers choices and discusses the consequences, is much more demanding on both patients and counsellors.

Dr William Glasser, the consultant psychiatrist originator of choice theory and reality therapy, a delightful man with a truly original mind, tells the story of a lady who plonked herself down in front of him and said "Let's do therapy!". I have a lot of time for that approach in so far as it implies that she herself might be actively involved in getting herself well.

Passive therapies of all kinds are immensely popular, but it takes only a moment's reflection to see that they could not possibly work for any emotional problem: we ourselves are the only people – through our own positive actions and through our choice of response to the actions of others – who can ever influence how we feel. The statement "He (she or it) *made* me feel..." is always untrue.

Dr Glasser himself coins new verbs from nouns in order to illustrate this point. Instead of acknowledging the clinical state "depression", he says that people choose the behaviour that seems most appropriate to them at the time – and hence "I depress" becomes a statement of choice. I depress when I believe that circumstances make it appropriate to depress. I depress when I cannot see what else to do. I depress in the hope of influencing others to help me. When they do help me, my choice of strategy is confirmed as beneficial and I remember it for further use at a later date. When people say "Pull yourself out of it", it confirms my belief that no one (yet) understands me. Then on to the scene comes the therapist, the magician, the healer, the shaman, the astrologer, and I am healed, if only temporarily, and I can say "There you are, I told you I was unwell". Bingo!

We see exactly the same in political terms, particularly on welfare issues, when people say "The Government ought to do something". In saying that, they lose sight of their own personal responsibility towards their fellow men and women and, by giving more power to the State, they erode their own freedom and that of everyone else. The principle of passive therapy is as dangerous in national and even international terms (when people look to their governments to solve domestic problems through taking national or international action) as it is in one-to-one therapy.

Dr Glasser also provides a very valuable insight into the motivation of human behaviour by saying that each of us carries in our heads two sets of pictures, the one describing the "how it is" world and the other describing the "how it should be" world. The mismatch between these two sets of pictures generates the sense of unease that leads us to make changes. Sometimes we try to change how things are in order to make them conform to how we believe they should be. At other times we modify how we believe things should be in order to make that conform to how things are.

This is exactly the process that takes place as addictive disease progressively tightens its grip. When addicts find that their behaviour repeatedly fails to conform to their values they eventually give up trying to change their behaviour and instead they modify their values. This is the origin of the cultural changes that one observes when addicts get together: they create a new system of values. In this way addictive disease progressively drives the sufferers down and down and further away from their previous values and behaviour. Inside them there is the terrible tussle between their former value system saying "Help me", while their addictive disease says "Get away from me".

Externalization, the process of believing that the true cause of a problem is outside rather than inside ourselves is a universal danger but it is a particular risk for addicts. Denial, the perception deficit in addicts by which their own addictive disease tells them that they haven't got it, insists that all life's problems are out there rather than in here. In a treatment centre, a whole group of such people trying to say that to each other simply doesn't wash: each may believe it of himself or herself but not of the others. It is on that principle of appropriate confrontation, and the principle of mutual support, that group therapy should be built.

One-to-one or group therapy

Furthermore, the personal secrets that each addict believes he or she could never divulge outside a one-to-one consultation often turn out to be common experiences among many addicts. It has been said that addicts are as sick as their secrets. By sharing these secrets with just one other person one may be inviting that other person to collude with the belief that one is special and different. By sharing one's innermost secrets with a group of other addicts, even a very small group of three or four people, the secrets lose their power to cause further damage. The commonality of addictive behaviour, and of the understanding of it and of what to do about it, are what binds the Anonymous Fellowships together and gives them the concept of fellowship.

It is often thought that group therapy is impersonal or that the purpose is to save time or make money. Those charges are possibly justified when there is no common psycho-pathology in the participants. There is no possible therapeutic gain from putting addicts into any form of group alongside general psychiatric patients. However, when addicts are alongside other addicts, and only other addicts, they are both mutually supportive and mutually challenging. They are individually expert at one-to-one manipulation but they can't take on the whole group. They get caught out and the whole group responds with the kind laughter of recognition of psychological games that all have played in the past. In such a group counsellors who are not themselves addicts are at a distinct disadvantage. The instinctive understanding, based on experience of their own addiction, gives recovering addicts a head start when they become counsellors. Further, they are instinctively trusted by the patients, whereas the insights and even the motives of other counsellors may be questioned.

The group, assisted by the counsellor's skills in helping them to work constructively rather than punitively, confronts denial, but at the same time provides support. In the very act of pointing out that someone is not special and different as far as addictive disease itself is concerned, the group is in effect also saying "the worst you have to acknowledge is that you're just like us". Again, this can only be said if the group is composed solely of people with addictive disease. Furthermore, the counsellor who is a recovering addict (working the recovery programme of the Anonymous Fellowships on a day-to-day basis) can demonstrate that he or she has personal, as well as professional, recognition of the difficulties involved in taking that first step of admitting that one is indeed an addict and that one's life has become unmanageable.

Powerlessness

Jacob (52) knew that first step from memory. He had recited it many times in meetings of Alcoholics Anonymous. Finding himself back in treatment for the third time in five years was more than a disappointment – it was infuriating. "I thought I'd got back my self-control", he said, remorsefully.

"Then what do you think it means in Step I when it says 'admitted we were powerless'?", asked the counsellor: "It doesn't say that you've lost a bit of power. You've lost all of it, just as a girl can't be a little bit pregnant: she is totally pregnant or not at all."

123

The point that the counsellor was making to Jacob is that he had never fully acknowledged his alcoholism as something that he is stuck with for the rest of his life. There is no point in him debating it or wasting valuable years of recovery in trying to find doctors or other people to confirm that he can go back to sensible drinking. There are plenty of doctors, and plenty of other people, only too eager to persuade him that he can return to sensible drinking and, in doing so, be normal. Alcoholics know they cannot – but, of course, they have first to know that they are alcoholics: this is the essence of Step I. Simply reciting Step I is not enough: one has to know its truth as applied to oneself.

The process of acknowledging that one is an addict of any kind is in fact a grief reaction. As such, it follows the pattern of any grief reaction: denial at first, minimizing or denying the problem altogether, then anger that one should be singled out and also anger at everyone else involved, then depression as the anger turns inwards, then bargaining as one begins to try to negotiate acceptance of one's problem on one's own terms, and, finally, full acceptance that the truth is the truth.

This process takes time. It isn't something that can simply be shrugged off or rushed through. It takes as long as it takes, depending on the severity of the grief. Recognizing that you really have lost the one you love is desperately painful at any time for anyone in any circumstance. When the love of your life has died, the situation is dreadfully sad. When the love of your life has left you for someone else, you are haunted each day. When the love of your life is still there, beckoning you on but then causing you catastrophic pain each time you have contact, what is that? That is the grief reaction of addiction.

Terence Gorski, president of the CENAPS corporation in the USA, is a widely respected researcher into all aspects of addictive disease and especially into relapse prevention. He, in line with the Steps of Change model, estimates that each addict negotiates his or her recovery for about two years before giving up and then for another two years afterwards. This is the duration of the grief reaction in addiction. This is generally the minimum time that it takes for any addict fully to accept Step I, the admission of total powerlessness over the use of mood-altering substances and processes and that his or her life really has become unmanageable. Dry drunk behaviour (experiencing the inner emptiness of addictive disease but denying one's self the former treatments) or going into other forms of therapy as an escape route, are no more than an extension of this period of negotiation before finally accepting Step I.

As if that wasn't bad enough, the whole process of the grief reaction has to be repeated, at differing levels of severity, with each addiction that the addict may have. Giving up drugs and alcohol produces one grief reaction, but giving up nicotine at a later date produces another. The prospect of having to look at one or more of the various remaining substance or behavioural addictions is understandably daunting. Our advice at the treatment centre is therefore that our patients should tackle all their addictions in one go. This produces a deeper initial grief reaction (which is why some counsellors, inadvisably in my view, suggest dealing with only one addiction at a time), but at least, under our regime, once patients have gone through it, that's the end of it.

Mary (25) successfully completed treatment with us for drug addiction and subsequently did so well in recovery, putting her life back together, that her mother began to look at her own alcoholism. Mary's mother Nancy (52) came into treatment and gave up alcohol and subsequently, a year later, gave up smoking as well. That second grief reaction caused her such pain that she now makes a point of coming back to the treatment centre periodically to speak to current patients (we have such visits as a formal part of the treatment programme in the evenings each weekend) in order to encourage them to take the opportunity to give up smoking at the same time as everything else while they are in treatment with us.

In addition, in order to avoid having to go through further grief reactions, the other reason for giving up all one's addictions at once is that there is no point in hanging on to a potential focus for addictive disease to lead one back to subsequent relapse.

Intuitive counselling

I visualize each of us having an identical internal magical glass container for our senses, feelings and values. I see it as a straight-sided tall glass. Floating in the air inside this glass are the whole range of human senses, feelings and values, not as solids or liquids, but as images like three dimensional holographs with associated sound, smell, taste, touch, vibration and the capacity for resonance with others. The magical glass is empty in the way that an organ pipe is empty but, whereas the organ pipe can produce only sound, the magical glass is sensitive to all the senses, feelings and values. This is where the wonderful abstracts (such as hope, trust, honour, innocence, love and beauty) all live and bring value and purpose to our lives. I suppose, all together, I would call these abstracts the soul.

Some glasses have bits of junk in them, representing unresolved trauma: the debris of our childhood, grief and resentment that has not been sufficiently processed, disappointments that have not been laid to rest, anger that is rekindled when a current event reminds us of a previous one or when a new relationship is dogged by memories of another. A glass so full of junk has little capacity to create its special magic.

Then into this glass is poured a liquid (that I visualize looking like molasses) that represents addictive disease, not the specific addictions that result from it but the evil underlying cause of all of them. Just as oil can be processed into aviation fuel, plastics, and a wide range of specific substances, so this evil liquid addictive disease has the potential to form many specific addictions. This addictive disease liquid clogs up the magic glass so that it cannot function effectively to bring out our full range of feelings and resonate sensitively with others. The addictive disease liquid is replenished by any active addiction in the same way that a daffodil bulb produces a flower and is subsequently replenished by it and made able to multiply itself.

The process of recovery is comparable to getting rid of the junk and stopping the production of the evil liquid. The glass becomes progressively emptier and its beautiful magical functions are restored.

There is considerable debate in Minnesota Method treatment centres on what one should tackle first: the junk or the evil liquid addictive disease, or perhaps just one specific addiction. Whole treatment philosophies differ over which of these we consider should have priority. There are treatment programmes that are based on first getting rid of the junk, in particular the trauma from early childhood. I believe this approach to be mistaken because it so easily leads back to blame and self-pity, the prime nutrients of addictive disease. The time to look back is when one is already in firm recovery from all one's addictions. Then one can see the junk clearly and look at it with understanding and even, at appropriate times, with humour.

Correspondingly, I personally believe that one should look at all one's addictions all at once, so as to stop the continuing reproduction of the evil liquid addictive disease. It never dies but it can be put into remission in limbo. It cannot touch us so long as we remain aware of its existence and do not release it by refeeding it.

Recovering addicts as counsellors

The reason that recovering addicts should never begin training as counsellors for three years or more after getting into recovery is because putting down all one's addictions, so as to turn off the production of addictive disease evil liquid, and then dealing with all the junk, takes at least that length of time. Also, one needs to live a bit in the real world, so as to have the experience and understanding that provide a firm base for the future. (There is more to life than simply getting into recovery: that is only the starting position, enabling us to gain new experience and understanding in the same ways that normal people do.)

When recovering addicts have clean magical glasses that are capable of resonating with those of other people, then they are ready to begin training as counsellors. If their own magical glasses are in poor condition they will project into patients, or into other people or institutions, the problems that are really inside themselves. They will not be able to be sensitive to what is happening in other people's emotional lives because their own magical glasses are incapable of sensitive resonance. For exactly this reason I believe that many existing counsellors should stop doing this work altogether and not consider returning to counselling work at all until their own magical glasses are free from all addictive disease evil liquid and all junk.

Tony (35) is a registered mental nurse and, as such, has a broad range of training and experience in dealing with emotionally disturbed patients. In his nursing training he had been taught counselling skills so he considers himself to be a counsellor. His whole life is dedicated to helping other people. As a student he used a variety of drugs, as many students do as part of their culture. He married and divorced and has a teenage son. Thus, he has human experience as well as some significant professional skills. As a counsellor, however, he was a disaster. He had not matured beyond his student days, still considering the occasional binge on drugs or alcohol to be "fun", even while working in a treatment centre. He had not dealt with the disappointment of his divorce and was on the lookout for new conquests in a far from appropriate manner. When his son suffered a particularly stressful incident, Tony went completely to pieces. He remains talented, likeable, committed, all sorts of things – but he should not work as a counsellor for several years, if at all.

The selection, training and supervision of counselling staff is the foremost responsibility of the director of a treatment centre or of any organization employing counsellors. I do not believe that counsellors should ever work on their own (they usually call themselves therapists or even psychotherapists when they do: their grandiosity goes with the isolation) because all counsellors need constant, rather than periodic, supervision. The work is hard, dealing with the madness day after day. The emotional demands are considerable and, when things go wrong, the risks to patients are immense. Then, most commonly, the damaged (and damaging) counsellors sometimes have the nerve to refer to "burnout" as if it was an infliction from outside, rather than a disease from within! Counsellors have a responsibility to take care of themselves. This does not mean that they require lengthy holidays or that they should be cosseted and pandered to by supervisors. It means that they have a fundamental responsibility to ensure that they themselves remain abstinent from all mood-altering substances, processes and relationships. When they are fully abstinent, the work is no more stressful, but a great deal more stimulating and rewarding, than any other occupation. Otherwise, the stress that they feel will be from living a lie: teaching one thing but living another.

Teresa (38) has a lot of skill. She has been in good recovery from alcoholism and drug addiction for six years or more. She went through her counselling training successfully and was able to preserve a lightness of touch and a sense of humour. In this she is rare. She is friendly and absolutely devoted to caring for patients.

Then where and why did it all go wrong? The end result was easy to see, and it came on suddenly, but where did the decline begin and could the senior staff and supervisor have observed it earlier?

The end result was seen in three separate ways: she was too thin, she had a flurry of arguments with other counselling staff and she declared undying love for one of the patients. I believe that all three of these events are in fact interrelated and that they came from one common source.

Firstly, it had been noticed that she was getting thinner and her colleagues had commented on it, pointing out that they were not making personal remarks nor, as she might have hoped, were they being complimentary. They had also noticed, and told her, that she tended to be less direct than other counsellors when dealing with patients with eating disorders. She let the patients get away with things and they thought she was wonderful. She made the public observation that maybe the treatment of eating disorders in that particular treatment centre was too rigid and that perhaps there were several different kinds of eating disorder requiring different approaches.

Secondly, she had been on the receiving end of a lot of back-biting when she refused to get involved in an earlier episode of madness among some of the former members of the counselling staff of that centre. She had become isolated but she had never really come out of that shell when new staff were taken on.

Thirdly, she is becoming increasingly aware that she is getting older. She is lonely and she wants to get married, settle down and have children before it's too late. There's nothing strange in that but the potential for damage depends how the urge takes her.

Behind these three strands is, I believe, one common source: the individual therapy that she had been having from a "therapist". In focusing on her individual guru she lost sight of the general principles of the Twelve-Step programme and of the HOW (honesty, open-mindedness and willingness) of continuing recovery. By becoming enmeshed in "issues", particularly those concerning her early childhood, she made a mess of current personal and professional relationships.

By assuming that her recovery was secure, because she still goes to appropriate Anonymous Fellowships for her alcoholism and drug addiction, she left herself vulnerable to her addictive disease letting rip with an eating disorder, with the result that she had to modify her attitude towards patients' problems in order to accommodate her own.

In becoming progressively more emotionally isolated, she came to believe that a specific solution (the discovery of a new love in her life) was an act of God. In personal terms it could be. It is not for anyone else to judge. In professional terms, however, her declared love for a patient was incompatible with continuing as a member of the counselling staff in her treatment centre and she was referred to us for treatment. Irrespective of whether love had resulted in sexual activity, she could not have been sufficiently emotionally stable to be trusted with patients' lives. It's a tough world and there was no responsible choice other than to suspend Teresa from counselling work. Nevertheless, she should be seen as being unwell rather than unethical or deliberately undermining or destructive. She therefore had to be helped to find appropriate support outside her own treatment centre, preferably in one where she can be completely anonymous, just like any other patient. Like sufferers from any other illness, she can go back to work when she is finally well.

But who looks after me? I am myself an addict. I work under enormous strain. I do two full-time jobs (my general medical practice and helping to run the treatment programme in the treatment centre and counselling centre) and I get tired. I have constant financial concerns and political battles to fight. I have personal and professional worries and preoccupations, as we all do. Our dog died a dreadful slow death. My parents both died in recent years. My work is mostly dismissed by my professional colleagues as being misguided and I am more often seen as a flamboyant nuisance than as a serious thinker. I have plenty of problems and if I go crazy then a lot of people can get hurt. How do I know that I am right in my insights and decisions?

The answer to that question is that I don't know, which is precisely why I work as one of a team of counsellors, rather than on my own. Even management decisions are discussed with senior counselling staff. I believe that my principal fault in my management of the treatment centre over the years is that I have sometimes been too prepared to listen and too slow to make firm decisions – but that's what I would say, wouldn't I?

The answer to the first question (who looks after me?) is that I look after my addiction in the same way as other addicts, by going to regular Anonymous Fellowship meetings (three a week – and that's a very small price to pay for what they give me) and I look after my own madness by working the Twelve-Step programme on a daily basis, I read the Fellowship literature, and I have a Fellowship sponsor to guide and cajole me. I remain abstinent from all mood-altering substances and I examine (and sometimes rationalise) my addictive behaviour. I also have a professional supervisor. I do all this to influence the plasticity of my brain.

Fallibility

But most of all – the absolutely most important feature of all – I do make mistakes. That, I believe, is my greatest security: I know that I am fallible. This is the essential message of all the Twelve Steps for continuing recovery from addictive disease and it's a good principle for living a healthy life, even for non-addicts. When counselling staff acknowledge fallibility, it could be argued that we spread an air of insecurity among the patients. The important fallacy in this is that perfection is impossible in any activity. Strange though it may appear, perfectionism is an addictive characteristic, to the extent that if something cannot be done perfectly then it is deemed best not attempted at all. In this way perfectionism goes hand-in-hand with procrastination, another addictive characteristic. Thus, acknowledging fallibility is a mark of recovery, along with punctuality and the completion of projects to which we set our hands. Recovering addicts are not perfect. We make mistakes, acknowledge them and try to remedy them, but, nonetheless, we give life our best shot. We no longer sit back, pronouncing on the imperfections of the world and all other people in it. We get up out of our chairs, get involved in life, take appropriate risks – and acknowledge when things go wrong. Then we start again.

In the introduction to our counsellors' handbook in the treatment centre, I have stated that it is deliberately loose-leaf rather than bound. This enables us to be challenged on our ideas and see where they can be improved. At any one time we have to have an agreed set of policies because otherwise we would have loose cannons going off all over the place and the patients would soon divide and rule. Nevertheless, those policies are flexible, rather than cast in stone, and we need to consider alternatives if we are to progress. If we do not acknowledge our capacity to make mistakes, we can never grow.

Trust, risk and share

This process is mirrored in the encouragement given to new patients in the group: "trust, risk and share". Learn to trust that you are in a safe place among friends who have similar experiences, take the risk of letting us see your pain and fear (there is no point in bluffing because we know about it anyway because we ourselves have "been there, done that and got the T-shirt") and share your feelings and experiences with us, so that we can help you to bond with us and learn how to move forward towards recovery. This is the very opposite of being told what to do by knowledgeable experts, especially when they play cognitive behavioural mind games, as if addicts don't know that A leads to B. Addicts of all kinds know perfectly well that A leads to B, but they don't know how to stop doing A and then stay stopped.

A new patient entering the group feels a sense of shame and failure, often showing itself in anger and defiance. In fact these new patients should be given credit for the courage that they have shown in fighting the impossible battle of trying to prove to themselves and everyone else that they are not addicts. This courage has enabled them to survive, even while driving themselves further into the clutches of their disease. Indeed they have failed – but what a magnificent failure!

Lilly (41) was in trouble with alcohol, but she was damned if she was going to admit it. Anyway, she knew the solution to the small problem that she did have with alcohol: transcendental meditation. She showed me an article that proved how successful TM is in curing alcoholism. Impressive graphs illustrated before and after. I assured Lilly that I very much support the idea of meditation as a part of the recovery process, helping to settle oneself and develop an awareness of wider perspectives than one's day-to-day preoccupations.

"No", she said, "it's not that. It says here that it cures alcoholism."

"Nothing cures alcoholism, as I fear you will have to find out for yourself", I replied.

"I'll show you that I can drink just a bit when I want it and no more", replied Lilly. "When I was in the day-care programme, trying to be totally abstinent, I found that the pull of alcohol grew and grew in my mind. It's much better – and less extreme – to know that I can have just a little when I want it."

A month after this conversation, I received a letter from Lilly's family saying that it was scandalous that we had charged so much for her treatment when it hadn't worked. She was back on a nine-day binge, drinking more than a bottle of vodka a day. The concept of passive therapy, the belief that we are, or someone is, responsible for doing something to Lilly, dies hard in Lilly and her family. The truth is that there is nothing that we can do to her at any time. We can work with her but not on her or for her. There is nothing we can do until she acknowledges that her own chosen therapeutic methods of treating alcoholism are a total and absolute failure.

Failure

The concept of failure being a tragic and shameful event is deeply ingrained in our society. I recall this being challenged brilliantly by the Harvard theoretical sociologist, Professor Robert Nesbitt, in a talk at the Queen Elizabeth Conference Centre in London. He cited that great philosopher Shulz, the creator of the "Peanuts" strip cartoon:

Charlie Brown is attending the psychiatrist, Lucy.

"Well, you know how it is, Charlie Brown," she says, "You win some; you lose some."

Charlie Brown, who has never won anything in his life, replies: "Oh that would be wonderful!"

Professor Nesbitt uses this story to illustrate that we train our children to admire success in a competitive society. Yet success is so transient and rare, whereas failure is an everyday occurrence for all of us. We should help our children to understand and accept failure as no big deal.

My brother and I play tennis. He wins. My son Robin and I play tennis. He wins. Anyone wins when playing me at tennis. So what? I still enjoy it. I used to enjoy drinking alcohol but I'm no better at drinking than I am at tennis and, try though I might, I couldn't get better at it. I always went for the sweet drinks: Sauterne, Bristol Cream sherry, Benedictine, Cointreau and they sparked off an eating binge, not because of the alcohol as such but because alcohol is a refined carbohydrate and those substances have a mood-altering effect on me. (This is why we recommend all eating disorder sufferers not to drink alcohol.)

I have to accept that I am a failure when it comes to managing my consumption of sugar and refined carbohydrates. Others have to accept that they are failures at drinking alcohol without it damaging them. So what? Where's the big deal? Interestingly, some people might smile at my persistence in playing tennis, even though I enjoy it, whereas they might feel very uneasy at my acceptance that I just don't drink because I'm not good at it. I don't mind if other people drink but I myself choose not to. Why should Lilly, and others like her, feel such a sense of failure at not being able to drink sensibly? Why should it matter to other people?

In fact I find that it really doesn't matter to the vast majority of other people at all. It really isn't of more than fleeting interest to them whether I eat sugar or drink alcohol or not, unless these substances have the same central importance to them that they used to have for me. Lilly's concern is that she will lose her friends and stand out as an oddball in her society if she doesn't drink. That may well be true because she has probably surrounded herself with people who have the same vital relationship with alcohol as she does.

Coming into treatment, Lilly and others like her have the opportunity to see that they are not the only ones to discover that they cannot control their use of mood-altering substances and processes any more. There is no disgrace in that, no sense of failure: it's just a fact for some people.

The early days in treatment have several simultaneous functions: detoxification where necessary, combating the denial, bonding with the other members of the group, and gaining a sense of hope for the future. Of these, detoxification is the most straightforward. The other three simultaneous functions are more complex and require considerably more skilful management.

Group power

Combating denial cannot be done by saying "Surely you can see that you are an addict? Look at what you do and look at the consequences". That obviously rational approach doesn't get through to an irrational disease. Denial is not an avoidance mechanism, any more than it is simple stupidity. Denial is the genuine belief that there is no problem or, at the very least, that such problem as there may be is not of great significance and certainly nothing to do with addiction.

Simon (16) says he is not a compulsive gambler: he says he simply steals money in order to play on slot machines.

Jean (40) says she is not an alcoholic: she says she is simply lonely and depressed and drinks for comfort.

Eric (25) says he is not an addict: he uses only cannabis and he's sure that's not addictive.

Paul (35) says he is not an addict: he uses cocaine, but he says he only uses it – he's not addicted to it.

Serena (22) says she is not anorexic: it's simply important to be slim and she hates feeling fat.

Johnny (40) says he is not an addict of any kind and he finds it highly offensive to be thought of in these terms at all: he smokes forty cigarettes a day simply as a bad habit.

Put all these people in a group and they can see the shallowness of each other's defences and hence gradually develop the insight that their own defence may be equally shallow. That is the way to combat denial: leave it to the patient, in an appropriate group setting, to come to his or her own conclusions.

Bonding with the other members of the group is a vitally important aspect of early recovery. Patients are allocated a "buddy" from amongst the other patients so that simple questions are easily answered. Staff members may be too far ahead in their own recovery, let alone too busy on other matters, to have the insight into how strange and fearful the early days in the treatment centre can be. Another patient, who has only just gone through the process, remembers it only too well. Patients in the detoxification cubicles in the nursing station are visited by the other patients from day one so that they do not become isolated. As soon as they are capable of standing up and walking around they are transferred to the main house and are expected to take part in all-group activities, even while still feeling rough, still on medication and having to attend the nursing station for regular check-ups.

All the bedrooms in the treatment centre are shared and patients go to them only in order to sleep at night. Again, this is to combat the terminal uniqueness that is so terrible a part of the disease: addictive disease drives patients to isolation, to despair and ultimately towards suicide. Allocating a special nurse to monitor the potentially suicidal patient twenty-four hours a day is a totally misguided approach. Firstly, it medicalises both the problem and the solution and creates an inappropriate dependency. Secondly, it underestimates the potentially suicidal state of all patients at this stage. Thirdly, it fails to use the supportive resonance that is already available (the other patients) and which, in due course, will always be available through membership of the Anonymous Fellowships.

Initially people often complain about the prospect of sharing bedrooms but, very rapidly, "room-mates" become the most effective instruments of recovery. It has been said before that the real work of a treatment centre begins after the counselling staff go home in the evenings.

By the same method of leaving patients to learn from each other, they gain great hope for the future.

Hester (22) was terrified of food. She had been for years. In hospital, when she was off the drip-feeds, they sat her down with the nurses so that every mouthful was supervised. Now, in our treatment centre, she ate with everyone else (although initially her portions were plated for her by the kitchen staff who have special training in preparation of food for eating disorder patients) and she was most definitely not monitored by staff or by other patients. Meal times are for fun and conversation, not for the torture of monitoring one's self or others. Hester learnt most from Janie (24) who had been in treatment for six weeks.

"I don't really have a problem with food", said Janie encouragingly, "I have a problem with me."

I could say exactly that to Hester myself – and have done so – but I don't get through to her in the way that Janie can. Patients get enormous encouragement from each other and they readily believe that each can do what the others can do, whereas they may be daunted by the counselling staff, let alone by the medical or nursing staff.

Our counselling staff, even with the advantage of personal experience to help them in understanding the patients, focus their attention on helping them to bond with each other rather than with various members of staff. The "nutrient-authoritative" or "re-parenting" approach, often seen in eating disorder units, is, in effect saying "I can be a better parent than your own parents". This is highly disrespectful, arrogant and undermining: hardly the best clinical and personal principles. In general, patients are more respectful and sensitive to each other and this is what should be encouraged because of its therapeutic potential.

Life story

Getting to know each other begins by each patient telling the others a half-hour "life story". This has two advantages, firstly purely social but secondly clinical: patients can sense what has been left out of the story or glossed over or rationalized away. "You didn't mention your husband at all" or "Did alcohol come into any of this?" or "If it was all so perfect what are you doing here?" are comments that patients will usually accept from each other, but might initially find intrusive from counselling staff.

In due course, when patients are more familiar with the honesty that is expected of them, they are asked to present "A day in my life", illustrating just how crazy this could be. Again the purpose is to use the group to combat the denial. People do not come to treatment centres without good reason. They might like to believe that they had "just a little bit of bother over the last few months", but it cannot possibly be true. By working in group, each patient discovers not only that it is impossible to bullshit a whole group of experienced bullshitters, but that it is helpful to tell the truth and learn from the experience of the group: collectively they know a huge amount about addictive disease and are daily learning progressively more about the early stages of recovery.

The phrase "collectively they know a huge amount about addictive disease" is every family member's nightmare, rather than reassurance. This is because of the contrast between what they know about their own relative and what they think they know, primarily from press reports, about addicts in general. Certainly a group of addicts or sufferers from any compulsive behaviour, put together, can get up to a great deal of mischief, learning all the devilish tricks of the trade from each other. This happens not only in prisons or ghettos but in hospital wards or eating disorder units. To some extent it can happen in a Minnesota Method treatment centre, but it should be possible to smell it out. When abstinence is the common goal, any addictive behaviour is a risk to the entire group. A new sense of loyalty is therefore instilled: loyalty to recovery rather than loyalty to the disease. Patients learn to confront (appropriately, with concern and support rather than with hostility) any suggestion of residual addictive values or behaviour in each other. Again, the strength of this process lies more in the group of patients than in the staff.

Monitoring the patients

Nonetheless, it has to be acknowledged that no therapeutic environment, or school or prison or any establishment whatever, can be totally free of all addictive behaviour at all times. Outbreaks of using behaviour among a few patients, colluding with each other, are bound to happen occasionally.

Peter (42) developed a particular fondness for walking in the country lanes near the treatment centre, accompanied by Nancy (30) and Gillian (21). A stroll round the fields and back through the village seemed a good, healthy contrast to sitting around in the grounds of the treatment centre day after day. Patients are allowed out in groups of three in the belief that this reduces the risk of collusion. Not in this case. Gillian lived locally and on one trip they left some money behind the village telephone box. On the next trip they collected the drugs dropped there by a dealer whom they had contacted by telephone.

The end result of that escapade is that it became rapidly apparent that the three of them were not making any progress in their recovery. They contributed little to group and complained of being confused. (As a rule of thumb we know that "confused" means "used" – something addictive.) They were generally argumentative. The suspicions of the group were aroused and the two girls walked out of treatment, complaining that they were not being treated fairly. Nancy regretted it and the whole business came to light. Peter was discharged from treatment and fairly soon afterwards I received a remorseful letter from him in prison. Nancy came back into treatment and did well. Gillian is still out there, doubtless still fidgeting irritably as she used to do in group. Doubtless, she still believes that she is too young to be an addict and that we are stupid to say that she needs to give up alcohol as well as all drugs even though she has never had a significant problem with alcohol. Doubtless she still believes that we don't know what we're talking about.

Sometimes we use urinary drug screens, but most commonly the group does the diagnostic work for us, as it does, for example, when anorexic patients form a vipers' nest together. To refer to their interrelationship as a "vipers' nest" may seem a bit strong for these perfectly behaved waifs. Anyone who has ever tried to confront an anorexic patient directly on eating behaviour or on body weight, however, will know that just one viper can cause plenty of trouble, let alone a group of them. Yet, again, the desire for recovery in the group (because they can see it in a Minnesota Method treatment centre, whereas they may never have seen it previously) is ultimately stronger than the resistance of a few individuals.

The fear of family members is often that their own sweet, innocent child will be corrupted by other patients. Indeed this can happen, as it can anywhere, but we tend to find that the family who is most concerned about this problem brings in a right pest to an otherwise peaceful house.

Angie (25) is wide-eyed and petite; a little angel. As her mother said, it was so sad that she had been influenced by other girls at work. Her mother was very concerned that Angie, who had bulimia, might be led into really bad ways by the addicts and alcoholics in the treatment centre. In due course we learned that in the psychiatric unit, from which she had been transferred to us, Angie had offered sexual favours to all and sundry in exchange for drugs. It became apparent that her bulimia was not her only addictive tendency and that she simply is not the sweet, innocent, child that her mother believes her to be.

Despite these startling or racy stories, the vast majority of our patients are straightforward men and women whose greatest risk is to themselves rather than to each other. The early days in recovery can leave a great sense of raw emptiness, particularly when several addictive tendencies are tackled at once, as I believe they should be. This rawness is the core of addictive disease, the loneliness that patients have been trying to treat in their various ways with mood-altering substances, processes and relationships. Will it ever go away? What could possibly take the place of the previous addictions? The immediate answer to this question is sometimes seen across the room.

Bernie (26), tattoos stretching and relaxing themselves on his biceps below his T-shirt, says that he needs to talk about his sexuality, having lost touch with it while in prison.

Chloe (21), cashmere pullover from Harrods, blushes demurely. Saints alive, what now? If Chloe's mother gets a whiff of this it will be the end of our referrals from anywhere in South East England. She'll tell her husband, the company chairman; he'll have a word or two with the family doctor; the buzz will go round the Chelsea Clinical Society, and we're done for.

Mercedes (22) says she can't stay in treatment any more. She has developed the hots for my son, Robin, the in-patient director.

Robin knows perfectly well how to look after himself in such circumstances and is concerned more for bed-occupancy figures in the treatment centre than for the prospect of his own bed being invaded.

Jack (30), his pony-tail swishing across his shoulders, says "I can't handle this stuff about not having any new close relationships in the first year or two of recovery."

Matilda (25) looks him up and down.

Belinda (36) bursts into tears and leaves the room.

There are times when the treatment centre seems more like a dating agency. There are treatment centres where the sexes are kept strictly apart. I believe this to be unrealistic. Patients need preparation for the real world. The risks in early recovery from forming and breaking close relationships are very real and these need to be discussed, hopefully without too much practical demonstration, while patients are in treatment.

The feelings of raw inner emptiness cry out to be filled by anything or anybody taking the former place of addictive substances and processes. These feelings simply have to be survived. It's tough but that's the way it is, if one wants to avoid developing another addiction. Whatever it is that one has given up, there are bound to be, not only the initial cravings of withdrawal (which are easily covered, where appropriate, with detoxification medication), but also the subsequent sense of emptiness. Furthermore, addiction suppresses the pain of the normal human experiences of growing up and of reacting to the difficulties and tragedies of life. When the agents of this suppression are withdrawn, the addicts are suddenly faced with the prospect, often for the first time in many years, of having to face the full range of human feelings as well as take on the normal range of adult responsibilities. All the pain and learning processes of adolescence have to be experienced. They were only postponed and cannot be avoided.

On the other hand, the joys of recovery are as intense as the sorrows. Whereas in active addiction the good feelings got closed down along with the bad, now in recovery the good feelings re-emerge at the same time that bad feelings have to be faced. In short, the addict emerges from the anaesthesia of addiction to the full experience and passion of human life.

Maggie (36) was insufferable. She had had a sparkling personality all her life. She had absolutely no need to take anything to get high. She was high by nature. However, behind the sparkling front was the inner emptiness of any addict and this had led her to alcohol and drugs, particularly cocaine. Life was one long party for Maggie and she enjoyed it and her friends enjoyed her company. In addiction, inevitably, all good things come to an end and Maggie was eventually indistinguishable from any other addict. In place of the sparkle was a brittle, critical, self-pitying mess. Her boyfriend of the last seven years gave up on her. This was the best thing he could have done for her because within a few months she was so lonely and desperate that she sought treatment. Within three weeks she was bubbly, sparkling, fun to have around the place, and totally insufferable to anyone who wanted to be gloomy and pathetic.

"Do you want to go back to drugs now?" I asked her.

"I never want to see another drug in all my life", she replied.

Many patients say that and think they mean it, but the resolution rarely survives the acute crisis that they are in. They take the next opportunity they have to use drugs, and they relapse. They still see life without alcohol and drugs as boring and depressing and life with them as fun. In Maggie's case the opposite was true. She didn't want the fun that alcohol and drugs had brought her. It wasn't fun at all. It was degrading, depressing and dangerous. She wanted to be herself again.

"I believe you", I said, "It is quite clear from your sparkling nature that you have genuinely turned the corner. You've had enough. That's why the patients who still resent giving up their addictions find you insufferable!"

It is interesting that addictive behaviour is so commonly represented in the press as being fun – until it eventually gets out of control. I was recently asked to write a comment on an article giving the story of a man who claimed to have had three thousand sexual partners by the age of thirty-two. I wrote about the happiness that one gets from having just one sexual partner. The editor didn't want to know. All he wanted was an account of how one identifies sex addiction. The happiness that one can get from developing just one relationship is not good editorial copy: it is boring, self-satisfied and, frankly, a turn-off that won't sell magazines.

Daisy (36) *the exact same age as Maggie, came to my office in London in a terrible state and said "I've been injecting cocaine all night. I've got to have something to help me. I'm going to die".*

"What sort of help do you want?" I asked her, knowing only to well what the answer would be.

"Drugs."

Rock bottom

The essential difference between Maggie and Daisy is that Maggie has had enough and Daisy hasn't. This needs to be emphasized because the concept of what constitutes a rock bottom in addictive use (after which one wants to turn the corner to get into recovery) is much misunderstood. Daisy was in a far worse physical, emotional, mental and social state than Maggie, but still fighting to prove to herself and to the world that she could do things her way. Maggie had had enough of that futile battle. Her rock bottom was at a much higher level than Daisy's. The level of each individual's rock bottom varies. Some have had enough pain fairly early on; others seem to need to get fairly close to death's door; and it can be anywhere between these two extremes.

The members of the Anonymous Fellowships who believe that one has to lose absolutely everything before getting into recovery are wrong. Only too often that principle leads to loss of life. The only thing that an addict needs to lose is the determination to prove that he or she is in control. This is precisely why the concept of helping alcoholics to return to sensible drinking is such a tragic, even criminal, misunderstanding of the nature of addictive disease. The concept of harm minimization in drug use is equally fallacious and dangerous. The harm for an addict is in using any drugs at all.

As family members, friends, employers or colleagues at work, doctors or other members of the helping professions, we all have enormous potential to do harm to alcoholics, drug addicts, eating disorder sufferers, compulsive gamblers and addicts of any kind. We risk their lives by doing too much to help them. By taking responsibility for them we reduce the likelihood of them coming to the point where they recognize the need to take responsibility for themselves.

Addicts of all kinds (if we want to be truly helpful to them) are best left to get into the whole range of problems to which their addictive behaviour leads them. This concept of "tough love" goes against the grain, but it works. This is what brought Maggie into treatment and what kept Daisy on the streets. Daisy is surrounded by "helpers", whose personal and professional helping brings her death closer each day.

By now Daisy has major medical problems that have to be helped. These medical problems could have been avoided if only people close to her had allowed her to get hurt from her own actions, rather than kept forever bailing her out and hoping that she would "see the error of her ways" or respond to some good sensible advice, tender loving care or (saints preserve us) "counselling". The best counselling of all is to stand back and do nothing whatever and let the addict experience the full consequences of his or her own behaviour. We do not need to create trouble, the addict can be guaranteed to achieve that on his or her own. What we need to do is the easiest thing to understand but the most difficult thing to do in practice: leave him or her in pain. This works for one simple reason: the only thing that ever motivates an addict to change his or her behaviour is pain. That sentence is worth repeating so that its full significance sinks in: the only thing that ever motivates an addict to change his or her behaviour is pain.

Maggie had had enough pain. She didn't want the life she was living. It hurt too much. Daisy might have changed earlier if she had also been allowed to feel the pain of her addictive behaviour, rather than have one person after another respond to her blaming and self-pitying bleats by "helping" her. Now she really is in danger, as she herself fears, of losing her life. Her only chance now, in my view, is in a residential unit that can cope with her medical condition and with her addictive disease and recovery. Simply helping her through the medical crisis will not be enough, however many wise words of caution, encouraging hugs, improving homilies or heaven knows what else are given to her by people who believe these processes to be helpful. They are not. She needs the understanding and example of other addicts who know how to guide her first faltering steps in a Twelve-Step recovery programme.

Dick (32) is the subject of a television documentary. The television company hawked him around various treatment programmes. He became a star. His whole emotional investment was in showing how difficult he is to treat, because he is "special and different" (that phrase again). He decides what treatment is appropriate. He decides when something is too emotionally painful to contemplate. He knows that the cameras will follow dutifully wherever he leads. On the standard naive pretence that the press only report but never create their stories, the producers watch him, fascinated by his self-destruction and conscious of their viewing figures. In my view, Dick will get better only when he is in sufficient pain to want the recovery programme for himself, not for fame or fortune.

__Robin__, our son (p.65 and p.92–3), was given the choice of being drug-free in our house or of having his drugs but finding somewhere else to live. He left. We knew perfectly well the risks that an out-of-work drug addict would inevitably run but we also knew that for us not to leave Robin to his fate would cause even bigger risks later on. We got on with our own lives, going out to our favourite restaurants, cinemas and theatres, playing tennis (badly, as before) seeing our friends and talking on every subject under the sun except addiction and never on what Robin might be getting up to. Then, later, when Robin did re-establish contact he saw the quality of our lives and what he had been missing in contrast to the sad emptiness of his own life. He asked for help.

Let's hear it again, one more time: the only thing that ever motivates an addict to change his or her behaviour is pain. Not only is there no need to cause pain, because the addict has plenty in his or her own life provided that one does not go to the rescue, but perhaps the greatest pain, and therefore the greatest influence towards changing behaviour, is the contrast between the quality of his or her life and other people's. When an addict sees other people getting on with their lives and being genuinely happy, while he or she feels wretched and miserable inside (whatever is said or put on for other people on the outside), that is pain.

No addict can afford to be allowed or enabled to be special and different. Only when he or she is out of the limelight (of the family environment, hospital ward, television studio or wherever) and treated as just another person or patient, with a very particular type of illness requiring a very particular type of treatment, will he or she be able to begin the painstaking but infinitely rewarding process of becoming an individual human being again.

In group all patients have equal status. That is the therapeutic strength of the group. Outside issues are left outside. Financial or professional status are outside issues. Race and sexual preference are irrelevant issues. Marital status, age, physical characteristics or illnesses, are all outside issues. The one and only inside issue is the desire for recovery from addictive disease.

__Tony (50)__ is a professional musician. I grinned at him over the orchestra rail at a concert recently. It had taken him weeks to get the confidence and dexterity to be able to play again when not under the considerable influence of alcohol. He had had to learn his craft all over again when he got sober. The sight of me in the audience was not, perhaps, his greatest moment of inspiration!

Tony told us the story of the two brass players (a notoriously inebriated section of the orchestra) checking-up on their performances the previous evening:

"Did I play okay last night?"
"I've no idea... Was I here?"

Eileen (40) *could have had a solo career as a cellist but alcohol was the stronger pull.*

Frederick (35) *gave us an amazing interpretation of the first movement of the Bartok viola concerto. In his fourth week in treatment, I had asked him to play it so that we could see his soul at work. He had no music; of course not – he's a professional. He had no accompaniment either. Nor even did he have a viola. He mimed it – and we saw his soul at work. I'll swear we heard the music, or at least we felt what it was that Frederick believed Bartok wanted to say.*

All these professional musicians could have assumed that their problems related to being professional musicians. They do not, any more than the problems of drunken or drug-addicted doctors relate to the stress of their particular profession. Our patients are musicians, doctors, accountants, housewives, students, unemployed mechanics, professional thieves or whatever else when they are outside the treatment centre. Inside it they are addicts and they share the common bond of the group, hearing each other, supporting each other, challenging each other, living with each other, loving each other. That's the way they get better from addictive disease: by focusing on each other rather than on themselves.

I consider that all the real work in the treatment centre is done in group. I have myself given over a thousand lectures in the in-patient centre and I also do one a week in the out-patient programme in London. Some of these have been videotaped so as to provide a basic introduction to the concepts of addictive disease and recovery. As such they have some value – but no more than that. They merely inform; they do not help to get anyone better. We have a video library of other people's lectures, including many brilliant contributions from the doyen of all specialists in alcoholism, Father Joseph Martin, from Baltimore, Maryland, USA. He informs, encourages, entertains, inspires – but he doesn't get anybody better any more than I do or anyone else does. He tells the story of the young man who calls out to God that he wants to be a doctor. A voice from heaven replies, "Go to medical school". Addicts have to work for their own recovery. As Father Martin himself says, "Action is the magic word."

Twelve steps in group

In treatment, after telling his or her life story, the first working group in which a patient will be actively involved is a Step I group. In this he or she gives details of how his or her life has been damaged by the uncontrollable force of addictive disease. (Step I is "I admitted that I was powerless over my addiction and that my life had become unmanageable.") The other patients respond by saying where they have identified with the story and they give corresponding examples from their own lives. Thus, all group work serves to bind the group together, to make the patients interdependent rather than self-sufficient or dependent upon the staff.

A patient may need to do several Step I groups if he or she needs to look at a number of different addictive tendencies, or if the other patients do not feel that he or she has looked at a problem in sufficient depth. In this way patients get to know each other very well, they learn how to appraise each other and see past the denial system of defences, and they also learn how to accept and learn from the feed-back given to them by their peers.

The function of the staff is to keep the group on track, to keep it moving, and to make sure that all patients are treated with respect and dignity. Essentially, however, the various Step groups work themselves, through the contributions of the patients. If the counselling staff say nothing at all in these particular groups they have still earned their wages – perhaps especially so.

In our treatment centre we work through all of the Twelve Steps of recovery and do all of them in group. This is unusual in that most treatment centres work on only the first three or, at the most, five and usually get the patients to look at them mostly in one-to-one sessions. Our reasoning is that Step I takes two years to grasp in its full significance and therefore anything that is done in a treatment centre is no more than providing a basic familiarization. The advantage of working, to some degree, on all the Steps is that the patients know that everything they have done in treatment is no more than the beginning: the real work begins again in the Anonymous Fellowships and world outside. We work the Steps in group so that each patient gets the encouragement and support of the others.

Jonathan (35) was very angry when he learned that we had changed our policy so that we now work all the Twelve Steps in our treatment programme rather than just the first five. More than that, he was furious at the prospect of patients doing Step V (Admitted to God, to myself, and to another person the exact nature of my wrongs) in group. We assured him that our procedure was that each patient could choose from among the others a few whom he or she trusted. These, along with a counsellor, would form the particular group for that patient's Step V. We do not require everyone to tell everybody everything. That could be too risky in terms of confidentiality. But, through long experience, we have come to believe the saying that "addicts are as sick as their secrets". Further, as mentioned previously, we have come to believe that sharing a secret with only one other person can be almost as sick as keeping it to oneself. It forms a collusive relationship, keeping the secrets from everyone else.

The purpose of working the Twelve Steps is to acknowledge that the power of addictive disease depends largely upon its capacity to isolate us spiritually from other people. By contrast, also through the Twelve Steps, we learn that other people and a "Higher Power" (than self) have the capacity to help us. The more we share with other people, and the more we acknowledge our essential commonality with all other addicts, the more we accept that our addictive disease led us to do terrible things, and the more we accept the need for a Higher Power than self. (Step II: Came to believe that a Higher Power than self could restore me to sanity.)

Thus, our decision in the treatment centre to work Step V - or at least its first preliminary attempt - in group is in fact an illustration of the acceptance of Step II: as recovering addicts we have to accept our need for other people and acknowledge their collective power to help us.

None of these explanations satisfied Jonathan. He knows better. He is a member of an Anonymous Fellowship and he believes that he knows the way things should be done. Perhaps he is unaware that even Alcoholics Anonymous, the most successful of all the Anonymous Fellowships, believes that it has a success rate of little more than 30 per cent. The primary, if not the sole, function of treatment centres, to my mind, is to see how we can help more people to benefit than would otherwise do so. If doing Step V in a selected group seems to work then that is what we'll do. If it doesn't we'll change again - and risk upsetting Jonathan all over again.

This trial and error principle was exactly how the Twelve Steps were first formulated. They work because they work. Men and women tried them and tested them with their lives. "These are the steps we took…" means exactly that: they were the result of experiment, the discovery of what actually works. When treatment centres stay static, doing the same things this year as last, or as they did ten years ago, they betray their inheritance.

The Twelve Steps themselves need no modification whatever. That research work has been done already and doesn't need to be repeated. Modifying the therapeutic environment, however, so that the Twelve Steps have a better chance of working, is in my view precisely what treatment centres should be for. We have the resources to do the research: this is our prime responsibility. If we focus simply upon making money then we have lost sight of the essential spiritual nature of the programme. If we focus simply on ticking over and getting a few people better we might ask ourselves what we can do that the Anonymous Fellowships cannot do on their own. It is only when we take on the challenge of researching anything and everything that might improve the long-term recovery rate that we justify our existence. Thus, our principal research is our continuing trial and error research in daily clinical practice, keeping our minds open to new ideas by recognizing that every one of our existing ideas and clinical procedures, particularly those we hold most dear, could be wrong or might benefit from modification or refinement.

Research

In addition to outcome studies, following up our former patients to see what became of them, our formal research department, headed by Professor Geoffrey Stephenson, emeritus Professor of Psychology at the University of Kent in Canterbury, has produced the following papers:

"Social psychological analysis of a Minnesota Model Centre for Addiction: patients' beliefs and attribution and post-treatment outcomes" (University of Kent, Canterbury 1994)

"Addictive behaviour: predictors of abstinence intentions and expectations in the theory of planned behaviour" (in D R Rutters and L Quine (editors), *Social Psychology and Health*, Aldershot, Avebury)

"The Minnesota Model in the Treatment of Addiction: A social psychological assessment of changes in beliefs and attributions" *(Journal of Community and Applied Psychology, vol 2, 25–41, 1992)*

"Excessive Behaviours: An archival study of behavioural tendencies reported by 471 patients admitted to an addiction treatment centre"

(Addiction Research, 1995, vol 3, No 3, pp 245–265)

"Some antecedents of "Hedonistic" and "Nurturant" addictive orientations in relation to gender: an archival study" *(Issues in Criminology and Legal Psychology,* 27: 23–33)

"Diaries of Significant Events. Socio-linguistic correlates of therapeutic outcomes in patients with addiction problems" *(Journal of Community and Applied Social Psychology,* 1997, Volume 7: 389–411)

Current research projects are, firstly, looking at the behavioural differences between male and female alcoholics and, secondly, clarifying our observation that patients who remain stuck in their heads have a worse outcome in our follow-up studies than do patients who express their feelings either positively or negatively.

The purpose of our research department is to study the process and outcome of our treatment programme. Certainly we have a lot to learn, as our patients on occasions are the first to tell us:

Jimmy (32) walked out of the treatment centre at midnight on a freezing cold morning in early January. He had been in treatment for only two days on this occasion and he was still being detoxified on Methadone after a six-month wild relapse on sex and drugs. He stole money from other patients and he left behind a letter:

"I simply cannot tell you just how awful it is here. The whole régime has changed. Robert seems to have become an even bigger guru than before. The groups are wishy-washy. There is nothing much I can learn here."

June (56) had severe liver problems as a result of her alcoholism and she also had whiplash injuries to her neck following a serious road accident. After leaving hospital she came to us. She was prepared to acknowledge that she had liver problems and whiplash injuries but not that either could possibly be related to her alcohol consumption. She left treatment in a storm of abuse when she discovered that my letter to her lawyers, prior to her prosecution for dangerous driving, did not present her medical problems as she had wished. (When preparing medical reports I always have the prospect of a hostile cross-examination in the witness box in my mind so I write only what I know I can justify.)

Subsequently, she returned a circular letter to all ex-patients with this note stapled to it: "Do not ever communicate with me again. Delete my name and address from your mailing list. Your so-called 'counsellors' very nearly destroyed me."

These two letters may give an accurate assessment of the staff and of our therapeutic programme. We have to be aware that we ourselves can go off the rails and that our patients are likely to be the first to tell us. On the other hand it is reasonable to take the critics' own state into account. Jimmy was still high on drugs and June was resentful that I did not perjure myself on her behalf. Neither wanted help for addiction. Both wanted somehow to blame us for their condition, irrespective of the state that they were in before they came to us. It is this belligerent attitude that makes addicts of all kinds so difficult to treat: they attack the very people who are trying to help them. No wonder doctors are generally so reluctant to take on this area of work.

However, the challenges and rewards of looking after addicts come in equal measure.

Rory (39) *blasted off a shotgun through a relative's window, not knowing who might be inside. He was fighting drunk at the time, as he was when he was subsequently arrested and as he was again when I saw him for an assessment in our flat in London late one evening. He took a swing at the friend who had brought him. The friend eventually gave up and left him in the street.*

In due course Rory was sentenced to community service and put on probation and given a recommendation that he should have treatment for his various addictions. This was not what he wanted and he left nobody in any doubt about that. His early days in the treatment centre were stormy. He was not physically violent in any way (we have had virtually no episodes of violence in fourteen years of operation of the treatment centre: addicts behave responsibly when treated responsibly and when drug-free) but his bitter resentment towards the whole wide world, and everybody in it, glowered out of him.

A year later I still see him in weekly aftercare sessions, despite the completion of his probation order. He has a responsible job. His principal concern is that he is sad that his long-term girlfriend is still on drugs and therefore simply not safe company for him. He would like to get her into treatment but he knows that he can not force her. He simply waits and hopes that one day she will want what he has now: full recovery and all the wonderful things that go with it.

When receiving letters like Jimmy's or June's or when dealing with really difficult verbal or even physical hostility in active addicts, I know, from the experience of working with Rory and literally thousands of others like him, what they can be like when they are well.

The art of working constructively and happily with a group of addicts of all kinds in a treatment centre depends upon being absolutely convinced of their potential to get better. This conviction is transmitted, probably more non-verbally than verbally, to the patients and they also come to believe it of each other. Even when people relapse, and become critical and resentful, it need not be for ever.

The symptoms and signs of acute appendicitis can be physically dramatic. The symptoms and signs of addictive disease can also be dramatic in all sorts of ways. As counsellors, we come to see appendicitis and addictive disease as having a great deal in common. They are both conditions for which the sufferer is not primarily responsible (although addicts are certainly responsible for behaviour affecting other people) and they are both capable of full recovery when given the appropriate treatment. It is this vision of commonality between those clinical conditions that needs to be taught in medical schools and postgraduate centres so that addicts can get the appropriate treatment for their clinical condition: group therapy alongside other addicts in specialist treatment centres that base their therapeutic programme on the Twelve Steps.

Counselling skills

The foremost skill in counselling is in managing a general process group, where there is no advance agenda: patients are encouraged to say whatever may be uppermost in their minds. The skill of the counsellor is in enabling the patients to speak freely, to express feelings appropriately and to be able to learn from each other. To achieve these three goals, while ensuring that all patients are actively involved and that the group deals with important issues of therapeutic significance (and while keeping within a one and a half hour timescale), takes a lot of learning and a lot of practice.

Most of our counsellor trainees are university graduates and some have previous counselling training and experience. Nevertheless, we ask them to stay silent in group for the first few weeks of their training so that they can learn to observe the process, rather than simply hear the content. Afterwards we ask them to comment on both the process and the content. Only when they can do that effectively are they allowed to begin to contribute.

Desmond (40) had been in analysis for many years and had worked in an analytical group therapy-based programme for nine years before joining our staff as a trainee. "I sense that you don't like me", he blurted out to a patient in the middle of one group. On another occasion, when a patient was telling us about the sexual abuse that she had endured as a child, he gave the opinion that young children can be very sexually attractive and may almost invite physical contact. Interestingly, Desmond was both surprised and hurt when told that his traineeship was terminated.

Angela (32) came to us after working in the prison service. Despite that brutalizing experience, she had a keen sense of humour and a thoughtful mind. She was a knowledgeable and skilful counsellor but she was too knowledgeable, too skilful and too professionally therapeutic. She treated patients as pieces on a chess board. She had all sorts of group skills that she had learned in various training courses but she still had no natural "feel" for the work, no innate personal skill. She also left us at my request.

Anne (30) *had three years of experience in working in a unit for disturbed teenagers and had all the paper qualifications you could name. I came to wonder how that establishment had ever distinguished between patients and staff.*

Beyond their initial training, counsellors also have to re-examine their own ideas as time progresses and treatment methods advance. Time and again we have outgrown some of our own counselling staff and they have had to go. As emphasized previously, the primary purpose of a treatment centre is to do what cannot be done in the Anonymous Fellowships alone. We must constantly re-examine our ideas and practical procedures. Counselling staff who are not prepared to do that have no place being counsellors.

The personal responsibility of each member of the counselling staff is to develop, progressively, the following:

- a securely-established recovery from all his or her primary addictions and from compulsive helping.
- professional understanding of addictive disease and recovery.
- sensitive human insight, based upon increasing clinical and personal experience.
- clarity of personal and professional values.
- technical skill and breadth of professional awareness.
- resilience in the face of personal and professional challenges.

Professional development and individual recovery from addictive disease have one fundamental process in common: they depend absolutely upon putting down self-pity and blame and, in their place, focusing upon how we can be genuinely useful to others. Counsellors should be judged primarily by their actions.

Patients need to be guided and encouraged, not helped or forced. Their own work is what will stand the test of time. Counsellors may know all about the technicalities of counselling (reflecting, interpreting, the theoretical aspects of group processes, co-counselling, being non-directive, and heaven knows what else). They may know the technical stuff (the Karpman triangle of victim/persecutor/ helper, the ins and outs of object relations theory, the stereotypical family positions of hero, scapegoat, lost child and mascot, the concepts of completing the gestalt, the techniques of empty chair work, the concepts of open doors, target doors and trap doors and of existential positions underlying ulterior transactions, and so on and so on), but they still may be absolutely useless when it comes to running a group and helping patients to work with each other in order to get better and learn the inter-personal skills that are going to be some use to them in the real world.

My own experience of employing and training counsellors over the last twenty-two years leads me to the conclusion that counselling is one of the most demanding professions of all and that effective counsellors are born rather than made, even though they then require specialist training. Counselling is essentially a practical skill allied to a sharp mind and a warm heart. To describe it in theory misses most of what actually happens. It has to be seen and experienced.

Any description of what actually happens in a treatment centre is therefore inevitably inadequate. How could one possibly record the interplay between thoughts, feelings and actions of a whole group of people? It can't be dissected theoretically without killing the subject. Suffice it to say that counselling skills in an addiction treatment centre need to be broad-based (some patients respond to intellectual challenge, others to emotional stimulus, some understand when they see things drawn out on paper, others when they experience acting it out) and that no single therapeutic approach gets through to everybody. Variety and spontaneity are the spice and essence of counselling. Mere education and encouragement of patients, important though they may be, are totally insufficient therapeutically. If addicts could change their behaviour simply through education and encouragement, or merely through talking about their feelings and experiences, they would have done so long before needing residential treatment.

Most of all, counsellors have to be intuitive as well as well-informed, appropriately trained and technically skilled. They need a sixth sense and would be lost without it, just as much as they would be lost if they relied only upon it. They need to have their own internal spiritual glasses empty of junk, and of the evil liquid molasses of active addictive disease, before they can begin to resonate with others. Then they need training and then they need experience, day after day after day after day after day.

Edward (52), in the course of his addictive disease that had progressively destroyed every value that he held dear, had repeatedly sexually abused his own daughter. What do you say to him, counsellor?

Jocelyn (20) worked as a homosexual prostitute and is HIV positive. What now, counsellor? What are your goals, beyond the trite advice to look after his health and practise safe sex?

Sandy (25) was often beaten by his father with the buckle end of a belt when he was five years old. His mother showed him an aborted foetus when he was ten. Both his parents are doctors. Do you believe that, counsellor and, if so, what do you do about it that will truly help Sandy?

Joanna (50) has left her husband for another woman. Does it matter to you, counsellor? What sort of family conference would you discuss with Joanna?

These examples are taken from the sharp end of clinical practice. They don't turn up every day in general medical practice, but they can do so in an addiction treatment centre.

John (20) died (overdose).

Stephen (41) died (heart attack following repeated use of cocaine).

Timothy (28) died (suicide).

Miranda (50) died (fell downstairs at home in an alcoholic stupor).

Kate (24) died (road accident after a rave).

...All in one year. If addiction counsellors can't take this heat, they shouldn't be in this particular kitchen.

Psychodrama

Perhaps the most demanding, effective and rewarding of all therapeutic approaches is psychodrama. Its originator, Jacob Levy Moreno, created the concepts of group therapy, psychodrama (acting out a situation so that one can see the patient's perception of reality) and sociometry (a system of measuring preferences within a group so that people get as near as possible to their wishes). Two therapists whom Moreno influenced were Fritz Perls, who went on to create gestalt therapy and Eric Berne, who went on to create transactional analysis.

Moreno's influence has been immense and yet few practitioners have followed him and become proficient in the art that he introduced. Perhaps the best insight into his ideas and clinical practice comes from his own words when he met Sigmund Freud, "Dr Freud, you analysed their dreams; I try to give them courage to dream again".

I believe that the reason Moreno is so little known, and psychodrama so relatively little practised, is that it requires skill. So much therapy is what Terry Pratchett's wonderful character, Granny Weatherwax, calls "headology". Certainly, to have a good head is important for a counsellor but it is far from sufficient. What Moreno achieved was to create a therapeutic approach that involves thoughts, feelings and actions all at the same time. By representing his or her own perceptions in a practical drama, the patient is in control of the content: we see his or her reality and thereby reduce the number of false assumptions that we make. If the patient is crazy we see his or her craziness and why it appears to be sane to him or her. Here indeed is the way into the madness.

Directing a psychodrama involves the capacity to be spontaneous and creative in structuring the drama from the material presented by the patient. At the same time the director has to judge the patient's capacity and readiness to move forward in thoughts, feelings and actions. The psychodrama may look backwards or project forwards in a patient's life or may look at a current situation. It may look at a broad picture of a patient's life, or only a tiny part of it. It may involve a major production employing props and many characters over an hour or more, or it may be a vignette, highlighting one issue or relationship in a few minutes. It helps patients to see their own dilemmas and consider how they might resolve them.

By getting into the realm of feelings and actions in addition to thoughts, a psychodrama is immensely powerful, and therefore as potentially dangerous as constructive. It requires both training and natural skill to be able to direct a psychodrama and it is essentially a practical art. As Moreno said, "Don't talk about it: show me".

*Patricia (35) is severely anorexic. Her husband despairs of her, as do countless other people who have tried to help her. In due course we ourselves may fail, but at least we can try a different approach to the analysis, cognitive behavioural therapy and punishment/reward techniques that have been tried on her before. I got **Catherine (22)** (another anorexic patient further along in treatment) to stand on a chair and represent the great goddess "Thin". Catherine gave out her commandments (coming off the top of her head from her own anorexic experience): "Thou shalt not eat anything that might be fattening, thou shalt burn off calories with exercise, thou shalt not get emotionally close to other people..." and so on. Patricia saw the goddess that she had been worshipping. She also saw how this distanced her from her husband, Richard, (played by **Julian (35)**, another patient). Finally she saw **Jake (25)**, a male anorexic patient, try his hand at confronting the great goddess "Thin" and then **Henrietta (23)**, an anorexic ballet dancer just completing her treatment, who told the goddess exactly what she thought of these commandments that had caused so much destruction in her life.*

Peter (38) is a professional singer and, by now, a professional alcoholic. I stood him on a chair and we all gave him a round of applause... and then another. It was what he had been used to in a distinguished career. His addictive disease knew that and turned it to its own advantage, isolating him from other people. He made his own choice to get down from the chair and rejoin the group as representatives of the human race in general.

*John (25) could sell his grandmother and has quite possibly done so several times. He is a street trader. I got him to sell a fir-cone, a bill clip and a bunch of keys. (The fir-cone was in the fireplace and the others came from my own pocket: one doesn't need elaborate props for psychodrama.) He sold them to **Colin (33)** whom I then asked to reverse roles (a standard psychodrama technique) with John. In this way John was on the receiving end of his own sales patter, now repeated by Colin. In fact Colin embellished it and was extremely funny. I then pointed out to John that his addictive disease also knew how to sell him any drug or any idea: it would find a way of convincing him that it was a* *reasonable purchase. He needs to be aware that his own professional skill could be, and probably has been, corrupted by his addictive disease for its own ends.*

__Brian (40)__ is separated from his wife and sick daughter. They would all like to get together again but Brian is frightened of it all going wrong again. He chose someone from the group to represent his wife Polly, and another to represent his daughter, Samantha, whom we put in a bed made from two chairs. He himself first played their parts to show us how they relate to him. The two patients then took over their roles as wife and daughter and, with a bit of whispered prompting from me, used every possible emotional twist that we could think of. If he can come through that, he should certainly be well prepared for the real situation when it arrives in due course.

__Susan (50)__ is the despair of her family. Her two children have said that if she drinks yet again they want nothing to do with her. Her mother says she needs a psychiatrist and some real treatment, and her husband has given up and simply gets on with his work. I got other patients to play each of those roles and they were shown their basic characteristics by Susan herself. I then got yet another patient to take on the role of Susan. I led the original (real) Susan away from the tableau so that she could see herself and her family dynamic from the outside. She came to see how the whole family revolves around her alcoholism and, in some strange way, almost expects her to occupy the role of family scapegoat. Getting sober will be only the first hurdle that she has to surmount. At least she now knows what she is up against and that she has to take things one stage at a time: getting sober first of all, then taking full responsibility for all her own behaviour and apologizing for the trouble her alcoholism has caused to other people, and only finally having the reasonable expectation that other members of her family might examine their own behaviour.

At the end of these vignettes each patient "de-roled" themselves from the parts that they had played (so that other members of the group would no longer see them in those roles) and each patient spoke about where any of those little psychodramas had impinged on their own lives. The entire group therapy session involving all six psychodrama vignettes took exactly an hour and a half, an average of fifteen minutes each. Twenty-two patients were involved in all and I had to be aware of all of them so that nobody got hurt: one can be as much affected by watching psychodrama as one is by participating in it. I do not believe that that amount of therapeutic work can be achieved in any other way so intensively for so many people in such a short space of time and with such potential for insight and change in patients' lives.

I should emphasize that these psychodrama sessions that I run in the treatment centre each Sunday morning follow a general process group of one and a half hours (after a 15-minute break), so that the group is already "warm". By the time they finish at half past twelve (I always have to keep an eye on the time) we have all of us earned our lunch.

I myself have had the privilege of attending workshops run by Zerka Moreno, the widow and collaborator of the great man, and have had training sessions with Carl Hollander, Kate Hudgins, Marcia Karp and others of his pupils and followers. Psychodrama is not something that should be tried simply because it sounds fun. It is fun but it is also extremely demanding, certainly the most challenging process in which I have ever been involved in my entire life, except perhaps for conducting three performances of *La Bohème* for the United Hospitals Operatic Society, which I founded but which promptly died, yet another illustration of the triumph of hope over experience in my life.

The reason that I mention my own artistic background is that I believe that it is extremely relevant to this work in psychodrama and, indeed, to all counselling work. Firstly, I believe that counselling and conducting have a great deal in common: the skill is not so much in doing a performance as helping others to interpret and create. Secondly, I believe that the only way to get inside the madness of addictive disease is to be more of an artist than a scientist. To be sure, one needs a scientific approach as well, but one is completely lost without equivalent artistic insight and practical skill. This, I believe, is why Moreno's work in particular is so neglected and why the treatment of addictive disease is shunned by so many doctors and therapists of one kind or another. "Headology" is fine but it isn't enough.

Not that I believe that psychodrama itself is essential in the treatment of addictive disease: I don't. However, I do believe that we can only get inside the madness by looking at the soul of the patient, not just his or her mind. Mindfulness, Cognitive Behavioural Therapy and Cognitive Dialectical Therapy are all excellent therapeutic approaches but they are insufficient for addicts. In a one-to-one consultation or group session a whole series of points may be made but how many of them will be remembered? In my psychodramatic vignettes the therapeutic points were simple and easily memorable because they were acted out rather than simply talked about. Further, in a one-to-one consultation only one person gets the benefit of those insights whereas in a psychodrama any number of people may benefit simultaneously at some level. A one-to-one consultation may reach great depths but in a full-length psychodrama, working primarily with just one patient for the hour and a half, there is ample opportunity to look in even greater depth at the psychological and personal problems of that particular patient. In psychodrama there is always some level of therapeutic insight for each of the other patients: in any story there is always something that resonates with the lives of each of the onlookers and this is what they tell each other about at the end of the session. Again the capacity of psychodrama for depth and breadth of therapeutic work all at the same time is unique.

Whereas dreams have been described as the royal route to the subconscious, I see them as no more than the brain doing its housekeeping. Analysing dreams may even cause further dreams so that the whole process becomes thoroughly self-indulgent and self-perpetuating for both the patient and the therapist. I agree with Moreno: the art of helping patients is not in analysing their dreams, but in giving them the courage to dream again through psychodrama.

Sheila (32) was upset by dreams of cupboards, carpet rolls and other items of furniture falling down on her. She didn't understand these recurring dreams and they disturbed her.

I got Sheila to lie on the floor at the feet of three men standing in a line. On my count of three the men fell forward over Sheila, catching themselves on their outstretched arms.

"That's just it", said Sheila, "that's just how it feels".

We did it again and then I took one man away and got another man and woman to stand behind the remaining two men. This time, on my count of three the new man and woman pushed the original two men over so that they fell down as before. I then asked Sheila who she thought the new man and woman were.

"The man is my ex-boyfriend, Jack, and the woman is … yes, the woman is my mother."

We then examined these relationships one at a time. First we got Sheila to reverse roles with the patient playing the part of Jack so that she could show us how he behaved towards her. She (in the role of Jack) produced a storm of criticism and suspicion. Reversing roles back again, the patient playing the part of Jack now reproduced that stream of invective and Sheila, amazingly, just took it. I asked her to pick someone else to play her own self and I brought Sheila over to stand by me to watch as Jack repeated the insults yet again to "Sheila". The real Sheila, seeing the situation from the outside, wasn't standing for that and cried out "No!" and went over, on my instruction, to show "Sheila" how to stand up to Jack and give him a piece of her mind. "Sheila" learnt well and did just that.

Then we looked at the relationship between Sheila and her mother, using the same techniques of role reversal and mirroring (seeing the situation from outside). In this relationship Sheila's mother was pleading with her to change her addictive behaviour and initially Sheila herself was demanding to be given more space and less hassle. Seeing the relationship from outside, however, Sheila recognized that she herself, rather than her mother, needed to change. She then rehearsed her double, the patient playing the part of "Sheila", in how to do that so as to build a better relationship with her mother in future.

We then went back to the original scene with Sheila lying at the feet of the three men representing various items of household furniture. This time, before the count of three was up, Sheila called out "Stop!" … and the psychodrama ended, with Sheila recognizing that she has the capacity to take effective control of her life and therefore to be rid of these troublesome dreams.

I don't know how Sigmund Freud would have analysed Sheila's dreams, but I suspect it would have taken an awfully long time and have had all sorts of sexual significance. This psychodrama lasted just over an hour, from start to finish, with all the participants de-roling themselves and each of twenty-one patients in all telling Sheila the resonance of her psychodrama in their own lives. Analysts might well argue that we simply skated over the surface of Sheila's problems. I think not. We looked into her own perceptions (none of the psychodrama was actually created by me: I simply enabled her own creativity) and we helped her to clarify her confusions, resolve her indecisions – and to dream again, peacefully.

Edward (34) had continuing daily nightmares (preoccupation with grief) from an elder brother who died of a heart attack. Edward was with him the day before he died but not on the evening itself. He still blames himself for his brother's death, believing that he might have been able to help him if he had been there.

I laid three large sofa cushions in a row on the floor and got another patient, representing the dead brother, to lie on them. I placed a handkerchief over his face. Edward spoke to his "brother", saying how much he felt he had let him down. From behind the handkerchief, a voice said that he had done no such thing: only God determines the time of our death.

At that moment I heard tears from behind me. Kim's brother had died in a fire from which she herself had escaped. She joined me, sitting on the floor on the opposite side of the "body" from Edward. I asked Edward and Kim each to choose two special friends from the group to sit beside them for support. I then asked Edward and Kim how much longer he or she wanted to keep the brother's spirit in torment with their own grief. After all this time (three years in one case, four in the other) it was time to let all the spirits (their own as well as their brothers') be at peace. The memories and the loss would still be there but the crippling grief should be resolved appropriately so that each spirit, in his or her own world, can move on.

After a time I asked Edward and Kim to close their eyes and I took away the handkerchief, beckoned the patient playing the part of the "body" to return to his place in the group, and I then took away the sofa seats. Edward and Kim remained supported on each side by their friends. Then they opened their eyes and gently re-entered the real world of the treatment centre. They stood up and hugged each other.

I knew that Mohamed's brother had died in an air crash and I saw how the psychodrama had affected him and I got him to join Edward and Kim. Then Sophie, who had lost her sister and Belinda, who still grieved for her mother, joined them. Then Roland, who had played the part of the dead brother, joined them because (as I knew) he had himself lost a brother. Then Chloe, whose father had recently died, joined the group in the centre of the room in an ever-expanding group of mutual understanding, comfort and support. I checked on all the other patients in turn but no one else acknowledged similar pressing grief.

We stayed in silence for a time and I then suggested that the group in the centre should say the first part of Reinhold Niebuhr's Serenity Prayer that is a Fellowship favourite (to the extent that many people erroneously believe that it was written by the founders of Alcoholics Anonymous).

"God grant me the serenity
To accept the things I cannot change,
Courage to change the things I can
And the wisdom to know the difference."

The group in the centre then returned to their original places in the wider group and I connected all the group together by saying that we all grieve in our own way. Addiction causes terrible damage in our lives. We grieve for being singled out in this way and we grieve for the hurt done to ourselves and to others.

Again we sat in silence for a few moments and then we closed the group, as we always do, by all saying the Serenity Prayer again.

A harrowing group session such as this one looks at the real issues of loss and emptiness, in this case not only the actual loss of loved ones, but also the deeper inner emptiness of addictive disease. This is what we primarily deal with in the treatment centre, not merely the effects of the mood-altering substances, behaviours and relationships with which addicts try to "treat" the inner emptiness that was there long before any specific episodes of loss and grief. Examining and helping the inner emptiness, and guiding patients towards the continuing use of the Twelve-Step programme as the effective continuing way of treating it, is the essence of all our counselling.

I personally favour psychodrama as my own preferred therapeutic approach, but each of our counsellors uses his or her own training and experience in the way that he or she finds most comfortable and effective. Throughout all is an undercurrent of cognitive behavioural therapy, despite its primary ineffectiveness in treating addicts. This paradox is explained by the fact that addicts will generally change their behaviour according to their feelings rather than their thoughts. Explaining something rationally to an addict will often get absolutely nowhere. Nonetheless, when he or she feels something (most commonly through an experiential rather than analytical therapeutic approach) then understanding and behavioural change may follow. Thus, our work is cognitive behavioural in effect, but it can only be approached through the patients' feelings.

Eye Movement Desensitisation and Reprocessing (EMDR)

EMDR is the brainchild of Dr Francine Shapiro, a research psychologist from California. She discovered that alternating stimulation of one side of the body or the other (through vision, sound, touch or vibration) could lead to both the thinking brain and the feeling brain being active at the same time. Getting the patient to follow the movements of the counsellor's hand, sweeping from one side to the other across the patient's field of vision, enables previous haunting images, self-talk, emotions and body sensations to be resolved and replaced with the appropriate responses that one should give to traumatic circumstances. In particular, the negative self-image that often accompanies trauma is dissipated. Although primarily used in the resolution of post traumatic stress disorder, EMDR has widespread applications throughout all areas of psychological distress. It does not heal an addictive tendency – only the Twelve Step Programme can do that on a continuing basis – but it resolves the trauma that can be a contributory cause to the progression from the genetic predisposition to the precipitant cause of overt addictive behaviour. It is an exceedingly valuable therapeutic intervention.

Neuro Linguistic Programming (NLP) and Hypnotherapy

Neuro Linguistic Programming (NLP) is the creation of Dr Richard Bandler and Dr John Grinder. It studies the way that the conscious and unconscious aspect of the brain are programmed through the use of language, not only the rational meaning of the sentences but also the unconscious interpretations imparted through using hypnotic techniques created by the authors and evolved from those established by Milton H. Erickson. These fascinating insights enable the brain to be reprogrammed so that phobias and other inappropriate debilitating thoughts and patterns of behaviour can be resolved effectively and rapidly. As with EMDR, special training is required and it is probable that relatively few practitioners develop skills that are sufficiently honed to be of therapeutic value. However, that value can be very considerable. Also, as in EMDR, NLP and hypnotherapy cannot cure an addictive tendency but they can go a long way towards facilitating the effectiveness of the Twelve Step Programme.

Stages of Change and Motivational Interviewing

Carlo di Clementi's Stages of Change refer to therapy needing to be targetted to where patients are in their progress from pre-contemplation through to action. William R Miller's Motivational Interviewing techniques, of reflective listening, similarly build on accepting the patient's initial ambivalence and then supporting self-efficacy and developing discrepancy between current behaviour and future goals.

Expressing feelings

Helping people to express their feelings appropriately is a serious responsibility for any counsellor and I fear it is much abused. Simply telling someone to "let the feelings out" is often little more than an instruction to cry. The resulting catharsis is assumed to be helpful. At times it may be but at other times it may be humiliating and hurtful.

The whole process of helping patients to cry, or to express their feelings in other ways, is fraught with danger for both the patient and the counsellor. It is said that geese chicks will identify as their mother the first living creature that they see after hatching from the egg. The same principle can occur in counselling: patients may idolise the counsellor who gets them to express feelings. At the moment of acute vulnerability they cling to the counsellor – and get stuck in a new dependency. Mature counsellors should be sensitive to this risk. Those who themselves are emotionally immature may even believe that they are doing good work when the glassy-eyed patients look at them in wonder, love and praise. Being deified can be fearfully seductive.

Barry (35) finally admitted to John, his counsellor, the secret that he had hung on to through two previous treatments and relapses: throughout his marriage he had also had a homosexual affair on the side. John replied that his secret was safe with him and that he would not tell the other counselling staff. This secret now locked the two of them together, preventing any further growth. The shame remained but now the collusion between patient and counsellor meant that Barry, although he had shared it, still couldn't deal with it. Far from realizing that addicts do all sorts of things in their quest for mood-alteration, he remained thinking that he is exceptionally depraved or diseased and that only this wonderful counsellor, John, could possibly be so understanding and generous. John preened himself. Subsequently, a further relapse revealed both secrets.

This *folie a deux* is totally destructive. Barry and John are as sick as each other and they feed each other's respective illness of being "special and different" from other addicts or counsellors.

I recall working in a therapy group, in Rapid City, South Dakota, USA that was billed as psychodrama but which I subsequently termed psychotic melodrama. Patients were encouraged to recount stories of their childhood, act them out, and then beat cushions with a bataka (a pole with a thick foam rubber surround, looking like a massive cylindrical lollipop) while screaming at the top of their voices.

The suppressed anger was supposed to be felt first of all in the pit of the stomach, then rising through the chest and finally popping out of the mouth. Believe it or not, that was the therapy. It struck me that all that occurred was that patients became good at beating cushions and screaming, while fuelling their resentments and self-pity even more.

It was suggested that I should beat a cushion labelled "mother" because my mother had abandoned me when I was young. In fact my parents were missionaries in India and they sent me to school in England in order to give me a better school education than was available in India at that time. Far from abandoning me, they did what they thought was best for me. I said I wouldn't object to beating a cushion labelled "mother's ideas" but I found that I hadn't got the heart even for that. This was interpreted by the counsellor as severe repression of feelings on my part.

What happened then was not simply bizarre but, I believe, wicked. Having placed three couples, representing my three successive childhood guardians, in three corners of the stage with their backs turned on little Robert (another of the patients chosen to represent me at the age of ten), the counsellor then invited me to observe little Robert and feel his pain and loneliness. I did: I remembered the real thing only too well... "That's enough for today," said the counsellor and closed the session, leaving me to wander in the woods, collecting my own thoughts and feelings. On each of the subsequent three mornings the counsellor asked how I was and responded to my "OK" by saying that I didn't look it. He then ignored me for the rest of the day. On the third day I responded to him that he had no chance whatever of breaking me down: anyone who can endure persistent bullying in a British private school knows how to survive.

At a later date, doing genuine psychodrama with the amazingly gifted Kate Hudgins in Black Earth, Wisconsin, I was able to look back at childhood traumas and lay them to rest. This contrast between a malicious fool and a clear-sighted, firm but gentle, genius has remained clear in my mind ever since. Counselling has immense capacity for harm, perhaps especially in the hands of those who, like the counsellor in Rapid City, have all the paper qualifications and licences but no basic love of humanity. Conversely, in Kate's hands (I don't worship her: I respect her professional skill), there is great opportunity for healing.

Empathy, of itself, is not enough. Counsellors need kind hearts and good minds. To nod one's head in understanding of a patient's feelings is pathetic and an insult. At the treatment centre we have a constant stream of therapists applying for employment on our staff in the belief that they know what to do for addicts. Art therapists, music therapists, occupational therapists, flower arrangers, potters, weavers, dancers, masseurs of one kind or another, acupuncturists, herbalists, homeopaths, neuro-linguistic programmers, hypnotherapists and all sorts of other hopefuls know what to do for addicts. These various therapists are well-intentioned no doubt, just as are the medicating doctors, but it takes a lot more than all of this put together to get inside the madness of addiction. We ourselves might use some of these approaches in our work in the treatment centre, but we would do so only in order to provide variety in the patients' day, rather than as any form of therapy.

Angus (50) is a local government official. Falling into a drunken stupor while actually conducting a council meeting didn't do his reputation any good. Nor did burning his house down when he fell asleep while smoking a cigarette. He turned up in my London office one hot summer afternoon in his shirtsleeves.

"I need help", he said, succinctly.

"Then go and get it, if you really want it", I replied.

He did just that. He walked to the station, caught a train, and then walked from the other station to the treatment centre, still in his shirtsleeves.

Initially he was forlorn and ponderous and he needed to be prodded into life and to have a bit of fun. Two of the women patients were asked to dress him up as a punk. They provided an appropriate hairstyle and make-up. (He told us subsequently that he now has two photographs of himself on his office desk: one in all his robes and the other as a punk!)

We also asked him to do a collage, made from magazine pictures, to illustrate what was really going on behind the official front in his life. He produced a splendid creation with doors emblazoned with coats of arms. The doors opened to reveal the bottles and garbage and broken dreams that litter any alcoholic's life.

Collage

The therapeutic principle behind a collage is very simple: "tell it how it is". We choose the subjects of the collage in order to help patients through particular emotional blocks with which they may be struggling: "My hope and my Higher Power", "Permission to love", "Holding me back". There is no profound analysis of interpersonal relationships or other favourite therapeutic subjects, although it is surprising how much patients see in their own collages and in each other's when they come to be presented to the group. Patients remember – and often treasure – their collages because they were actively involved in their creation and in feeling and thinking about what they symbolized.

Writing

Writing things down can be a therapeutic process in itself and we use this process particularly when we ask patients to write letters (not to be posted, but to be read to the group) to various significant people in their lives.

Meg (ageless), my wife, worked a great deal ten years ago on her relationship with her father. She has come to understand his pain as well as her own. She sees what he gave her as well as what he took away in his decline and death by suicide following many years of active alcoholism. He died more than thirty years ago but still lives in her head. She has been able to change their relationship, very much for the better, by working on her side of it, in part by writing to him.

Writing things down at the end of each day is what we encourage patients to do on a "significant feelings sheet". They recount their vision of the day and what it meant to them. These are read by the counselling staff each morning and the patients' comments give insights not only into their own lives but often into us. I may give what I think is a stimulating lecture or run a constructive and challenging group, yet there may be no mention of either by any patient in the significant feelings sheets. It does us no harm at all to realize how small a part we play in patients' lives, and that's exactly as it should be.

In the early days in treatment the patient's feelings are all over the place. They are depressed, frightened and lonely, suffused with guilt and shame. Then, at one moment, they feel part of the group and have a sense of hope for the future. They move from being sensitive (precious and easily offended) to being sensitive (caring and considerate). The next moment they have lost it all and want to run off again, believing that the old times were not so bad after all. These emotional fluctuations level out gradually as time goes on.

Mini groups

Patients help each other to come through the bad moments and sometimes do so formally in unsupervised mini-groups in the evenings (sometimes at our suggestion and sometimes at their own). Particular concerns or events may be talked about without any formal structure to the group. Sometimes we select the participants whom we believe would benefit from sharing a common focus of attention in this way. At other times patients select their own group members, perhaps a single-sex group or a single-issue group, for example one concerning specific difficulties at home or at work, or with recovery issues such as difficulty with the concept of a Higher Power.

During the normal working day we ourselves may split the group into supervised mini-groups. Sometimes we look at a particular addiction, such as sex and love addiction, so that patients can share intimate details that they might find difficult to share in a larger, more general, group. At other times we may look at a subject such as grief, guilt or shame (guilt over what we have done, shame over who we are; the difference often needs to be spelt out). These mini-groups provide the opportunity to work in greater emotional depth than in a larger group, although that is not necessarily so. Some of the most moving, challenging and healing groups are when the whole house works together to support someone in particular pain.

Colleen (30) was adopted. She got on with her adoptive parents but never felt really close to them. In adulthood, she searched for and found her real mother. Eight years ago they met. Her mother was by now married with four more children. She explained that she had felt forced to give up Colleen because she came from an Irish Catholic background and did not have family or social support as a single parent.

Meeting so many years later was a very special event for Colleen, who had always dreamed of a real family. She asked her mother if she could meet her half-brothers and sisters but her mother said she didn't want them to know about her.

As if this further rejection was not enough, Colleen's mother has now written to her (what a sad and bizarre method of communication on such a subject!) to say that she has now, after all, told her other children about Colleen's existence.

At every turn Colleen is made to feel excluded. She wept, as well she might. The group were immensely supportive of her and we helped her to see that her mother clearly had problems too. Psychodramatically, we were able to influence Colleen's attitude towards her mother, healing the relationship to some degree, without ever meeting the mother. We were also able to show Colleen that no person or event ever makes us feel anything: our perceptions depend upon our feelings and understanding.

Barry (40), at the time of his mother's death, while he was in treatment with us, was told by his father that he didn't want him to come to the funeral. His father said that he would kill him if he did attend. The shame of Barry's alcoholism was too much for his father, along with the grief of losing his wife.

It was as if Barry had lost both parents at one go. He was in trouble enough with his own feelings of grief, guilt and shame without having them compounded by his father. We were able to help Barry to see the situation from his parent's perspective, without in any way discrediting his own. But the principal support for him came from the group, with one after another patient sharing his or her own experience and reaching out to Barry.

A large part of the healing process from the madness of addictive disease is the recognition by group members that they are just like each other in spirit, even if their personal experiences and specific addictions may differ. Marital status, employment state, race, age, sexual orientation and any number of other factors that may cause divisions in the outside world have no relevance in the treatment centre. Patients join with each other in a common bond and with a common purpose. The best thing that counsellors can do to facilitate this process is to stay out of the way. Again and again it is the group that heals itself and this miraculous activity would be hindered by one-to-one consultation and intellectual analysis.

Kevin (38) is a well-known actor. He had begun to use cannabis at drama school. As with other soft drugs and alcohol, cannabis was part of theatrical culture. In Kevin's case his drug use rapidly progressed to intravenous heroin and he had eight years of progressive destruction. That came to an end ten years ago when he went to a Twelve-Step treatment centre and got clean. Initially all went well, he remained clear of drugs and he became progressively better established in his profession. In fact he did so well that it was difficult, so he said to himself, to get to meetings of Narcotics Anonymous. They were in the wrong place at the wrong time.

Playing opposite a beautiful young actress he let the author's fantasy become his own reality and left his wife for her. Four months later he realized his mistake and was eventually able to persuade his wife to take him back. He decided that he should go into therapy and work on "relationship issues". He has been doing just that for four whole years ever since.

He came to me in my medical practice, complaining of occasional episodes of dizziness. I found nothing whatever on physical examination and all his various test results were negative except that an x-ray showed sinusitis, for which I gave him the appropriate treatment. He returned a few days later, convinced that he had disseminated sclerosis. After further examination I assured him that I saw no sign of it. Another few days later he was absolutely certain that he had Creutzfeld Jacob syndrome from BSE. He hadn't. Then he came back with his wife, who told me that Kevin had been progressively troubled by similar fears for the last four years, ever since they had got back together again.

A continuingly successful career and two lovely children became a source of further fear rather than reassurance: suppose it was suddenly all taken away from him just when everything was going so well? I found out that he had not been going to Narcotics Anonymous meetings at all from before the time of the affair, nor during all the time that he had been in therapy. It therefore did not surprise me that his emotional and spiritual life had fallen apart at the seams. He had not relapsed back to alcohol or drugs – but it might almost have provided him some relief if he had. This is the classic dry drunk syndrome that families (and doctors) find so difficult to understand.

We took him into the treatment centre and on his very first day, a Saturday morning, I did a psychodrama vignette with him, showing him (and the group) how his drugs, his affair, his therapy and his phobia were all substitutes for intimacy: the actor was frightened of being himself. Addictive disease had parasitized his professional talent for imagination and brought him to his knees in a jumbled heap of fear and confusion.

After the group session he sought me out.

"Please write down on a piece of paper that I really do not have a serious disease. Then I can look at it during the afternoon", he implored, his eyes desperate for reassurance.

"No, that wouldn't be right", I replied firmly but, I hope, with understanding of his plight. "Your method of doing things hasn't worked in the past and it won't work now. Don't try to work things out for yourself. Let the group look after you."

I gave the "group leader" (this appointment changes each week and is often used as a method of helping reclusive patients to come out of their shells) the instruction to ensure that Kevin spent time with one patient after another during the afternoon and evening. Then I went home.

People who have relapsed, or who have had a spell as a dry drunk as Kevin did, often find great difficulty in asking for help again. They feel guilty for failing and, more than that, their addictive disease does everything it can to drive them away from further treatment, emphasizing that treatment didn't work and that it probably never would for them. Nevertheless, people who have survived the "field research" of one relapse or dry drunk episode often find it a very valuable experience because it teaches them that they really are powerless over addiction: it wasn't just a glib phrase.

Family groups

While Kevin was in treatment, his wife, Jackie, went to our family groups that are run primarily by my wife Meg, but also contributed to by a number of our married counselling staff. I find that junior counselling staff, who have no marital experience of their own, often want to get involved in family groups. I suspect that what they want to say to the families is, "This is what it is like to be an addict and this is what you could do to help." The family members would love that and it is exactly what they do not need to hear; they need to focus on their own feelings and behaviour. As with the addicts in treatment, it is helpful to give them some basic information on the nature of addictive disease and recovery, but the most helpful process is sharing experiences (of their own madness and recovery from it) with other family members. There is never a right thing for a family member to do for an addict, other than to leave him or her alone to understand the consequences of his or her behaviour and subsequently to encourage all positive steps towards recovery.

For family members to go with the addicts to open meetings of the Anonymous Fellowships is fine on one occasion purely out of curiosity. (Doctors would also benefit from doing this.) Beyond that would be intrusive and unhelpful. Family members need to learn about themselves and about the dynamics of addictive families and, where appropriate, go to their own Anonymous Fellowships for family members.

Sylvie (45) wanted to know all about our treatment programme because she needed to know that we were exactly the right place for her daughter. That's fair enough to some degree but Sylvie took it too far: she wanted to be able to control her daughter's treatment. She had worked out for herself exactly what would work and she was determined to find someone to do it for her. In this respect she was making exactly the same mistake as Kevin: they were both trying to do things in their own way, despite years of experience that their own way doesn't work.

"But I'm only trying to help my daughter", said Sylvie, defiantly.

"By looking after yourself, as I have had to learn for myself, you will do exactly that", replied Meg.

Family members learn from each other that there is nothing whatever that they could have done to stop the addicts from using addictive substances, behaviours or relationships. Addiction is primary, not secondary to something else. Some people just are addicts: it's the way they are made. They don't become addicts as a result of personality inadequacy, stupid experiment, stressful events or anything else.

"I don't want your husband mentioning any of his ideas on genetic inheritance to my daughter", said Sylvie, "She'll run a mile."

In fact her daughter never did come to see me. I suspect she never even heard about me, let alone about my ideas on genetic inheritance. Her mother probably never told her: we didn't give her what she wanted, so I anticipate that she will go on looking for someone who will – and her daughter can sit back, confident in the knowledge that her mother is doing everything for her; she herself doesn't have to do anything.

Just as no one makes someone became an addict (addicts themselves often try to blame other people for their own behaviour), similarly no addict makes a family member, or other significant person in his or her life, feel or do anything. Each of us (other than very young children) is totally responsible for our own thoughts, feelings and behaviour. Even traumatized young children can grow up to become responsible for themselves: they don't have to remain traumatized for the rest of their lives.

Mary (45) was in no doubt about the cause of all the problems in her adult life.

"You see, doctor", she confided, "it's all because I had an unfortunate sexual experience when I was young."

"Didn't we all?" I inquired, trying to do so (perhaps impossibly) supportively rather than dismissively.

I am very well aware of instances of persistent systematic sexual abuse of children (whatever the false memory syndrome people may say) and they require extremely careful management. In Mary's case, however, she blamed all the problems of her subsequent life on just one instance of sexual contact with another girl of her own age at school.

Blaming childhood experiences, and going into therapy in order to deal with them, can be totally counterproductive. At what point is the past the past? At what point are we responsible for our own thoughts, feelings and behaviour, irrespective of what may have happened in the past? At what point do we let go of the previous hurts in a relationship and see what we can make of it today? Do we have to have counselling for absolutely everything that ever happened to us?

Certainly, in our work we deal with traumatic childhood experiences, but only to help patients to live in the present. The more people examine the past, the more they become stuck in it and the less they feel empowered to deal with the present. Nobody makes us be or do anything today, whatever may have happened in the past. The whole purpose of treatment, both for addicts and for family members, is to help them to move on. Delving into the past in greater and greater depth runs the risk of producing an analysis paralysis: the centipede when asked which of its legs it moved first, thought about it so hard that it couldn't move at all.

Throughout treatment we try to have family conferences with the addicts and their family members so that we can help them to move forward. Far from allowing them to blame each other (or even encouraging them to do so, as I have seen in hospital-based programmes), we try to help them with developing the skills to look after themselves first, before learning to communicate with each other. Indeed, the phrase "We don't communicate" is usually code for "She won't do what I tell her" or "He won't accept that black is white".

*Philip (51) had sexually abused his niece **Barbara (22)** on several occasions when she was a young child. This was not a case of false memory syndrome: he himself told us about it eight years ago when he was in treatment for alcoholism and he had felt deeply saddened and guilty about it.*

Now, Barbara was in treatment for bulimia and shopping and spending addiction and she also felt saddened and guilty. (Children who have been sexually abused often do feel guilty over it, which is doubly sad for them.)

One Sunday afternoon, after the family group session that Meg and David and I run together, I brought the two of them through to a private office and helped them to talk to each other about it. (To do so in a full group would risk re-traumatizing other members of the group, as well as re-traumatizing these two, and the risks of failure of confidentiality would also be too great. They can take that risk together at a later date if they so wish, in order to encourage others to take the risk of being truthful to each other in order to acknowledge the past and heal the present – but that is up to them.)

I helped each in turn, niece and uncle, to say how sad they were over the past, and then helped Philip to say how sorry he was to Barbara. I emphasized to Barbara that she was under no obligation to accept the apology. She needed to acknowledge – for both their sakes – that what was done was wrong and she needed to express her feelings about it and then decide what to do. After many tears on both sides over the next hour, I left them together in the office, so that they could gradually readjust to their new lives and support each other in their mutual, brave, recovery.

__John (35)__ and __Annabel (32)__ sat down with me one Saturday afternoon in Robin's office. Annabel had found out before John came into treatment that he had been having an affair with a mutual friend. She had said nothing until now because she didn't want to do anything that might lead to him changing his mind about coming into treatment. Now she had her chance to say how hurt she had been. John had no choice but to take it on the chin. The purpose of this exercise was not to humiliate him but to let Annabel say what needed to be said so that the relationship can now move on.

I suggested to Annabel that she might now wish to draw a line across anything that happened before John came into treatment, including things that she may not yet have discovered. To John I suggested that he should make amends to his wife in three ways: saying sorry (in his own way in his own time), asking Annabel what she might like as an amend and, most importantly, committing himself to not doing it again. He also needs to be as understanding and forgiving to Annabel, if she ever goes off the rails some time in the future, to the same extent that he hopes she will be understanding now. The relationship needs to be mutually understanding and considerate if it is to survive, and hopefully flourish, in the future.

Then I left them together in the office to talk to each other. In my experience, counsellors tend to do too much. As I see it, our function is simply to establish general principles, to guide the patient's and family member's initial faltering steps, to ensure that no further damage is done by the counselling session itself – and then to get out of the way while they heal themselves.

People cannot communicate with each other unless they have a common agenda. As Dr William Glasser points out, the first requirement of therapy is that the people concerned should be in the same room. However, even if they are together, simply to talk at someone is not communication at all. Communication is what arrives, not what is put out. We therefore need to be aware of the various filters (educational, cultural, emotional, experiential) through which other people process what we say to them. We need to adjust the way that we approach them if we genuinely want to communicate with them. Equally, we need to be aware of our own filters if we are ever to increase our awareness of the thoughts and feelings of other people and of the world around us. Helping patients to do this is the basis of our individual family conference sessions and of the conjoint family groups that Meg runs with other counsellors.

These group sessions can sometimes reveal some real goodies:

"John told us that Robert said that cannabis isn't addictive."

"Mary said that you told her to tell us not to come to the treatment centre."

"Julie said that it is part of your policy to encourage patients to learn to drink sensibly."

"Peter is adamant that you suggested that he and I should get divorced."

"Patrick said that your consultant psychiatrist said he should be on antidepressants and should be treated in a psychiatric hospital rather than here".

These examples of the lies that addicts will sometimes tell, in order to try to involve us in their madness, illustrate the value of the conjoint family sessions. Not only are the lies busted for that particular family, they also serve as examples for the others. I believe that these various subterfuges are designed to protect the addicts' escape routes. When family members, friends, teachers, politicians, doctors and the world in general really do understand addiction then they will become immune to the addicts' attempts to blame anybody and everybody else for their own problems. When addicts try to undermine their own treatment, and keep visitors away from getting involved in the work of the treatment centre, they are trying to set up a future situation, after they have left treatment, in which they cannot be contradicted when they say, "These people are no good: they don't know what they're doing." Again, it is a measure of the fearful nature of addictive disease that it does everything it can to push help away.

More positively, however, addicts and their families who do get involved in the conjoint family groups can see how other addictive families, who are further along in treatment, are learning to recover as a family as well as learning to accept their individual responsibilities. As a general principle, the more family members involve themselves in the recovery programme, the more likely it is that the addict will get into recovery and the more likely it is that the family will heal itself thereafter. We even encourage children to get involved in the recovery process. After all, they were very much involved when the disease process was rampant in the family. Meg sometimes runs a short group for juvenile family members before she does the conjoint family group for adults in the treatment centre on Sundays. Other staff run the full juvenile in-patient treatment programme for those juveniles who themselves have an addiction problem.

In London, Meg and one or another counsellor (to single out any of then by name would be disrespectful to the others: we work as a group for a group of patients and we take credit – or blame – as a group and not as individuals) run two weekly one-and-a-half hour sessions and monthly four-day family workshops that very often include people whose addicted family members or friends have yet to contact us. They come wanting to know how to stop the one they love, or are concerned about, from drinking, using drugs, bingeing or starving or whatever. What we hope to show them gently is that they can't. However, we can show them what to do to make that event more likely – and that usually involves doing the opposite of what they have tried in the past or expect to be told to do now.

Beatrice (39) is in love with her alcoholic employer. She looks after him both at home and at work. We were absolutely clear in our advice to her:

"When he upsets a client, let him know it and get him to face the full consequences and see the damage that he is doing to the company. Don't cover up for him. Covering up for him will make things worse in time, both for him and for the company.

If he comes home drunk, knocks over the table, vomits on the carpet and falls asleep on the stairs, leave him there, leave it all alone: leave the mess, let him wake up in due course in yesterday's clothes and see the disaster for himself. If you put him to bed and tidy up all the mess he simply won't believe you when you tell him about it in the morning."

In due course he came home and vomited on the carpet and did all the other things that active alcoholics do.

"What did you do?" I asked hopefully.

"Well I had to tidy it up. I couldn't stand the mess and the smell and it wouldn't be kind to him", said Beatrice.

He's still drinking to this day.

Patients and their families often believe that relationship problems should be dealt with first of all, perhaps in the hope that the problems with alcohol, drugs, food or other addictive substances or processes will then go away. This is the wrong way round: addiction is primary, all other problems come secondarily from it. Indeed, when patients do get into recovery from their various addictions they become different people and their close relationships inevitably change. If the family members themselves do not make equivalent changes in their own thoughts, feelings and behaviour, the relationships can come under severe strain in early recovery. Family members need to see just how much they have been caught up in their own madness (running life around, or even for, the addict) as well as caught up in the madness of the addict.

Thus, both the addict and the family members have to examine their own thoughts feelings and behaviour first of all, and only after that can they begin to build a new relationship together. Even so, things don't always go smoothly and sometimes the damage is simply too great for a new start to be considered worthwhile.

Richard (50) had suffered recurrent relapses in his alcoholism and his wife Pamela (46) had given him an ultimatum: one more drinking spree and that's it. He drank again and was readmitted to our treatment centre. Pamela refused to come to our family programme (on a previous occasion one of our counselling staff had referred to her as an angry lady and she never forgave us for that) and in fact she refused to come to the centre at all. Twelve weeks went by without any contact whatever from the family. It would appear that the verdict of our counsellor may have been correct. However, I myself did not live with Richard during his years of drinking: I know only the lovely person that he is now, when he is sober. I am therefore in no position to judge anyone else's behaviour. Even so, it is sad when a potentially perfectly good relationship falls apart.

Ironically, I have known a wife divorce her alcoholic husband as soon as he got into recovery and then promptly marry another drinking alcoholic. The madness is not always one-sided.

Magic fixes

Perhaps the most helpful thing we can do for families is to show them that the various things that "everybody knows" are helpful for addicts are in fact almost insignificant. Healthy exercise is fine in so far as recovery should include having a healthy body as well as a healthy mind, but it is a pointless end in itself: it never prevented anyone from being addicted, nor helped anyone out of it. We have recreational facilities in the treatment centre, but only in order to provide variety in the long working day, not as part of the treatment programme as such. Healthy nutrition is sensible for everyone but, as with exercise, it can become obsessive in its own right. Getting a good job builds self-esteem but, while still actively addicted, it is like turning on the bath tap while the plug is still out: eventually all the hot water (or the beneficial effects of the job) will run away. Moving to the countryside, or even to another country, is no help whatever: addictive disease goes wherever the addict goes. These false hopes are known as "geographical cures". Living in a "therapeutic" community of addicts, doing healthy physical work by day and (in some cases) praying to God by night, is fine while it lasts – but what then? Healthy living is a worthwhile goal in its own right but it has nothing to compare with the development of healthy values through the Twelve-Step programme.

Magic fixes, be they social, financial, geographical, marital, educational, religious, medicinal, therapeutic, political, ancient or new age philosophical, or anything else provided by other people, simply don't work for addiction or, for that matter, for anything else.

Sue Ellen (52) is a new patient in my general medical practice. She is American. She takes Prozac. I do not yet know her well enough to have a sense of whether or not she is an addict of some kind. She shared a confidence with me and, so it seems, with anyone else who would listen.

"I was telling my nutritionist this morning, after I'd worked out with my personal trainer, that if my husband (her third) pulls off the deal he's been working on for the last six months, I want two million dollars in my own bank account. I'm not prepared to let him risk it on any other deals."

She appears to put nothing into the marriage, except her excessively pampered but inevitably ageing body, yet she proposes to emasculate her husband. I anticipate she will shortly be hunting for her fourth. Whatever else Prozac and her various other magic fixes (nutritional, physical, marital, financial) have done for her, they certainly have not helped her towards developing a mature philosophy.

The same general principle (magic fixes don't work) applies as much to our patients in the treatment centre as it does to Sue Ellen but it is even more vital to addicts than it is to Sue Ellen.

The Twelve-Step programme

It is only when the addict accepts full responsibility for his or her own thoughts, feelings and behaviour, and treats his or her addictive disease with the Twelve-Step programme on a daily basis (just as wearing glasses or contact lenses on a daily basis counteracts short sight) that he or she will get better.

The Twelve-Step programme has to be worked on a continuing daily basis for life. Addictive disease cannot simply be cut out and thrown away like an inflamed appendix. Similarly, one cannot simply learn about addiction, as one would learn a foreign language, and hope that the problems will go away. Knowledge and determination are no match for the incessant, overwhelming, power of addictive disease. If one wants to stay drunk one has to stay drinking. If one wants to stay in recovery from addictive disease one has to stay working the Twelve-Step programme. Only this therapeutic approach acts as a life-enhancing mood-altering process that will fill the inner emptiness appropriately one day at a time so that one never returns to the use of damaging mood-altering substances, processes or relationships, nor gets stuck in a miserable dry drunk state, nor lives only by courtesy of the pharmaceutical industry. The Twelve Steps are for life: a good life. If the prospect of doing something for life seems daunting or even overwhelming, the addict should remember the Chinese proverb that a journey of a thousand miles begins with a single step. Focusing attention primarily upon what needs to be done today is all that any addict need be concerned about. Yesterday has gone and tomorrow will benefit from getting today right.

A further insight from China is that the Cantonese word for crisis is the same as the word for opportunity. People in general, and addicts in particular, often imagine that opportunities come from outside: that particular speakers or therapists have amazing insights, that particular treatment centres (usually a long way away, preferably in another country) have the only true understanding of a particular problem, and so on and so on. In reality, opportunities are self-generated: if we truly want to examine and change our thoughts, feelings and behaviour we will do so, whatever our circumstances. Once in recovery, the addict is free to choose any personal relationship, professional opportunity, social environment, political or religious creed, standard or alternative philosophy or anything else. While still addicted, there is no choice: the addiction will always come first and everything else will be pushed out of the way.

Living by comparison with other people is commonplace in everyday life, not simply in advertisements for washing powders, and, again, this is utterly destructive and yet almost universal. Whole political and social philosophies are built on envy, greed and malice: the Twelve-Step programme is almost unique in its focus on responsibility for self rather than on the expectation that "the Government (or someone) should do something". Yet the Twelve-Step programme, through focusing on the spiritual paradox that one keeps only what one gives away, is also the most compassionate and socially cohesive, rather than divisive, philosophy. Political, religious, traditional and alternative philosophies and therapeutic practices tend to be exclusive: they shut out the non-believers. The Twelve-Step programme, as a philosophy for life rather than merely a treatment for addictive disease, is inclusive: it teaches acceptance of other people, whatever their beliefs or behaviour. As such, it goes beyond the divisions of religion, politics or therapeutic beliefs and is a force for acceptance and healing rather than further rejection and damage in our society.

Mark (55) is exceedingly angry with me and, I gather from several sources, loses no opportunity to blacken my name. As he told me himself, "You completely misdiagnosed my ulcer. I complained to you about the pain in my back and all you wanted to do was put me in your bloody clinic. You must be a millionaire by now but you're getting nothing from me."

Mark's sudden bleed from a gastric ulcer caused him to lose two thirds of his total volume of blood in a few hours. The acute hospital to which I referred him saved his life. I assume that he has now gone back to "social" drinking, the cause of his ulcer in the first place. Doubtless the hospital will have to "save his life" again soon.

Walter (62) is a dear friend. He gave me an enduring love of poetry and one cannot be more generous in life than that. He smoked no more than fifteen to twenty cigarettes a day but I couldn't persuade him to stop. He developed cancer of the larynx and he had a series of surgical operations, each one hopefully the last but turning out not to be so. A total laryngectomy left him speechless, an utter tragedy for a poet who believes that poetry should be lived through speech, not merely passively read. Yet even that was not the end of it. One night he coughed up some blood and took himself to the hospital. While there he suddenly had a massive haemorrhage. The emergency team intubated him to provide artificial respiration and packed his throat solid with gauze to provide direct pressure on the bleeding point. I joined the surgeon in the operating theatre and for two and a half hours watched him tie off the right carotid artery, the one whose pulse can be felt in the side of the neck. In the course of the operation twenty units of blood were transfused into his groin to replace that same quantity that was bursting out of his neck. He survived long enough after the operation to take peaceful leave of his family, and they of him.

"If you can help people to give up smoking" said the surgeon to me afterwards, "you will save more people from cancer than I ever can."

I acknowledge and accept my failure in my clinical management of both Mark and Walter. Mark hates me for getting the real diagnosis (alcoholism) right and he does what he can to damage me. Walter's family say that I am wonderful – but I failed him just the same. Yet, even so, I know that telling this story of Walter's life and death will not in fact influence anyone else towards giving up cigarette smoking, the most vicious, destructive and widespread addiction of all. Addicts do not change their behaviour as a result of intellectual awareness. They change when they themselves are in pain: sometimes too late.

Unsafe drugs

When pop singers or other young "celebrities" say that ecstasy or cannabis are relatively safe drugs they are telling the truth. It *is* responsible for me to say that. I am not condoning the use of any drug at any time. I spend the larger part of my personal and professional life dedicated to telling people about the dangers of all addictive substances, particularly in children, who know only too well when one is merely preaching to them or trying to frighten them. Ecstasy and cannabis certainly do cause considerable damage, but I tell children what I tell anyone: the most damaging addictive drugs by far in our society are alcohol and nicotine. Neither is essential to normal social life. Both come with a terrifying price tag.

Far from suggesting that people should use cannabis and ecstasy and even heroin (which, again, is medically a relatively safe drug in comparison with alcohol or nicotine: its risks come from overdose or from the transmission of diseases through needle use) in place of alcohol or nicotine, I emphasize that one doesn't need any mood-altering substance or process to be normal – one needs the opposite. Even so, I am no prohibitionist: I know that I cannot stop people doing what they want to do. Conversely, as far as drugs are concerned, I am no libertarian: there is no liberty in the compulsion of addictive disease. The consequences of use (including legal consequences) can help to combat denial and move the sufferer closer to the acceptance that he or she has addictive disease and needs to seek help.

What we try to provide for our patients in the treatment centre is an awareness that they are particularly at risk from any mood-altering substance, behaviour or relationship. We try to show them that, as far as their addictive disease is concerned if not necessarily in other aspects of their lives, self-reliance has to be replaced with interdependence with others. The self-help groups (the Anonymous Fellowships) are really for mutual help. Fellowship members do indeed help themselves, but only through reaching out to help each other and by sharing their experience, strength and hope with each other. By accepting and coming close to each other, they understand addictive disease and see how it drives lovely people to do terrible things to themselves and to others.

Gradually, in recovery, they create for themselves a new set of values: they learn to replace resentment with gratitude, blame with understanding, shame with acceptance, and despair with hope. As they accept other people so they come to accept themselves, seeing all addicts as ill rather than intrinsically bad, even though they may do bad things. They learn to take responsibility for their lives and take back their proper place, with all its duties and obligations, in their families and occupations. They make amends for the harm and hurt they have done to other people. They get rid of the garbage of self-pity and blame and they look forward to whatever each new day may bring. When things go badly that's just too bad. As Scarlett O'Hara (an addict if ever there was one!) in Margaret Mitchell's *Gone with the Wind* says, at the end of heaven knows how many pages, "Tomorrow is another day"!

Love

Thus, the purpose of treatment is far more than simply learning how to be abstinent from mood-altering substances, behaviour and relationships. That is only the beginning of the journey towards peace of mind in spite of unsolved problems, mutually happy and rewarding and fulfilling relationships, and spontaneity, creativity and enthusiasm in personal and professional life. These are the essence and purpose of recovery. In the course of treatment patients first learn to accept the love of others, then they learn to love themselves and, finally, they reach out in love for others. This is the love that conquers all.

At the end of our treatment programme, each patient has a "burning ceremony", when his or her full set of significant feelings sheets are put on a bonfire. I don't know how that ceremony came about. I suspect that one patient decided to do it as a rite of passage to mark his or her departure from the supervision of the treatment centre and re-entry into the sphere of individual responsibility in the outside world – and it simply became a tradition. The following morning, in a "goodbye group", the staff present the leaving patient with a medallion and each patient in turn says something personal about his or her relationship with that individual. Then off they go to the outside world, or to the less structured supervision of the daycare programme or weekly aftercare sessions. But even then we offer patients the opportunity to come back to the treatment centre for a weekend for several months after they have left treatment. This helps them to keep in touch with the ideas and principles of the centre, as well as with their friends, and it gives them an opportunity to recharge their emotional batteries after what may have been a very challenging time. More than that, however, it is also encouraging for our existing patients to see others, whom they knew in treatment, now doing well in the outside world.

I've seen miracles with my own eyes. I take no credit for them. I simply provide the environment: the patients do their own work for their own recovery. It's a miracle that anyone at all gets better from addictive disease but some patients are particularly memorable.

Tim (28) lived with his mother and an aunt. They loved him but it didn't appear that anyone else did and one can well understand why. In addition to his addictive disease, which led him into any number of drugs and varieties of mischief, he was also completely barking mad. There is no reason why addicts should be immune from mental illness any more than they should be from appendicitis or diabetes. Tim was absolutely away with the fairies. At first we wondered whether he was simply illustrating the effects of too many hallucinogens (LSD or ecstasy) or amphetamines or cocaine or other drugs, but he was no different off the drugs than on them.

We referred him to the psychiatric hospital in which he had been seen before and he was given appropriate medication. As soon as he was stable they let him go back into the community (they said it was wrong for us ever to have seen him in the first place) and he went straight back on drugs. The consultant psychiatrist who worked with us at that time said that we should not readmit Tim and there was nothing we could do about it. I am not a psychiatrist and I cannot go against the clinical decisions of my own consultant staff. I explained this to Tim, his mother and his aunt, and I feared that that would be the end of it and possibly of him.

I was wrong. Tim had seen enough of recovery while he was with us and he decided that he wanted it for himself. He got himself off the addictive drugs (addicts do that all the time: it's no big deal) while staying on the appropriate prescription drugs and he started going to regular meetings of Narcotics Anonymous. A year later he came to see me in London and asked me if he could stop taking his psychiatric medication as he now felt so well. I said absolutely not: it was still too early. In our current state of knowledge of his particular problem (paranoid schizophrenia) he might need to take medication for life. However, I myself am not convinced of this and I hope that in due course Tim will be able to become totally free from all drugs.

He now lives in his own accommodation, provided by the State, and is attending educational courses (the first of his life), because he says he wants to learn psychology so that he can be a counsellor. I'll bet he does just that.

He came back to the centre to talk to our patients and I gather that many were reduced to tears of wonder as well as sadness.

As it happens, our present consultant psychiatrists are not only brilliant in their own field of expertise, but are also open-minded to our ideas because they see them working in practice. We have an increasing number of other psychiatrists, general medical practitioners, specialists of one kind or another, psychologists and other medical and para-medical people who appreciate what we try to do. Any innovation threatens the established order, so it is not surprising that we have ruffled a few feathers in the past, but now our time has come. We have significant published research studies and our annual reunions are packed out with former patients who come from all over the country, and even from abroad, just to be together on that special day. Looking out from the podium on to a sea of happy, addiction-free faces, I feel grateful for the opportunity to hand on to others what was given to me and to see, one day at a time, a little bit more inside the madness of my own and other people's addictive disease.

Part IV
Recovery

STEP I for mood-altering substances, behaviours, relationships and compulsive helping; STEP II for mood-altering substances, behaviours, relationships and compulsive helping; STEP III for mood-altering substances, behaviours, relationships and compulsive helping; STEP IV for mood-altering substances, behaviours, relationships and compulsive helping; STEP V for mood-altering substances, behaviours, relationships and compulsive helping; STEP VI for mood-altering substances, behaviours, relationships and compulsive helping; STEP VII for mood-altering substances, behaviours, relationships and compulsive helping; STEP VIII for mood-altering substances, behaviours, relationships and compulsive helping; STEP IX for mood-altering substances, behaviours, relationships and compulsive helping; STEP X for mood-altering substances, behaviours, relationships and compulsive helping; STEP XI for mood-altering substances, behaviours, relationships and compulsive helping; STEP XII for mood-altering substances, behaviours, relationships and compulsive helping; Relapse to mood-altering substances, behaviours and relationships and to compulsive helping.

Multiple addictions have probably been around for ever and certainly since the time of Bill W. and Dr Bob, the cofounders of Alcoholics Anonymous. Bill W. dabbled in the use of LSD, may possibly have been a sex and love addict, and died a dreadful death from emphysema, a consequence of lifelong nicotine addiction. Dr Bob also had a dreadful death from the consequence of lifelong nicotine addiction: he died of cancer.

But, leaving aside the possible causes of our eventual death, the use of mood-altering substances, behaviours and relationships and their counterpart, compulsive helping, damages the quality of our lives here and now.

Frail though they may have been (we all are), Bill W. and Dr Bob bequeathed to us the Twelve Steps, the fundamental basis of recovery from any or all addiction. Professional therapies and religious beliefs were around before AA, and have been since, and may provide help and support to some, although they may discourage or even damage others. The Twelve-Step programme, through being suggested by addicts themselves, and by emphasizing that each one of us is free to choose the God or Higher Power (than self) of our own understanding, provides an opportunity for recovery that is not only specifically tailor-made for addictive or compulsive behaviour, but is freely available to everyone.

As a medical doctor I am familiar with cognitive behavioural therapy and other standard psychiatric, psychological and pharmaceutical approaches towards treating addictive or compulsive behaviour. From various training courses outside my medical experience, I have some familiarity with analytical psychotherapy, rational emotive behaviour therapy, reality therapy and choice theory, gestalt therapy, transactional analysis, person-centred counselling, psychosynthesis, psychodrama and other professional therapeutic approaches that can be helpful to those who are beset with the troubles of life. Any one of these therapies (and many others) can be useful in helping addicts with those aspects of their lives that they share with non-addictive people. Indeed, we use many of these therapies in our work at the treatment centre and counselling centre: each member of the counselling staff brings his or her own training, experience, insight and skill. Yet I believe that only the Twelve-Step programme tackles addiction at its source.

But if abstinence from alcohol alone was good enough for Bill W. and Dr Bob, why should any of us want more? Surely, those of us who are addictive by nature have to be addicted to something? In answering these questions I can speak only for myself and from my own experience. I want more: I want to be me. I don't want my life ruled by addictive cravings of any kind. I want open and loving, rather than manipulative and resentful, relationships. I don't want to be the person I was: I want to be the person I am now, happy and creative despite all sorts of problems in my life.

Professionally, as the director of the treatment centre and counselling centre, I want to do whatever I can to reduce the terrible toll of relapse. As I see it, the only function of a Twelve-Step treatment centre is to help a larger number of people to get better than would have been likely to do so through the Anonymous Fellowships alone. However, times change and just as we now have greater insight into multiple addictions than was possible sixty or more years ago at the birth of AA, so we also have to recognize that residential treatment centres are expensive and therefore unavailable to many people. Furthermore, the Twelve-Step approach is not without its enemies (as can be seen from the original book reviews of "Alcoholics Anonymous" in the medical press reproduced in Appendix I) and never more so than today. The problems of addiction in our society are increasing every day, yet Twelve-Step treatment centres are being destroyed by the politics, philosophy and economics of people who oppose them even while having no understanding or experience of them.

Such is life – but it need not be death. It is up to those of us who work in this field to find inexpensive and politically immune ways of helping addicts to recover. Relying upon charitable donations is fine for some at the expense of others: spending other people's money is a curious virtue and the resource is in any case limited. Relying upon the State is even more dangerous as policies change with governments and because the short-term economics of pharmaceutical treatments tend to be convincing to bureaucrats. Further, we have to accept that addicts of any kind are not generally the recipients of clinical or personal understanding. Our addictive behaviour tends not to induce sympathy in doctors, nor in the public at large. We are our own worst enemies and, as a result, we are on our own.

Yet so were the co-founders of AA – and look what they achieved with no resources and with very considerable cynical opposition. We should be so lucky to have been handed on what they gave to us!

My aims in writing these Twelve-Step work-sheets (which are simply my own personal interpretation of how the Twelve Steps should be worked) are, firstly, to pay homage to Bill W. and Dr. Bob and all the others who originated and carried the message of recovery to us; secondly, to defy those who believe that destroying Twelve-Step treatment centres destroys their ideas; and, thirdly, to encourage those who want happier lives, free from all addiction.

If working the Twelve Steps is hard, that's just the way it is – but it's better than the alternative.

Addicts of any kind will tend to believe that our use of mood-altering substances, behaviours or relationships is not significantly different from that of many other people. Thus, in this respect, we deny our own personal problem. The commentaries on each step for addicts have therefore mostly been written in the first person in order to encourage individual awareness.

Compulsive helpers will tend to believe that what we do is simply a personal choice rather than an addictive behaviour that is seen in many people. Thus, in this respect, we deny our commonality with others. The commentaries on each step for compulsive helpers have therefore been written in the plural in order to encourage corporate awareness.

Step I for mood-altering substances, behaviours and relationships

Step I: I admit that I am powerless over the mood-altering substances, behaviours and relationships that affect me and that my life has become unmanageable.

Core beliefs:

1. The neuro-transmission systems in the mood centres of the brain act as chemical junctions between the electrical pathways between neurones (nerve cells). If these neuro-transmission systems or other structures in the mood centres are defective, the basic level of mood is disturbed so that the sufferer feels constantly anxious, depressed or emotionally empty. Mood-altering substances, processes and relationships act on the process of neuro-transmission in various ways so that there is increased stimulation by the neuro-transmitter chemical molecules. Thus the mood-altering effect is actually produced by the neuro-transmitters themselves. This again demonstrates the commonality of all addictions.

2. There is increasing genetic and epidemiological evidence that the neuro-transmission systems in the mood centres are defective in some people (giving them excessive appetites for mood-altering substances, behaviours or relationships), but not in others. It follows that addictive disease can neither be prevented nor treated through love, education or punishment. Genetic inheritance implies that the sufferer is not personally responsible for having the condition as such, although still fully responsible for all his or her behaviour towards other people. Genetic inheritance does not imply inevitable onward transmission to children or that the parents or grandparents of the sufferer necessarily had similar compulsive or addictive tendencies. They may have had other outlets for addictive disease or may simply have carried the tendency to addictive disease in their genetic material without ever developing the disease itself.

3. Our own research studies have shown that addictive behaviours commonly come in clusters:
   a. "hedonistic": the determined search for pleasure.
   b. "nurturant" (of self): soothing one's self.
   c. "compulsive helping": to satisfy the need to be needed.

   Both "hedonistic" and "nurturant" addictive tendencies lead the sufferer to use substances, behaviours or relationships on the basis "I need you to fix me". In compulsive helping the addictive relationship is used on the basis "I need you to need me". As these tendencies are the mirror image of each other, it is common for compulsive helpers to marry "primary" addicts ("hedonistic" or "nurturant"). Thus, addictive disease is perpetuated down the ages even though it probably affects only 10 per cent of the population.

It is not true that all people have a tendency to be addicted to something. Addicts can be differentiated from the general population through self-assessment using the questionnaires in Part II (Specific Addictions).

The healthy use of mood-altering substances, behaviours or relationships is when they are used for their normal function rather than specifically for their mood-altering effect on that individual in order to quell emotional cravings. It is also not true that addiction is caused primarily by physical, emotional or social trauma in childhood or merely through exposure to addictive substances, processes or relationships. What is probably true is that addictive or compulsive behaviour has a threefold origin:

a. Genetically-inherited defect in the neuro-transmission system, or other structures in the mood centres, causing a basic defect in mood;

b. Emotional trauma that sensitizes that defect and sets up a craving for mood-alteration;

c. Exposure to substances, behaviours or relationships that have a specific mood-altering effect for that individual.

Many people have experienced similar trauma or have been similarly exposed, yet I believe that they develop no addiction whatever because they have no underlying genetically inherited addictive disease.

Some sufferers from addictive disease have one addictive cluster ("hedonistic", "nurturant" or "compulsive helping"). Some have two. Some have all three. Some people who come from addictive families have no addictive outlet whatever, although they may carry the latent tendency to addictive disease in their genetic material even though they do not suffer from it themselves.

4. Environmental factors may have an influence upon which particular addictive substances, processes or relationships become the particular addictive outlets for each sufferer from addictive disease.

5. Addictive disease also affects the perception mechanisms of the brain so that sufferers are in denial: they are unable to see and accept their own problem. This denial may be increased when sufferers from addictive disease cannot conceive what life would be like without the

use of mood-altering substances, behaviours and relationships.

6. Denial is countered solely through the group experience of recognizing one's own behaviour in others. One-to-one therapy is counter-productive, tending to increase isolation and the belief that one is special and different.

7. There is no primary intellectual impairment in sufferers from addictive disease: cognitive behavioural therapy is unnecessary as well as ineffective in combating the condition itself, although it can be helpful in those aspects of life that sufferers from addictive disease share with other people. There is no psychiatric or psychological defect as such in sufferers from addictive disease. They may coincidentally have the same psychiatric or psychological problems as anyone else, particularly those from dysfunctional families of any kind. Thus, they may receive help for their general psychiatric or psychological problems through various therapeutic approaches but none of these will be any help whatever for the underlying addictive disease. Furthermore, once the sufferers are in appropriate recovery from addictive disease, there will be no psychiatric or psychological problem other than those from which they may suffer coincidentally. The underlying anxiety, depression and the emotional emptiness of addictive disease should resolve completely with the continuing application of the Twelve-Step recovery programme.

8. Addictive disease can be falsely treated by chemical (pharmaceutical or recreational) substances but, unlike the use of the Twelve-Step recovery programme, the therapeutic dose can never be finely adjusted to suit all human circumstances on a day-to-day basis, but only in a blunderbuss fashion.

9. Addictive disease is appropriately and effectively treated (and the dose adjusted as required on a day-to-day basis) through total abstinence from the mood-altering substances, behaviour and relationships that affect each individual and through the continuing mood-altering behaviour of reaching out to help other sufferers on an anonymous basis and working the Twelve-Step programme of the Anonymous Fellowships. The mood-altering effects of the Twelve-Step programme are transient and therefore have to be repeated on a regular basis. Abstinence by itself simply leads to the dry drunk syndrome in which the sufferer retains the mood disturbance but has no appropriate or even inappropriate outlet for it.

10. Professionals working with sufferers from addictive disease are not helped themselves for their own addictive disease through their professional work: they may even become grandiose (and the effects

of their addictive disease may become worse) because their work is not done anonymously. They need the same continuing appropriate treatment for their own addictive disease, through total abstinence and through working the Twelve-Step programme alongside other sufferers.

11. The purpose of working the Twelve Steps is more than merely to stop using mood-altering substances, behaviours and relationships. It is to develop an entirely new way of life, with the following characteristics:
    a. full responsibility for self, not expecting other people or the State to provide.
    b. contributing to society through gainful employment or through other positive contribution.
    c. mature stable relationships.
    d. peace of mind, regardless of unsolved problems.
    e. spontaneity, creativity and enthusiasm.

12. True recovery is seen rather than heard. It shows itself in the way people live their lives, rather than in what they say.

Step I Work-sheets for mood-altering substances, behaviours and relationships

1. My life is a mess and I have lost control of some aspects of it.
   i. What parts of my life are a mess (relationships, work, finance, home, legal, health, loss of interest etc.)?
   ii. Where have I lost control?

2. Some problems persist despite my repeated attempts (occasionally temporarily successful) to be in control.
   i. Which parts of my life have I tried hardest to control (occasionally successfully) only to find that I lost control again later?

3. In particular, I have attempted to use some mood-altering substances, behaviours and relationships in order to feel better.
   i. What do I use to make myself feel better, or less emotionally empty?

4. These attempts to comfort myself have eventually turned against me: the mood-altering effects have been progressively less successful, while the damaging consequences have grown.
   i. Which mood-altering substances, behaviours or relationships have I used in the past to make me feel better but now have much less positive effect?
   ii. What damage has my use of mood-altering substances, behaviours or relationships caused to me and to other people?

5. I have felt increasing self-pity, feeling that I deserve to feel better and

to have a better life, and have increasingly blamed other people, places and things for my pain, as follows:

- events in my life that have been particularly traumatic;
- my parents and my childhood upbringing;
- my school and teachers;
- my work and colleagues;
- the place where I live and the people there;
- doctors and others whom I feel have interfered in my life and failed to understand me;
- lawyers, police, the government and others in society whom I feel have made silly rules and got in my way;
- other people in general and in particular for not understanding and accepting my special needs.
  - i. What events have caused me pain that I feel other people have not fully understood?
  - ii. Who or what have I blamed for my pain?
  - iii. Have I justified my use of mood-altering substances, behaviours or relationships by blaming others and pitying myself?

6. I have used some mood-altering substances, behaviours and relationships, saying that I need them, deserve them, and could not reasonably be expected to do without them.
   - i. Which mood-altering substances, behaviours or relationships am I frightened of giving up or reluctant to give up?
   - ii. Which mood-altering substances, behaviours or relationships do I cling to because I do not know how I could possibly do without them?

7. Sometimes I have tried to give up a particular mood-altering substance, behaviour or relationship and have felt so bad that I "had to" go back to it, thus failing to acknowledge that the bad feelings are in fact the direct withdrawal effects from previous use.
   - i. Which substances, behaviours or relationships have I gone back to because I felt so awful without them?

8. I have blamed myself for being weak-willed and inadequate, despite plenty of evidence from other aspects of my life that I can be exceedingly determined and highly competent.
   - i. Over what have I blamed myself for being weak-willed and inadequate?

9. On the occasions when I have succeeded in putting down one mood-altering substance, behaviour or relationship, I have often increased my use of another.
   - i. What do I tend to use when I put down another mood-altering substance, behaviour or relationship?

ii. What last resorts do I cling to, and may even persuade other people to tell me that in early recovery I should not give up these particular mood-altering substances, behaviours or relationships?

10. I have continued my use of mood-altering substances, behaviours and relationships despite the repeated serious concerns of others, and I have justified my actions (to myself if not to them).
    i. What accidents and dangers did I get into as a result of my use of mood-altering substances, behaviours or relationships?
    ii. What concerns have other people expressed?
    iii. How did I respond to the concerns of others?
    iv How did I justify my rejection of their concern?
    v. What treatments (of any kind) have I tried but found unsuccessful?

11. My way of life sometimes illustrates the opposite of the characteristics seen in recovery.
    i. Give examples of where I have expected other people or the State to provide for me or to bail me out of my problems.
    ii. Give examples of where I have contributed progressively less to society.
    iii. Give examples of where my relationships have been immature (but I have expected other people to be sensitive to my needs and wants, irrespective of my behaviour towards them), and where my relationships have been damaged, or have broken down altogether, because of my behaviour.
    iv. Give examples of where my use of mood-altering substances, behaviours or relationships has led me to lose my peace of mind and my capacity to live with unsolved problems.
    v. Give examples of where my creativity and enthusiasm have diminished as a result of my use of mood-altering substances, behaviours and relationships (regardless of what I may have believed to the contrary at the time).

12. Give examples of where my words have not been matched by my actions.

13. Consider the extent of my addiction, i.e. the extent of false "treatments" for my addictive disease.

Terence Gorski, president of the CENAPS Coporation, describes Post-Acute Withdrawal (PAW) as follows: "PAW is a biopsychosocial syndrome that occurs after the acute withdrawal syndrome (the immediate affects of giving up alcohol or drugs) subsides. PAW results from the combination of damage to the brain and nervous system caused by alcohol and drugs, and the presence of the psychosocial stress of coping with life without drugs or alcohol."

He describes the six primary symptoms of PAW as:

- Thought disorders (difficulty in thinking clearly).
- Affective disorders (difficulty in managing feelings and emotions).
- Memory disorders (difficulty in remembering things).
- Sleep disorders (difficulty in sleeping restfully).
- Psychomotor disturbances (difficulty with physical co-ordination and accident proneness).
- Stress sensitivity (difficulty in managing stress).

He emphasizes that these symptoms can persist from six weeks to eighteen months after the last use of alcohol or drugs and that the syndrome is often unidentified because it can easily be mistaken for lack of motivation, denial and resistance, personality disorders and mental disorders.

I myself believe that PAW can be seen in any addiction and that we may try to treat our underlying addictive disease, or the PAW symptoms that result from giving up one addiction, by using another mood-altering substance, behaviour or relationship. Thus it is vitally important that we examine all our addictive tendencies, checking off the various addictive characteristics against each specific addiction. We can then see at a glance the overall spread and severity of our addictive disease (this can be determined from the questionnaires in Part II: Specific Addictions.)

14. The extent of my addiction, i.e. the extent of false "treatments" for my addictive disease is as follows:

- Alcohol
- Nicotine
- Drugs
- Caffeine
- Gambling and risk-taking
- Work
- Addictive relationships
- Sex and love
- Shopping and spending
- Exercise
- Prescription drugs
- Bingeing
- Starving
- Compulsive helping

Notes:
a. In relationship addictions we use other people as if they were drugs. In compulsive helping we use ourselves as drugs for other people.

b. Gambling and risk-taking includes the stock and commodity markets, property, bingo and lotteries as well as activities in the casino or betting shop.
c. Work includes hobbies and interests, cults or sects.
d. For a full set of questionnaires please consult Part II (Specific Addictions).
e. Four positive answers on any addictive substance, behaviour or relationship indicates a significant addiction.

The characteristics of any addictive behaviour are as follows:
i.   Preoccupation with use and non-use.
ii.   Preference for, or contentment with, use alone.
iii.   Use as a medicine to help relax or sedate or to stimulate.
iv.   Use primarily for mood-altering effect.
v.   Protection of "supply", preferring to spend time, energy or money in this way.
vi.   Repeatedly using more than planned. The first use tends to trigger the next.
vii.   Having a higher capacity than others for using this substance, behaviour or relationship.
viii. Continuing to use despite progressively damaging consequences.
ix.   "Drug" seeking behaviour and progressively rejecting activities that preclude use.
x.   "Drug" dependent behaviour, "needing" it to function effectively.
xi.   The tendency to "cross-addict" into other substances or behaviours when attempting to control use.
xii.   Continuing to use despite the repeated serious concern of other people.

15. Step I Questions:
    i.   Do I want to be rid of all my addictive outlets for my addictive disease or do I want to hang on to some of them?
    ii.   Am I frightened of change or of staying as I am?
    iii. Am I ready to take responsibility for my own life?

Step I for Compulsive Helping

Step I: We admit that we are powerless over other people's lives and our own compulsive helping and that our lives have become unmanageable.

Core Beliefs:
1. Compulsive helping is the mirror-image of primary addiction to mood-altering substances, behaviours and relationships. Whereas the primary addict seeks something "out there" to help him or her to feel better, the compulsive helper offers himself or herself (something "in here")

to other people (commonly to addicts), to help them and thereby the compulsive helper feels needed and valued.

2. The tendency towards compulsive helping is probably also genetically inherited rather than a product of up-bringing or personal behavioural choice. It is not caused by exposure to the addictive behaviour of other people.

3. Compulsive helping is not a pleasant, constructive, personality trait. It is unpleasant and destructive (however sweetly expressed and well-intentioned) because it patronizes, assuming that the recipient could not manage alone, and it gets in the way of people developing their own skills through learning from experience.

4. Compulsive helping is also highly destructive to the person who does it. Eternally seeking one's self-esteem from other people is exhausting and does not lead to the development of healthy relationships.

5. Compulsive helping is an addictive process, being progressive and destructive in the same way as any other addictive or compulsive behaviour. The "drugs" of compulsive helping are caretaking (far beyond normal caring) and self-denial (far beyond normal kindness or selflessness) and even self-abasement (to the level of stupidity).

6. Those of us who are both addicts and compulsive helpers will find that we tend to be the demanding and manipulating addict in some relationships and the anxious, pestering or long-suffering, compulsive helper in others. We tend to relapse into one addictive process on the pain of the other.

7. "Compulsive helping" indicates a specific problem in an indivdual, whereas "Co-dependency" means so many things (co-dependent with alcohol and drugs and other addictive substances and processes or relationships; co-dependent because one was brought up in an addictive family; co-dependent because one was abused or abandoned as a child; co-dependent because one is in a relationship with an addict) that it really means nothing at all.

8. "Compulsive helping" is not the same as "people pleasing", which is a manipulative behaviour that expects something in return and which anyone (addict or non-addict, compulsive helper or otherwise) can do.

Step I for Compulsive Helpers

Step I: We admit that we are powerless over other people's lives and our own compulsive helping and that our lives have become unmanageable.

How much do I assume that I know what is best for other people? How often do I take on their pain, bailing them out for the consequences of their behaviour and preventing them from learning from their own experience? How many of my relationships have followed similar patterns? How much do I consider my own needs?

How often is it my natural instinct to keep the peace, lower the tension, quench the tears, relieve the discomfort, soften the blow, find a compromise? At first sight these look like virtues – and that is exactly what they are individually on appropriate occasions. However, when they are put all together they can be seen to be based on superiority and interference.

Supposing we always impose a compromise in quarrels between two children. The child who was wrong gets away with his or her bad behaviour, while the child who was right is not rewarded and may in effect be punished for good behaviour. This is exceedingly unfair. We may believe that we are giving a message of tolerance whereas in fact it is one of injustice. If this principle holds for the upbringing of children, how much more true is it for adults, especially for addicts? By failing to have the courage to take sides, have a firm view and oppose tyranny, we may indeed temporarily keep the peace – but at a terrible price.

Compulsive helping is every bit as destructive in families as any addiction can be. The parent who is enabled to continue inappropriate behaviour is just as damaging to the children whether the parent is an active addict or a compulsive helper. Drunkenness, drug addiction, food obsession and the other primary addictive behaviours are damaging enough in one parent without the other parent making allowances for them instead of confronting them head on. Singling out one child for special attention and favours, on some pretext of special need, can at times be fearfully damaging not only to the other children but also in particular to that selected child.

The social effects of institutionalised compulsive helping, through the activities of various professionals, from politicians and social workers to teachers and doctors, can be utterly disastrous and divisive. Compulsive helping is not a virtue: it is a well-disguised (especially from ourselves) self-aggrandising, destructive vice.

Step I Work-Sheets for Compulsive Helping
This is the real nitty gritty. Are we powerless? Precisely where are we powerless over compulsive helping? Is life unmanageable? Please give specific examples for each question.

1. On what occasions have I been loyal to someone's illness rather than to his or her potential recovery? When have I inappropriately kept a secret for him or her?
2. When have I protected someone from the consequences of his or her behaviour? When have I failed to recognise someone's capacity to get

better, as a result of working through the painful consequences of his or her addictive behaviour, rather than helping him or her to avoid those consequences?

3. When, through my own self-denial, have I allowed myself to be dragged down in a direction in which I really did not want to go? When have I risked my own wellbeing and recovery in the process of "helping" someone else?

4. When have I "counselled", rather than simply identified with the other person's experience or feelings or confronted his or her behaviour?

5. When have I apologised for taking time (even in family therapy groups) for myself?

6. When have I explained away someone else's behaviour rather than let him or her see it for himself or herself and take the full consequences? When have I tried to lessen the feelings (sadness, fear, anger, loneliness) that he or she experiences as a result of his or her addictive behaviour, rather than let him or her learn from that experience?

7. When have I failed to recognise someone's need to surrender? When have I done things that may have protected him or her from the need to do so?

8. When have I been prepared to sacrifice myself so that I might eventually be left with nothing worth having or nothing to offer?

9. When have I used compulsive helping as a means of controlling my own feelings?

Step I Work-sheets for Compulsive Helping

A. Self-denial

1. Write down examples of when you last
    i.   went to the cinema or theatre or to a sporting event
    ii.   had some friends round for the evening
    iii. had a holiday away from home
    iv.   played any kind of game
    v.   read a book for fun

2. How much time would you spend on these preceding five things in an average week, month or year?
    i.   going to the cinema or theatre or to a sporting event
    ii.   having some friends round
    iii. having a holiday
    vi.   playing a game
    v.   reading a book

3. By contrast, write down examples of when you last
    i.   read an article on addiction.
    ii.   cancelled a social engagement, or abandoned plans for something pleasurable, because a problem cropped up with the addict in your

life or with someone else.

iii. stayed up late talking to someone who was under the destructive influence of an addictive substance, behaviour or relationship.

iv. stayed away from work or from some important personal activity in order to do something "necessary" for the addict in your life or for someone else.

v. gave money, goods or services which you could not afford to part with to the addict in your life or to someone else.

4. How often have you done these five things in an average week or month or year?

i. read an article on addiction.

ii. cancelled a social engagement, or abandoned plans for something pleasurable, because of a problem with someone else.

iii. stayed up late talking to someone who was under the destructive influence of an addictive substance, behaviour or relationship.

iv. stayed away from work or from some important personal activity in order to do something "necessary" for someone else.

v. given money or goods or services to the addict in your life or someone else when you could not really afford it.

5. Write down further examples of where you yourself are aware of episodes of self-denial in order to help the addict in your life or someone else.

B. Caretaking

1. Write down examples of when you last

i. provided food, clothing or other "necessities" for the addict in your life or to someone else who could not afford them (other than in an act of charity).

ii. gave money to the addict in your life or to someone else because he or she would be in trouble if you did not.

iii. provided accommodation for the addict in your life or for someone else who had nowhere else to go.

iv. told a lie in order to protect the addict in your life or someone else from getting into even worse trouble.

v. took personal or financial responsibility for something that had been done by the addict in your life or by someone else.

2. How often have you done these things in an average week or month or year?

i. provided food, clothing or other "necessities" for someone who could not afford them (other than in an act of charity).

ii. given money to someone who would be in trouble of some kind if you did not.

iii. provided accommodation for someone who had nowhere else to go.

    iv. told a lie in order to protect someone from getting into even worse trouble.

    v. taken personal or financial responsibility for something that had been done by someone else.

3. Write down examples of when you last
    i. took on extra work in order to provide something for someone else.
    ii. tidied up a significant physical mess left by someone else.
    iii. tried to soothe a damaged personal relationship of someone else.
    iv. tried to protect a professional or educational relationship of someone else.
    v. paid off the debts or fines or loans of someone else.

4. How often have you done these things in the last week, month or year?
    i. taken on extra work in order to provide something for someone else.
    ii. tidied up a significant physical mess left behind by someone else.
    iii. tried to soothe down someone else's damaged personal relationship.
    iv. tried to protect someone else's professional or educational relationship.
    v. paid off someone else's debts, fines or loans.

C. Powerlessness

1. Write down examples of previous relationships that have followed similar patterns to the one that you now have with the addict in your life or with someone else who currently receives your preoccupying compulsive help.

D. Unmanageability

1. Write down examples of any present or previous relationships where you have found that your own life has become significantly and progressively more chaotic and damaged because of that relationship.

Step II for mood-altering substances, behaviours and relationships

Step II: Come to believe that a power greater than myself could restore me to sanity.

My determination to do things my own way is my perfect right and has resulted in many fine achievements. Sometimes, however, it has gone so far that I have caused myself and other people a lot of damage that could have been avoided, if I had given up an impossible struggle earlier. I have difficulty in distinguishing between the battles which should be fought and those I should abandon. Often I have fought hardest to prove that I am right over something where I am obviously wrong. Anyone could tell me I was wrong – and often did – but I wouldn't listen.

I have protected my use of mood-altering substances, behaviours and relationships to the very last, despite the damage they have caused, because I could not believe I could do without them.

Sometimes, when I have tried to give them up, I found that I could not: I survived without them for a time – as any addict can – but felt dreadful and it was only a matter of time before I found a reason to go back to them. Then the damaging consequences of their use became even worse so that I couldn't live with the mood-altering substances, behaviours and relationships but couldn't live without them.

Even then I was only prepared to submit (acknowledge that I had lost a particular struggle) but not to surrender (admit that I had lost the entire war). I felt that if I were to surrender I would be finished.

The great paradox of recovery, however, is when we discover that it is only when we give up trying to control our moods that we do find peace of mind, through learning to distinguish the things that we can change from those we cannot. This paradox has been particularly well expressed in the statement "I could not help myself until I realized that I could not help myself". In other words, self-control and the determined exercise of will-power simply do not work, whereas working with others in the Anonymous Fellowships and applying the Twelve-Step programme does work.

Far from believing that the world and other people have problems and that we have the solutions, we find that we have problems and the world and some other people have solutions.

But which other people? Previously we sought out people who agreed with us. We closed our minds to ideas that differed from our own determined beliefs. Now we realize that, if we are ever to grow, we have to re-examine ideas that we thought stupid and to challenge those of our own ideas that we felt were most obviously correct.

Ultimately we recognize a profound truth that eluded us (as well as confusing many people who tried to help us) for so long: irrational behaviour cannot be changed by rational methods. If we could have "pulled ourselves together", "grown-up" or "used our intelligence or will-power", we would have done so and our behaviour would have changed. But the fact is that in this particular aspect of our lives (control of our mood) we could not, irrespective of how rational the rest of our lives might be and regardless of our various achievements and distinctions.

Other people's attempts to understand and help us were insane: we knew that. But how about our own determined belief that only we could ever understand and help ourselves? This flew in the face of all the evidence. Under our own custody our lives had got worse, not better.

Cynics like us were unlikely suddenly to flip over into religious belief, without at the same time fearing that we would lose all powers of rationality, and the concepts of "God" and "spirituality" seemed nothing if not religious.

Yet what are hope, love, trust, innocence and honour if not spiritual values? They do not necessarily coexist with fine intellect or even with religious belief, however much lip-service may be paid. These are what we had lost: we have a "spiritual" disease and these spiritual values are what we must find again. And what is God if not a concept of something greater than individual man? Clearly we also need to find a "God" or "Higher Power" (than self) of some kind.

But how? Certainly not through our own determined efforts: we know exactly where those led us. Then we met others who had also been in the pits of despair where we had been and who now had peace of mind, happy relationships and fulfilling, creative lives. Something had clearly worked for them (and they acknowledged that they had not achieved these things for themselves any more than we had) and we come to believe that a power greater than ourselves could restore us to sanity.

Step II Work-sheets for mood-altering substances, behaviours and relationships

1. Where have I been insane in my thoughts, behaviour and relationships in trying to prove that "black" is "white" regardless of evidence to the contrary?
   a. Thoughts
   b. Behaviour
   c. Relationships

2. What are my greatest talents and how has my compulsive or addictive behaviour turned them to its own advantage?

3. i. What in the past could I not live with but not live without?
   ii. What do I know I shall not be able to live with in the future (when the consequences mount up) but not be able to live without (because I am dependent)?

4. When, and over what, have I gone on fighting (even submitting for a time so that I can refresh myself and fight again) when total surrender would have been more appropriate?

5. Whom have I sought out to agree with me in my determined beliefs and where did I look for them?

6. i. Have I had enough pain?
   ii. Am I prepared to look at ideas that always seemed stupid?
   iii. Which ideas?
   iv. Am I prepared to reconsider ideas that I have believed are obviously correct?
   v. Which ideas?

7. When have I tried to "pull myself together", "grow-up" or "use my intelligence and will-power"? What happened?

8. What happened on various occasions when I was determined to be the only person who could understand and help myself?

9. What do I understand by "spirituality"?

10. What do I understand as a "power greater than myself"?

Step II for Compulsive Helping

Step II: Come to believe that a power greater than ourselves could restore us to sanity.

Initially one might assume that a compulsive helper would believe that everyone is a power greater than himself or herself. The opposite is true: the compulsive helper has an absolute conviction in the correctness of his or her own viewpoint and of what is right or wrong with and for the world. Though this is often supported by excellent personal and social values of honesty and consideration for others, there is a level of smug superiority in knowing what is best for other people. Even if that knowledge is justified by experience and practice, it is still destructive: people learn best for themselves. Furthermore, it is difficult enough to know even a small part of one human being (it would not say much for that person if one really did "know" all of him or her), let alone fully "know" many others or understand all human nature. Arrogance at this level is dumbfounding.

Compulsive helpers may profess the contrary but, in effect, we believe in the correctness of our own vision: we are our own Higher Power.

Step II Work-sheets for Compulsive Helping

1. What are my basic viewpoints on what is right or wrong with the world:
   i.   political
   ii. religious
   iii. family values
   iv. social responsibility
   v.   professional work ethic

2. Give examples of when I have tried to impress these viewpoints on others:
   i.   political
   ii. religious
   iii. family values
   iv. social responsibility
   v.   professional work ethic

3. Give examples of when even I acknowledge that I have gone too far in my determination to impress these views on others.
   i. political
   ii. religious
   iii. family values
   iv. social responsibility
   v. professional work ethic

4. Give examples of when my caretaking and self-denial have in effect meant that I have been trying to be a Higher Power for someone else.

Step III for mood-altering substances, behaviours and relationships

Step III: Made a decision to turn my will and my life over to the care of God *as I understand Him*

Without doubt our addictive disease, compulsive behaviour (call it what you will) "wants" us dead. The whole drive of addictive behaviour is towards self-destruction and death.

It might be helpful to imagine addictive disease being caused by a decaying process: it rots the mood centres of the brain so that spiritual values are progressively destroyed; it erodes the capacity for perception so that our self-awareness progressively diminishes. It is almost as if the most treasured aspects of our lives are being eaten by a parasite.

The most fearful aspect of all this is that the progressive effects of addictive disease come from within. They are not forced upon us by other people, places or things. They do not come from radiation or toxins. They are not due to dietary deficiencies or allergies. Like the effects of Alzheimer's disease, the origin is inside us; part of us. We do not become addicted as a result of injudicious experiment or wild over-indulgence. We are addicts by nature.

The emotional emptiness (regardless of our natural gifts or acquired comforts) of addictive disease leads us inexorably towards substances, behaviours and relationships that make us feel better about ourselves. If the alternatives are constant depression or suicide ("just say no" is fine in theory for those who have never experienced utter loneliness, desperate cravings or blind panic), then indeed we have taken the sensible option when we use mood-altering substances, behaviours and relationships to stay alive. When that use develops problems of its own then we are stuck and have nowhere to turn.

Yet still we turn to mood-altering substances, behaviours and relationships in the determined quest to recapture what they once did for us. After all, nothing else ever worked for us. Our families, our homes, our work and our possessions may still all be present. (Addicts do not necessarily lose everything; nor must they do so before recognizing their need for help.) But the emptiness persists and our former treatments are no longer as effective as before, if at all.

So what now? When there is nowhere to go, where do we go? The ultimate choice for us is simply death or life; nothing more complex than that. If we choose death – and many do, either physically or spiritually (with a fake life on constant medication) – then so be it and nothing more can be said. If we choose life, we have to recognize that our entire existence has to turn round and face in the opposite direction from previously. No more self-pity: only acceptance of whatever life may bring us. No more blame or resentment: only understanding and gratitude.

If the devil was death and destruction, then God is life and creativity. Only through total abstinence, welcoming life and creativity through reaching out to help others on an anonymous basis, can we counter our addictive disease each day by feeding it a positive mood-altering process.

Step III Work-sheets for mood-altering substances behaviours and relationships

1. How near to death have I come?
    i.   Physically
    ii. Spiritually

2. How determined have I been to use my will-power in various aspects of my life?
    i.   Physically to attain strength.
    ii. Professionally or mentally to attain power.
    iii. Emotionally to attain influence.
    iv. Spiritually to attain control.

3. I may have achieved control physically, professionally, mentally or emotionally, but did I ever achieve control over the loss of hope, love, trust, innocence, honour and other spiritual values?

4. How much do I welcome life and creativity?

5. Am I prepared to take the ups and downs of life as they come, doing my best but accepting my failures and those of others?

6. What do I understand by an attitude of gratitude?

Step III for Compulsive Helping

Step III: Make a decision to turn our will and lives over to the care of God *as we understand Him*.

There are none so blind as those who will not see. There are none so unteachable as those who know all the answers already.

Compulsive helpers usually have very clear principles and a well worked-out code of morals and ethics, often based upon a specific political or religious creed. With such firm convictions (obviously correct) we may believe that we already have a Higher Power and therefore no need of another.

The fundamental difference between a Twelve-Step programme and a specific political or religious belief is that the latter may sometimes tend to be exclusive (saying, in effect, "I am right and therefore you are wrong") whereas a Twelve-Step programme is all-inclusive. In the literature of all the Anonymous Fellowships the word "God" is followed by the italicized and underlined phrase "as you understand Him". Thus, in a Twelve-Step programme, a compulsive helper may gratefully cling to whatever personal beliefs he or she already has, but needs at the same time to acknowledge the spiritual right of others to have different political or religious beliefs or, more significantly, none whatever.

For compulsive helpers, letting go of knowing what is right for other people is exceedingly difficult. Leaving them to get into their own difficulties, work out their own solutions and learn from them, is desperately hard for us. "Suppose he or she is damaged...", we say, "I could never forgive myself". On such an altar more lives are commonly sacrificed than saved. Addicts never learn from their behaviour while we compulsive helpers tidy up their messes and take their pain for them. The way further into their hell is paved with our good intentions.

Step III Work-sheets for Compulsive Helping

1. What are the addictive or compulsive behaviours of other people whom I have tried to influence?
    i.   Individual person
    ii. Addictive or compulsive behaviour

2. However correct my vision of what is obviously right for other people in helping them with their additive or compulsive behaviour, have I succeeded in changing that behaviour?
    i.   Individual person
    ii.   Addictive or compulsive behaviour
    iii. My Intervention
    iv.   Result

3. Give examples of when I have found it difficult to stop trying to influence or even control another person's addictive or compulsive behaviour because I have said to myself "I could never forgive myself if he or she is damaged".

4. What are my feelings about myself when I have failed to influence someone else's addictive or compulsive behaviour?
   i. Failed intervention
   ii. My feelings about myself

Step IV for mood-altering substances, behaviours and relationships

Step IV: Make a searching and fearless moral inventory of myself.

Most of us look at this step in trepidation, seeing it as a fearful immoral inventory. But that isn't what it says. Our morals and ethics are the principles and values by which we live. They show themselves in our behaviour, both good and bad. Therefore if we are to examine our principles and values we have first to examine our behaviour. We have to look at this fearlessly (accurately) if we are to understand ourselves.

We sometimes like to believe that we do things because of our environment or because of what others do to us. We answer the telephone because it rings. We are unpleasant to someone because he or she was unpleasant to us. But we do have a choice: we don't have to answer the telephone and we do not have to behave unpleasantly, whatever other people's behaviour may be to us. In each and every case we act on our own belief system, often simply out of habit, because we never stop to think about it. We may never have asked ourselves whether we have to follow a particular course of action simply because we have always done so.

The fourth step inventory gives me an opportunity to look not only at the circumstances and events of my life, and at my actions and reactions, but also at the opportunity to see patterns in my thought process and behaviour.

Writing a lengthy narrative is probably not constructive (and it may be no more than a self-indulgent autobiography) because it does not put down the material in a form that can easily be examined for patterns of behaviour and underlying principles and values. Nevertheless, we each do our own inventory in whatever way feels most natural and appropriate for us. The important thing is to be honest and thorough rather than merely exhaustive, covering page after page with detail that actually obscures the true pattern of our behaviour.

One way is simply to make lists of circumstances and events and our actions and reactions in the various major stages of our lives and in our current significant relationships. I should at the end be able to see the overall shape of my life and be prepared to acknowledge that I myself largely shaped it that way (other than in early childhood) irrespective of events over which I had no control and irrespective of what other people did to me. By acknowledging my own capacity to influence my reactions to events and to other people, I begin to take responsibility for the one person I can change (through working the Twelve-Step programme): myself.

Step IV work-sheets for mood-altering substances, behaviours and relationships

Step IV: Inventory of both "good" and "bad" responses.
1. Early childhood
   i.   Events
   ii. My response, shaping my thoughts, feelings and behaviour

(Note: in these answers it is sometimes easier to record the behaviour first and then work out the thoughts and feelings and personal characteristics that led to it.)

2. Early school years
   i.   My thoughts and feelings and developing characteristics
   ii. My behaviour, affecting myself and others

3. Main school years
   i.   My thoughts and feelings and developing characteristics
   ii. My behaviour, affecting myself and others

4. Further years of education or training
   i.   My thoughts and feelings and characteristics and the principles and values behind them
   ii. My behaviour, affecting myself and others

5. Professional/Vocational/Personal adult life
   i.   My thoughts and feelings and characteristics and the principles and values behind them
   ii. My behaviour, affecting myself and others

6. Marriage or other close relationships.
   i.   My thoughts and feelings and characteristics and the principles and values behind them
   ii. My behaviour, affecting myself and others

Step IV for Compulsive Helping

Step IV: Make a searching and fearless moral inventory of ourselves.

Initially Step IV holds no fears whatever for a compulsive helper. We incessantly take our own inventory. We always wonder what we might have done wrong or could do better for other people. But in that very process lies the destructive power of our own addictive disease: through our compulsive helping we do not help others (in spiritual terms, whatever we may do practically) and we do considerable damage to our own lives both practically and spiritually.

Self-sacrifice is a desecration of our God-given lives, whatever our concept of God. To do something for others is nice and kind and helps to create a caring society – but only provided:

i.   that what we do does not damage someone else's capacity for growth.
ii.   that we do not damage or destroy the gift of our own lives in the process.

By saying "Oh, I don't matter" we sow the seeds of a vile creed: that individuals should not live for their own happiness, because happiness can only be at the expense of others, and that true happiness therefore needs to be interpreted as self-abasement. On such a philosophy (that our actions towards others should be determined by our own negative self-image), the inquisitions and mass murders of religious or political tyrants are based.

Respect for all life, including my own, is the central spiritual message of the Twelve Steps.

Step IV Work-sheets for Compulsive Helping Drugs of choice: "self-denial" and "caretaking"

1.   Early childhood/family background
    a.   Where was the addictive disease or stress in my childhood/family background
    i.   Father
    ii.   Mother
    iii. Brothers and sisters
    iv. Others

    b.   What do I remember of my caretaking for others even from a very young age?
    i.   Person
    ii.   Event

    c.   What do I remember of self-denial?
    i   My age
    ii   What did I do without?
    iii   My reasons

2.   School/College/University/Training
    a.   Where was the addictive disease or stress in my close surroundings?
    i.   Family
    ii.   Friends
    iii. Others

      b.   What do I remember of caretaking for others?
i.   Person
ii.   Event
      c.   What do I remember of self-denial?
i.   My age
ii.   What did I do without?
iii.   My reasons

3.   Adult Life
      a.   Where is the addictive disease or stress in my close surroundings?
i.   Family
ii.   Partner(s)
iii.   Others

      b.   What do I remember of caretaking for others?
i.   Person
ii.   Event

      c.   What do I remember of self-denial?
i.   My age
ii.   What did I do without?
iii.   My reasons

Step V for mood-altering substances, behaviours and relationships

Step V: Admit to God, to myself and to another human being the exact nature of my wrongs.

There is a lot more to Step V than simply reading out the negative parts of Step IV. All the steps are studies in honesty and humility but Step V is the first time that someone else is involved in the process.

To myself I have admitted many things many times, sometimes casually (almost jokingly) and sometimes seriously, most commonly in maudlin self-pity. To other people I usually bluff and posture, making out that I know more, do more and am more than is true. To God... well, that's another story... perhaps at the day of judgement...

The day of judgement is here now – and also the day of atonement. Step V, if I do it thoroughly and really mean it, gives me the opportunity to experience both the judgement and the personal penalty at the same time and then begin a new life.

The whole point of admitting something to God is that, whatever my concept of God, there is nothing to be gained by lying or by telling half-truths. If I am to get the full value of Step V, I can do so only by digging down past my pretences and justifications. The time for explanations and rationalizations is past.

The other person is necessary, partly to ensure that I do not duck the issue and produce yet another great performance that says everything and means nothing, and partly to enable the process to be a rite of passage: I go through it at a specific time and I come out different.

Step V enables me to get rid of the ghosts that haunt me. When I face up to them totally honestly, and accept my responsibility for them, they lose their power. They damaged my past but will no longer be able to damage my present and future. I clear them out of my head, leaving only the acknowledgement that, in Steps VIII and IX, I have to make total amends to those I have harmed. The more seriously I take Step V, the more I accept my responsibility for my behaviour towards other people, the more clear I shall be of crippling shame at the end of it. My life will be mine again.

One simple technique that may help me to gain maximum benefit is to make a short summary of the worst things I have done (the things I could never tell anybody) and tell these things first. When the worst is out, the immense sense of relief enables me to relax, slow down, go into more detail and get rid of it all, once and for all.

Step V Work-sheets for mood-altering substances, behaviours and relationships

1. What are the worst things I have done, about which I could never tell anybody?

2. What are the other things I have done, about which I am sad and ashamed? What pretences, justifications, explanations and rationalizations have I used?
    i   Behaviour
    ii Pretences, justifications, explanations, rationalizations.

    (Note: Sometimes we first have to look at our pretences, justifications, explanations and rationalizations before we acknowledge that a behaviour was in fact wrong.)

Step V for Compulsive Helping

Step V: Admit to God, to ourselves and to another human being the exact nature of our wrongs.

We compulsive helpers are delighted to admit our wrongs. When the addict acknowledges that he or she has stolen something or injured somebody, we promptly chime in that we too are criminals, as testified by a solitary parking ticket (incurred when helping someone else). Furthermore, we fail to understand the difference between compulsion and habit or temptation. In trying to empathize or sympathize with the addict, or encourage him or her, we do in fact patronise. Then, in self-immolation, we scan the seven deadly sins, or other behavioural check-lists, in order to work out how we can put ourselves into the worst categories.

That process itself is our own wrong: unintentionally (but factually nonetheless) we belittle other peoples' acknowledgement of their wrongs. By caretaking for them – trying to diminish their pain of self-assessment – we get in the way of their spiritual recovery. And by self-denial – taking other peoples' pain onto ourselves – we damage our own lives. Yet what is more God-given, and more to be treasured and nurtured, than our own lives?

At core is our misunderstanding of the word "selfish". We believe that caring for ourselves, expressing our own needs, is a vice perpetrated at other people's expense. Nothing could be further from the truth: it is in our self-interest to be kind and considerate to other people and also to ourselves. By treating ourselves differently from other people (rather than the same as other people) we set ourselves apart from them, above them. Such arrogance is unattractive.

Step V Work-sheets for Compulsive Helping

1. Give examples of where I have tried to diminish someone's pain by taking responsibility for his or her actions.

2. Give examples of where I have tried to make someone feel better about his or her actions by equating them with my own.

3. Give examples of where I have damaged my own life by trying to take on someone else's pain.

4. What do I understand by the word "selfish"?

5. Give examples of where I have a higher set of standards for my own behaviour than I expect of others.

Step VI for mood-altering substances, behaviours and relationships

Step VI: Become entirely ready to have God remove all my defects of character.

Steps VI and VII are the central spiritual steps of the Twelve-Step programme. They are commonly called "the forgotten steps" because they are often overlooked in the rush towards Steps VIII and IX so that we can make amends, solve our guilty consciences, and hopefully get some amends in return. But they are forgotten at our peril: if a Twelve-Step programme is not fundamentally spiritual it is nothing.

Our defects of character should by now be obvious. The advantage of doing Step IV thoroughly and methodically is that our defects of character (the misguided principles and values upon which our behaviour was based) now stare us in the face.

Wanting them to be removed is not as obvious as might at first appear. Some of them are so familiar through regular practice that we wonder who and what we would be without them. Others may be difficult to give up because, in fact, we are reluctant to give them up: we feel justified in our resentments and exasperated by any suggestion that we should change while others do not (or, at least, before they do). Further, we may quite simply not want to change: this is the way we are and other people can take us or leave us.

A complicating factor is that our family and friends may even implore us not to change too much. They explain this to us on the basis of reassurance that we are not all bad (we probably never thought we were) but the truth may be more sinister: they may like to keep us in the role of "problem" and they may even be concerned that they themselves might be next in line for self-examination.

At any stage in the Twelve-Step programme or in life, we can opt to make no further changes. But we shall pay the consequences of that stagnation. We grow or we shrivel; we change for the better or we regress. The world does not stay still, nor do relationships, and we cannot simply stay static. As with all living things, we change or die, in this case spiritually and therefore ultimately physically.

Our spirit reflects our whole life and every aspect of our life: physical, mental, emotional and practical. Our spiritual life is expressed in our behaviour towards ourselves and others. Defects in our character damage everything and taint every relationship. Is that really what we want to perpetuate?

One might say that, surely, all we have to do is to make up our minds to change and do so. There is an element of truth in that because no change will take place unless we make up our minds to change and take specific appropriate action. But we have made up our minds to change our compulsive or addictive behaviour many times before – and failed many times before. That means that we have failed so far to discover the specific appropriate action that works in the long term.

Asking for help is never easy. Recognizing the need for help seems humiliating. But it is not: it is simply an act of acceptance and humility and there is all the difference in the world between humiliation (being humbled by someone else) and humility (accepting that we ourselves are not omnipotent, infallible and impregnable – in short, not God).

Asking help from God requires the belief in some form of God who would listen, who would care, and who would have the power to act. Some people find this God in various religious beliefs. Others do not. The beauty and miracle of the Twelve-Step programme is that it accommodates both. "God, as you understand Him" is all that is required of belief in order to make the necessary acknowledgement "I am not God: I do not have all the answers myself: I cannot survive in isolation."

In the Anonymous Fellowships, in the very essence of their anonymity, there are people who will listen, who care (if only because their own continuing recovery depends upon reaching out to help others, thus "keeping what we give away") and who have the insight and power to help us through example.

If I want lasting recovery I have to take the specific appropriate action that works: reaching out to help others on an anonymous basis and with no thought whatever for gain for myself, other than the maintenance of my own continuing recovery.

If I want my inter-relationship with other people to be my God, the relationship has to be mutual. If I want a sense of love or hope or peace of mind, then I have to go to any lengths to provide these for others, taking my mind off myself (and all my woes and resentments) and concentrating totally on them. My action in reaching out to help others on an anonymous basis is God-like in itself and this helps me, provided that I am absolutely genuine in seeking help for others rather than acting out of smug self-satisfaction. By being selfless I discover myself and I am then able to attain my full potential in every aspect of my life.

The prize is there for the taking – but am I ready to take the appropriate action that leads towards it or do I want to go on doing it my way?

Step VI Work-sheets for mood-altering substances, behaviours and relationships

1. What are my defects of character that I can see from my Step IV inventory and what are the resistances that I put in the way of removing them?
   i. Defects of character
   ii. My resistances

2. What are the behaviours or characteristics that my family or friends say I should not change too much? e.g.
   a. Give up alcohol or sugar and white flour or cannabis and other "soft" drugs altogether, because that would be too extreme and I won't be any fun.
   b. Talk about "powerlessness" when all I really need is a bit more will-power.
   c. Go to Fellowship meetings and talk about God and spirituality instead of just sorting myself out and getting on with life.
      i. My behaviour or characteristics
      ii. Family or friends' attitudes

3. Which aspects of my life have been destroyed by my defects of character?
   i. Defect of character
   ii. Destruction

4. Which of my relationships have been damaged by my defects of character?
   i. Defect of character
   ii. Damage to relationship

5. When have I been determined to change a defect of character but failed to sustain that decision?
   i. Defect of character
   ii. Failure to sustain changes

6. When have I acted as if I were God, as if I knew all the answers and believed that only I could help myself?

7. What has happened to me (irrespective of what may have happened to the other person) when I have reached out to try to help someone else on an anonymous basis?

8. What are my woes and resentments that I believe others should listen to before I consider they really understand me or before I turn my attention to them?

9. What is my full potential that I would like to achieve in various aspects of my life?

10. a. Am I really ready to take my attention off myself and my woes and resentments and transfer it to others?
    b. Or do I want to go on trying to change everything to my way of thinking, in the same way that I have always tried, but now even more determinedly?
    c. What aspects of my life do I believe do not really apply to working a Twelve-Step programme?

Step VI for Compulsive Helping

Step VI: Become entirely ready to have God remove all our defects of character.

We compulsive helpers are almost eager to look at our anger, greed, deceit, depravity and all the defects of character that we find on addicts' checklists. The very fact that we look at their literature at all, very often before they look at it themselves is indicative of our own defects as compulsive helpers: caretaking and self-denial.

Are we ready to give up these defects of caretaking and self-denial? Can we live without them or will life lose its point? Supposing someone did get damaged, could we live with ourselves and the belief that we might possibly have done something to prevent that damage? Because of that fear (compulsion) are we never going to acknowledge how much damage our compulsive helping has done, both to others and ourselves?

Yes indeed, we may sometimes have been angry, greedy, deceitful, depraved and so on, and we can look at that. But, as with anyone who looks at the motes in other peoples' eyes rather than the beam in his or her own, when are we going to look at the real issue: helping is a virtue; compulsive helping is a vice or, at any rate, an illness.

Step VI Work-sheets for Compulsive Helping

1. On what occasions have I tried to help another person by learning as much as I can about his or her specific problem?
   i. Person
   ii. Problem
   iii. My efforts to learn about it

2. Where is the appropriate boundary between helping and compulsive helping?
   i   Person
   ii   Problem
   iii What anyone might reasonably do
   iv   What I did

3. What would be the opposite defect to my own compulsive helping behaviour? (e.g. total disregard for others would be the opposite of total disregard for self)
   i. Person
   ii. Problem
   iii. What I did
   iv. The opposite defective behaviour

4. What would happen to me if I give up compulsive helping and simply do the normal helpful things that anyone might do?
   i.   What close relationships would I still have left?
   ii. What activities would I still have left?
   iii. What value do I feel I would still have to other people and to society at large?
   iv. What value do I feel I would still have to myself?

Step VII for mood-altering substances, behaviours and relationships

Step VII: Humbly ask Him to remove my shortcomings.

Looking at my list of shortcomings, I can see that I do not need or want them any more. But supposing I swing to the opposite extreme. Is being creepy and wet any better than being arrogant and hostile? Humility is putting myself alongside other people, neither above nor below them. It is the process of rejoining the human race.

Step VII is first and foremost about balance. We all know people who have become single-issue fanatics. They are particularly unattractive companions because of their tense absolutism. Whatever the topic of interest or conversation they somehow bring it round to their own preoccupation. We know that discussion is pointless and argument unproductive. Is that what we want for ourselves – a closed mind and proselytising zeal? Surely not.

The Anonymous Fellowship slogans, such as "Live and let live" and "Easy does it", remind us to be tolerant of those who disagree with us. After all, we are more likely to learn from those who have a different perspective than from those who see things only as we do.

The Twelve Steps are practical rather than metaphysical and none more so than Step VII. If we come face to face with God only at the end of our lives, we might reckon on getting away with all sorts of things provided we say "sorry" at the last minute. However, if our God is present in the here and now, such as in our relationships with other people, then we are conscious of our behaviour all the time. With such a concept of God (the love and enthusiasm we find in our relationships with other people), our shortcomings have obvious practical damaging consequences.

Focusing on getting the best out of ourselves and other people in our relationships with them gives us a highly practical daily contact with the God of our understanding and a daily opportunity to be rid of our shortcomings. The quest for creativity in ourselves and in our relationships with other people reminds us that the derivation of the word enthusiasm comes from the Greek *en theos* (God within).

Step VII Work-sheets for mood-altering substances, behaviours and relationships

1. My shortcomings and the opposite extremes.
    i.   My defects of character as in Step VI
    ii. The opposite extremes

2. On what subjects am I in danger of becoming a single-issue fanatic?

3. When have I forgotten to "Live and let live"?

4. When have I forgotten "Easy does it"?

5. When have I realized that I was wrong and changed my mind and behaviour?

6. What are the good things I can see in the people I most resent or despise?
   i. Person
   ii. Good things

7. What are the good things I can see in myself?

Step VII for Compulsive Helping

Step VII: Humbly ask Him to remove our shortcomings.

Yet again, we compulsive helpers are prepared to go through the routine. Of course we are: we've done it all our lives. We've apologised, wondered how we could be so thoughtless and stupid, prayed for forgiveness, and so on, until by all accounts we should be whiter than white – and then some. Yet still the inner shame clings to us, however many times we acknowledge guilt for our actions.

Yet again we are on the wrong track. It is our preparedness for self-immolation, always putting ourselves at the bottom of the pile, instead of in whatever may be our appropriate or rightful place, that causes other people and ourselves so much damage. If we have natural gifts of intelligence, musicianship, or hand/eye co-ordination, do we believe it is truly helpful to anyone for us to deny these talents or pretend that everyone has equivalent attributes of some kind?

It is simply not true that everyone has talents of equal value, although differing in kind. If we have special abilities then we should use them to benefit ourselves and others – but we can only do so if we acknowledge and exploit, rather than deny, them. Equally, we can only be truly helpful to others if we acknowledge their limitations, not critically nor pityingly but with acceptance of reality.

Interfering in other peoples' lives because we have a great vision for them spells exploitation and, yet again, arrogance.

Step VII Work-sheets for Compulsive Helping

1. i. Give examples of when I have wondered how I could have been so thoughtless and stupid in getting something wrong when I tried to help someone.
   ii. Can I ever be forgiven?

2. Give examples of when I have denied my own talents or gifts.

3. Give examples of when I have exaggerated the talents or gifts of people I wished to help.

4. Am I now prepared to ask to have self-denial and caretaking, the specific damaging effects of compulsive helping, removed by the God of my understanding?

Step VIII for mood-altering substances, behaviours and relationships

Step VIII: Make a list of all persons I have harmed and become willing to make amends to them all.

Addicts rather enjoy this Step because we know that at some time in our list we can write the word "MYSELF". Oh the melodrama! Oh the self-pity! Oh yes, let's wallow in it!

The truth is that we certainly have damaged ourselves every time we hurt someone else, because we ourselves are part of each and every one of our relationships. The way to make amends to ourselves is therefore to make amends to the people we have harmed. When I have completed my amends to them there will be no need of further amends to myself.

As any addict worthy of the name will know, we are all capable of flying from one extreme to the other. In Step VIII we believe either that we have never harmed anybody at all (well, not intentionally anyway... and, well, they did in some ways contribute to it themselves... and, come to think of it, they caused me a fair degree of harm), or that we have harmed everyone we ever met (which is manifestly untrue and simply another defence, protecting us from facing up to the full reality of the harm we have done to particular people, especially those closest to us).

If we go back to our Step IV inventory and to the Step VI list of our defects of character, we can work out who we have harmed at each stage of our lives and as a result of each defect of character. We shall probably discover that it is largely the same people who get harmed time and time again. The sadness of that realization (that we hurt most the people we love most) is one of the most difficult moments of the entire recovery programme.

Nonetheless there are other people who are not as close to us, sometimes even total strangers, whom we have harmed by our compulsive or addictive behaviour, or through the preoccupations and self-obsession brought about by our character defects, and they need to be on the list even if we do not know their names. The process of recovery involved in Step VIII depends not so much on the practical possibilities of making amends (that is the subject of Step IX) but on my genuine and absolute willingness to do so.

Step VIII Work-sheets for mood-altering substances, behaviours and relationships

1. From my Step IV inventory, who was harmed (apart form myself) by my actions in various phases of my life?

    a. Early childhood
      i. Person
      ii. Harm
    b. Early school years
      i. Person
      ii. Harm
    c. Main school years
      i. Person
      ii. Harm

    d. Further years of education or training
      i. Person
      ii. Harm

    e. Professional/vocational/personal adult life
      i. Person
      ii. Harm

    f. Marriage or other close relationships
      i. Person
      ii. Harm

2. From my Step VI list of my defects of character, who am I aware that I have harmed?
  i. Defect of character
  ii. Person(s) harmed

3. Which people do I believe should make amends to me? Irrespective of their behaviour towards me, over which issues do I need to make amends to them?
  i. Person who owes me amends
  ii. Issue(s) over which I owe that person amends

4. How willing am I to make amends to others, regardless of what they may have done to me?

Step VIII for Compulsive Helping

Step VIII: Make a list of everyone we have harmed, and become willing to make amends to them all.

Learning to respond only when asked for help, and to offer only the facts of our experience rather than well-meaning advice, does not come naturally to compulsive helpers. Indeed we do rush in where angels fear to tread.

    The angels are right to fear treading on other peoples' lives. With new insight into compulsive helping as a progressive and destructive addictive disease, we can look back and see how much damage this process has done to the lives of others and to ourselves.

As compulsive helpers, the harm we have done to others is through doing too much:

i.   We have given them so much that they became dependent rather than developing their own capacity for independence.

ii.   We have bailed them out of their difficulties, buying into their own sob-stories or into the threats of others.

The harm we have done to ourselves is through doing too little:

i.   What time, money, energy and enthusiasm have we left for our own pleasure and personal development in the simple joys of living?

ii.   How much do we value our own lives, rather than some macabre concept of serving others to the extent of our own self-destruction and death?

Step VIII Work-sheets for Compulsive Helping

1. i.   Life event (from Step IV)
    ii.   Other person affected

2. i.   Life event (from Step IV)
    ii.   Damaging effect on myself

Step IX for mood-altering substances, behaviours and relationships

Step IX: Make direct amends to such people wherever possible, except when to do so would injure them or others.

There are clear stages in making amends. I need to follow them carefully and sensitively.

i.   Working out in advance precisely what I have done and what it is appropriate to say, bearing in mind the need to avoid making matters worse for the other person.

ii.   Contacting the other person and finding a time convenient for him or her. (If the person is difficult to find, imagine that he or she owes me a large sum of money!)

iii.   Getting straight to the point and saying what it is that I have done. (There is no need for any flowery explanation: a simple explanation that I have something on my conscience will suffice.)

iv.   Saying sorry.

v.   Asking what amends the other person would like. (At this point it is appropriate to say that it matters to me that atonement should be made. Money should be paid for things I have taken, even if the other person is rich. If I have no money then I can offer a skill that I do possess or I can offer time – a commodity that busy people might readily appreciate.)

vi. If the other person really does not want amends (and I should neither hope nor look for this) then accept his or her kindness simply and gratefully. If he or she reacts negatively to the information I have given him or her, that is his or her absolute right and I have to accept it as a consequence of my own previous damaging behaviour, rather than see it as a defect in that person.

vii. Do not do whatever it was again (perhaps the most important amends that we can make to those who are close to us).

When the person to whom I wish to make amends is unknown, I can do something anonymously for someone else.

When the person is dead or untraceable I can give something to, or do something for, another person or for a cause I believe that person would value.

The Twelve Promises (from page 83 of the *Big Book* of Alcoholics Anonymous) are often read out at meetings of the Anonymous Fellowships without any acknowledgement that they refer specifically to working Step IX: "If we are painstaking about this phase of our development..." I need to acknowledge that if I am to progress.

Step IX Work-sheets for mood-altering substances, behaviours and relationships

Step IX: Of all the Steps, this Step needs to be worked painstakingly.

1. i. Person harmed
    ii. Harm done
    iii. Date contacted
    iv. Amends made

2. Check whether the Twelve Promises are coming true in my life. If not, do further work on painstakingly making amends to those I have harmed.

    1. We are going to know a new freedom and a new happiness.
    2. We will not regret the past nor wish to shut the door on it.
    3. We will comprehend the word serenity.
    4. We will know peace.
    5. No matter how far down the scale we have gone, we will see how our experience can benefit others.
    6. That feeling of uselessness and self-pity will disappear.
    7. We will lose interest in selfish things and gain interest in our fellows.

8. Self-seeking will slip away.
9. Our whole attitude and outlook upon life will change.
10. Fear of people and of economic insecurity will leave us.
11. We will intuitively know how to handle situations which used to baffle us.
12. We will suddenly realize that God is doing for us what we could not do for ourselves.

Step IX for Compulsive Helping

Step IX: Make direct amends to such people wherever possible, except when to do so would injure them or others.

For compulsive helpers, making amends is certainly tricky and requires some thought. How does one say "I'm sorry I helped you"?

In fact that is not the issue, and looking at it that way simply perpetuates the myth that compulsive helping is good but has gone too far. This is exactly the same as believing that alcoholism comes from drinking too much, that drug addiction comes from unwise experiment, and that eating disorders are the consequence of childhood abuse, of reading fashion magazines, or of following the wrong diet. Compulsive helping is as different from normal helping as alcoholism is from normal drinking (which is because one likes the taste rather than because one wants to change the way one feels about oneself), or as different as any other addictive process is from the counterpart enjoyed by non-addictive people.

Thus we can readily say, "I think I damaged you by doing too much, by interfering in your life, and by not trusting you to find your own way through life's difficulties and I'm sorry for that".

We may or may not be understood – particularly not if the addict is still using mood-altering substances, behaviours or relationships and still relying upon us to pick up the pieces. Under such circumstances we may get a barrow-load of abuse along with spine-chilling stories of what will happen to the poor, defenceless, incapable, addict if we withdraw our support. Too bad. Even so, we need to be sensitive in making amends with love and understanding, rather than doing so as yet another act of proving that we know what is better for other people than they know themselves.

Making amends to ourselves starts first and foremost with the belief that we are worth it and with the acknowledgement that compulsive helping really has damaged our lives and that it is not a virtue that we have simply overdone. If we haven't grasped that (and it really is difficult to do so, not least because we really haven't done anything significantly wrong, in the legal sense, in this aspect of our lives) then we need to go back through the Steps again.

Step IX Work-sheets for Compulsive Helping

1. i.   Caretaking Event
   ii. Other Person affected
   iii. Date Contacted
   iv. Amends made

2. i.   Self-denial Event
   ii. Specific amend to myself through alternative behaviour
   iii. Date

Step X for mood-altering substances, behaviours and relationships

Step X: Continue to take personal inventory and when I am wrong promptly admit it.

Steps X, XI and XII are the "maintenance Steps" that we do every day in order to prevent relapse. We sometimes hear people emphasizing that they do Steps I, II and III every day, focusing on their powerlessness. Surely this should have been accepted long ago. The whole purpose of working through the Steps is so that we can move on and take full responsibility for our lives. Far from continuing to be powerless (except over the use of mood-altering substances, behaviours or relationships) we gain the power (or, to be precise, we are given it: the paradox of recovery is that it is a gift that we did not deserve and we did everything we possibly could to reject) to manage our lives appropriately alongside other people.

Just as people who wear spectacles can thereby overcome their short sight (and do not self-consciously show off the fact that they are doing so), people who work a Twelve-Step programme as a matter of course in their lives can trust its effectiveness. To discard the Twelve-Step programme after a time would be just as crazy and dangerous as discarding spectacles in the belief that one no longer needs them after using them for a long time.

The first part of Step X is easy: provided that I remember to do it as part of automatic daily discipline even when I am tired and fed up (or, for that matter, happy and exhilarated).

The second part is difficult. Admitting that I am wrong at the very time that I am wrong is fiendishly hard, until I discover how much other people appreciate it. The problem then is that my addictive nature will look for further opportunities to be whiter than white or holier than thou. Hence the need for daily vigilance. However long it may be since my last use of mood-altering substances, behaviours or relationships, my addictive nature does not go away. I may no longer have daily problems with the use of mood-altering substances, behaviours or relationships (although it should always be remembered that it says in the *Big Book* of Alcoholics Anonymous – hopefully not as an invitation to relapse – that "no one among us is capable of perfect adherence to this programme") but I still have a problem with me.

Step X Work-sheets for mood-altering substances, behaviours and relationships

Daily Inventory (to be kept by the bed and filled in at the end of each day).

My good behaviour
  i.   My action
  ii. Person affected

My bad behaviour
  i.   My action
  ii. Person affected

Notes:
  i.   Try to keep the columns more or less the same length: we are neither all good nor all bad.
  ii. Sometimes an event may be part healthy and part unhealthy. It can therefore be entered on both sides.
  iii. Look for patterns of behaviour or preoccupation with particular individuals and ask myself why this happens.
  iv. Make continuation sheets and use them as time goes on. There is never a time when we can afford to discontinue taking a daily inventory. Far from reinforcing our negativity and incompetence, this inventory retains our creativity and competence in our daily lives.

Step X for Compulsive Helping

Step X: Continue to take personal inventory and when we are wrong promptly admit it.

It is said that when compulsive helpers are drowning, someone else's life passes before our eyes. By the time we reach Step X we should have a better appreciation of the value of our own lives.

Those of us who are both addicts and compulsive helpers may believe, on reflecting over the course of our lives, that our primary addiction caused a great deal of damage to other people whereas our compulsive helping caused a great deal of damage to ourselves. In truth however, the more we take our inventory, the more we discover that both primary addiction and compulsive helping damage both ourselves and other people equally.

The purpose of recovery from any addictive process is to regain a normal life. Addicts will never be able to recapture the ability to use mood-altering substances (such as alcohol, drugs, sugar and refined carbohydrates) sensibly, because we never had that capacity in the first place: we were born with our addictive tendency. Addictive behaviours or relationships, however, are slightly different in so far as we have to retain the behaviour (exercising, risk-taking, shopping or spending, working etc) but learn to use it for its primary purpose rather than for mood-altering effect.

Correspondingly, compulsive helpers have to learn how to help normally and avoid being compulsive helpers. This process is easier than it first appears. All we have to do is to ask ourselves (and confirm in our daily inventory) if the purpose of a particular course of action is to be genuinely helpful and in response to a request, or whether our aim is to satisfy our addictive need to be needed.

When we do make an error and compulsively help, rather than respond appropriately to a request for help, do we now have the insight (and the guts) to see what we have done and promptly admit it, rather than find a worthy reason that justifies it to others and to ourselves?

Step X Work-sheets for Compulsive Helping

Daily Inventory (to be kept by the bed and filled in at the end of each day).

Compulsive Helping Behaviour
- i   Caretaking event
- ii   Person affected
- iii Self-denial event damaging myself

Recovering Behaviour
- i   Non-caretaking event
- ii   Person affected
- iii Self-enhancing event, being good to myself

Notes:
- i.   Try to keep the columns more or less the same length: we are neither all good nor all bad.
- ii.   Sometimes an event may be part healthy and part unhealthy. It can therefore be entered on both sides.
- iii. Look for patterns of behaviour or preoccupation with particular individuals and ask myself why this happens.
- iv.   Make continuation sheets and use them as time goes on. There is never a time when we can afford to discontinue taking a daily inventory. Far from reinforcing our negativity and incompetence, this inventory retains our creativity and competence in our daily lives.

Step XI for mood-altering substances, behaviour and relationships

Step XI: Seek through prayer and meditation to improve my conscious contact with God *as I understand Him,* praying only for knowledge of His will for me and the power to carry that out.

Anyone who has ever said "God help me" or "Good God!" or even "For God's sake" has, perhaps unwittingly, said a prayer. An acknowledgement of inability to control events, a statement of wonder, or even an imploring for something to happen or not, are all recognitions of something greater than self.

Anyone who has marvelled at a sunset, been mesmerized by a candle flame, or relaxed in a warm bath while listening to gentle music, has meditated. Taking a brief respite from the hurly-burly of the day and pondering the infinite is meditation enough, without the need for mystical performance and funny smells. Prayer and meditation, perfectly straightforward, normal, healthy activities, have been high-jacked by professionals and made to appear as if the rest of us can appreciate their beauty and wonder only on special licence. We need to reclaim them for ourselves.

Some prayers may have universal appeal, such as the prayer attributed to St Francis of Assisi:

> Merciful God, to Thee we commend ourselves
> and all those who need Thy help and correction.
> Where there is hatred, give love;
> where there is injury, pardon;
> where there is doubt, faith;
> where there is despair, hope;
> where there is sadness, joy;
> where there is darkness, light.
> Grant that we may not seek so much to be consoled as to console;
> to be understood as to understand;
> to be loved as to love.
> For in giving we receive;
> in pardoning we are pardoned;
> and dying we are born into eternal life.

and "The Serenity Prayer", the first part of a much longer prayer by Reinhold Niebuhr:

> God grant me the serenity
> To accept the things I cannot change,
> Courage to change the things I can
> And the wisdom to know the difference.

and also The Step III Prayer from the *Big Book* of Alcoholics Anonymous:

> God, I offer myself to Thee – to build with me and to do with me as Thou wilt. Relieve me of the bondage of self, that I may better do Thy will. Take away my difficulties, that victory over them may bear witness to those I would help of Thy power, Thy love, and Thy way of life. May I do Thy will always!

Each one of us may have favourite prayers, gleaned from religious texts of various beliefs. They may say something special to us or they may be comforting through familiarity. A poem or some other piece of literature may also be a prayer, in its expression of beauty and awe, despite being secular. A simple wish or a statement of gratitude can be a prayer (known as an "arrow" prayer because of its directness) and it is certainly no less of a prayer for being simple and straightforward.

Recitation has value if it acts as a constant reminder. It has perhaps less value if it is merely repeated without thought. Contemplation is an activity of a restful mind, but it is no less an activity for being restful. By contrast, the triviality of the quick fix is as much a cause for despair as its short-lived effects.

In reflecting upon the great mysteries of life (such as the three fundamental questions "Where did I come from?", "What am I doing?" and "Where am I going?") we can, if we so wish, turn to religious and mystical writings and practices if we find practical help in doing so.

Alternatively, we can write our own prayers and meditations, seeking our own personal spiritual goal.

Our Dog Phoebe
Our dog Phoebe is
loving and much loved,
enthusiastic and cheerful,
adventurous and brave,
clear and direct,
faithful and loyal.
I'd like to be like our dog Phoebe.

Darkness
My God, my God, why hast Thou forsaken me?
I mean well and I try hard.
I've made many mistakes and I've been silly and inconsiderate.
Sometimes I deliberately hurt other people; more often I try to help.
Now I'm defeated, destroyed, exhausted, sad.
My Son, my Son, when will you understand?
Life is the journey; not the destination.
Take the gift of this one day – and use it.
 Light
And God said, "Let there be light;

Light in your eyes instead of weariness,
Light in your heart instead of depression,
Light in your mind instead of confusion,
Light in your soul instead of emptiness.
Let your light shine to brighten each day."

The PROMIS Prayer
Help me, O God,
to be innocent and ignorant instead of all-knowing,
to be observant instead of arrogant,
to be questioning instead of certain,
to be able to be influenced instead of ever eager to influence others,
to be at peace with myself and others instead of ever critical.
O God give me the simplicity of spirit to be still.

The PROMIS Meditation
Be still and know that I am God
the crucible of creativity and the cradle of caring,
the home of happiness and the haven of hope,
the love of life and the life of love,
the glow of gratitude and the gentleness of grace,
the softness of simplicity and the serenity of silence.
Be still... and *know* that I am God.

This meditation can be used as a contemplative journey into one's inner self if it is read with four beats to the line, breathing in on the first and third beats and out on the second and fourth as follows:

	In		Out
	In		**Out**
Be	still	and	know
that	I	am	God
the	crucible	of	creativity
and the	cradle	of	caring,
the	home	of	happiness
and the	haven	of	hope,
the	love	of	life
and the	life	of	love,
the	glow	of	gratitude
and the	gentleness	of	grace,
the	softness	of	simplicity
and the	serenity	of	silence.
Be	still ...	and	know
that	I	am	God.

For each of us our concept of God will work for us when we feel that it is conscious and specifically relevant in our lives. Spiritual growth may be attainable through religious belief but the world's wars are often fought on sectarian divisions, and a modern scientific education does not look kindly upon mysticism, so some of us may choose to formulate our own spiritual path. If we do so, however, we need to be aware of the risk of returning to the arrogant belief of all using addicts: that we are right and everyone else is wrong. Seeking to separate ourselves from the rest of humanity is what we did before – and look where that got us.

Acceptance, tolerance, forgiveness, love, tenderness, gentleness, hope, trust, honour, innocence, happiness, peace of mind, confidence, ease and grace: these spiritual values are surely God's will for us – whatever our concept of God. Doing everything I can to bring these values into my own life is a worthy recognition of the gift of life itself.

My own daily prayers and my own daily meditations – seeking deeper values in my life than my professional and personal preoccupations – bring me closer to conscious contact with the God of my own understanding.

Do I have the power to achieve clarity of value and purpose in my life? Yes, indeed I do – if I get out of my own way.

Step XI Work-sheets for mood-altering substances, behaviours and relationships

1.   i.   Have I ever said "God help me", "Good God!" or "For God's sake"?
     ii.   If so, does the concept of prayer frighten, repel or confuse me?
    iii.   If so, why?
    iv.   Have I marvelled at a sunset, been mesmerized by a candle flame, or relaxed in a warm bath while listening to gentle music, or done something similarly contemplative?
     v.   If so, does the concept of meditation still frighten, repel or confuse me?
    vi.   If so, why?

2.   i.   Do I have any favourite prayers that say something special to me or are comforting through familiarity?
    ii.   Write them out here to remind myself:

3.   Write out some "arrow" prayers that I find myself saying, perhaps without realizing it at the time.

4.   i.   When have I been genuinely contemplative, rather than self-pityingly and idiotically drunk, stoned or otherwise blown out of my mind?
    ii.   When have I gone for the quick fix in various ways and with what result?
      a.   Quick fix
      b.   Result

5. i.   Write my own prayer:
    ii. Write my own meditation:

6. i.   Have I made my God my own so that I am conscious of the values and behaviours that bring me close to the God of my understanding?
    ii. What are these values and behaviours?

7. i.   Am I totally or largely tied up in my professional and personal preoccupations?
    ii. Which?
    iii. How do I propose to get out of my own way in such a way that peace of mind is easily repeatable day after day after day? (Keep it simple!)

Step XI for Compulsive Helping

Step XI: Seek through prayer and meditation to improve our conscious contact with God *as we understand Him,* praying only for knowledge of His will for us and the power to carry that out.

What is God's will for compulsive helpers? We always imagined that it was to serve others and to help to make the world a better place. So it may well be, but it is certainly not to be compulsive helpers, getting in everyone else's way with our self-righteous conviction of what is right for them and our determination to see our chosen path to glory through to the end, however much we ourselves may suffer in the process.

Control is the name of the game. Are we still determined to be in control or can we trust the God of our understanding to run the show? As compulsive helpers, can we get on with the straightforward practical business of running our own lives and leave others to run their own lives, make their own mistakes and learn from them?

Do we have the power to "Live and let live" and to "Let go and let God"? If not we had better pray for it (try it out in our relationships with others and ask other recovering compulsive helpers for their insight if we get into difficulty) and meditate upon it (take some quiet time for ourselves to ponder the spiritual abyss into which our addictive compulsive helping has led us).

When we have done that, might we allow ourselves to pray and meditate on the concept of happiness? Ultimately God's will for us (whatever our understanding of God) must be for us to live normal, healthy and happy lives. With our compulsive helping in recovery on a day-to-day basis, we can do so.

Step XI Work-sheets for Compulsive Helping

1. Write a prayer or meditation on "Live and let live".

2. Write a prayer or meditation on "Let go and let God".
3. What is my concept of a normal healthy happy life?

Step XII for mood-altering substances, behaviours and relationships

Step XII: Having had a spiritual awakening as the result of these Steps, I try to carry this message to others who still suffer and to practice these principles in all my affairs.

Those of us who have worked for a university degree and have also worked a Twelve-Step programme will often readily acknowledge that the degree was the easier task. This is because the Twelve-Step programme is not an intellectual exercise but a spiritual path. (There may be a few people who may be too intellectually impaired to be able to work a Twelve-Step programme but there are a considerable number who may be too clever by half.) To be sure, we have to think about it but, most of all, we have to do it: it is entirely based upon action. Running a marathon is easy by comparison: you train for it, run it in an afternoon and it's all over. Working a Twelve-Step programme takes a lifetime, one day at a time.

When we first come to meetings of the Anonymous Fellowships we may happily imagine that all we have to do is to sit back and let recovery come to us. Other people reach out to help us unstintingly, giving us the benefit of their experience, strength and hope. It takes time for us to realize that this is the way they get better and that we have to follow their example if we are to recover and keep our recovery.

The gradual and inexorable process of taking our minds off ourselves and on to other people is grindingly hard in working through the Twelve Steps and it is not over when it's over: it starts again each day. Granted it gets progressively easier as time goes on but, if we ever become complacent, we relapse. It's as simple as that, although not necessarily as immediate. It often takes quite some time to throw away our physical abstinence even though our value system and our behaviour towards others may decline very quickly.

A spiritual awakening may be a sudden process like a flash of light in the sky (although this is perhaps more commonly the result of a stellar supernova or the intra-cerebral perception of light caused by a detached retina), but it is usually experienced gradually and retrospectively. It is only when we look back over the mountain ranges that we have climbed that we realize that we have reached some sort of a summit – or at least we can see that we are higher up than we were before.

The development of Twelve-Step residential treatment centres has been a mixed blessing. They have the capacity to help people through the difficult initial days or weeks of timid recovery and thus they should at least double the number of those who would have got better through working the Twelve-Step programme in the Anonymous Fellowships alone and without further aid. However, treatment centres may have the disadvantage of putting an unjustified emphasis on professional therapy of one kind or another, rather than reinforcing our continuing dependence upon working the Twelve Steps. The *Big Book* of Alcoholics Anonymous is absolutely and specifically clear on this point: "These are the Steps we took..."

Most dangerous of all is the effect that providing therapy for others can have on counselling staff who are themselves in recovery. Failure to remember where we came from, and failure to work our own Twelve-Step programme anonymously alongside other addicts (irrespective of whatever we may have been doing all day in our professional work), spells grandiosity, dishonesty, resentment and disaster.

Carrying the message to others does not imply success. Very often we do not succeed in helping the other person. Yet still we succeed in our aim of perpetuating our own recovery by keeping what we attempted to give away. This same principle (keeping what we give away) is what we try to show to others but we have to remember that, although we may love them, we cannot do their loving for them: we can set an example of love and provide a loving environment but we can only do our own loving.

The Twelve-Step programme is practical to the very last. What use would it be if not to apply the principles of honesty, open-mindedness and willingness (the H-O-W of recovery) in all our affairs? To have one set of principles for Anonymous Fellowship meetings and another for home and the office would be both daft and impossible. The great truth and the great gift of the Twelve-Step programme is that it is a programme for life.

Step XII Work-sheets for mood-altering substances, behaviours and relationships

1. i.   What have I done in my life that required harder work than my Twelve-Step programme?
    ii. Have I been "fearless and thorough from the very start" in working my Twelve-Step programme.
    iii. Am I at times too clever by half to work a Twelve-Step programme each and every day?

2. Do I acknowledge my continuing need of the Twelve-Step programme?
    i.   What regular Anonymous Fellowship meetings do I attend?
    ii. What service commitments do I have to these meetings or to a Fellowship as a whole?
    iii. What is the regular relationship I have with my Fellowship sponsor?
    iv. What Fellowship literature do I read each day?
    v.   What regular attention do I give to the Twelve Steps themselves?
    vi. What mood-altering substances, behaviours or relationships do I still cling to?

3. What form has my spiritual awakening taken?

4. i. What professional therapy, and which professional therapists, do I credit with my recovery?
   ii. What will happen to me and to my recovery if I find that they have feet of clay?

5. If I myself am a professional in a Twelve-Step treatment centre what am I doing (outside my work) to ensure my own continuing recovery and spiritual health?
   i. What regular Anonymous Fellowship meetings do I attend?
   ii. What independent professional supervision do I receive?
   iii. What personal therapy do I receive?

6. For all recovering addicts, professional counsellors or otherwise:
   i. When do I give away my experience, strength and hope anonymously?
   ii. Do I avoid giving advice, other than to follow the Twelve Steps?

7. i. Do I set an example of love?
   ii. Do I provide an environment of love?

8. i. Am I able to let go graciously when someone does not want what I have to offer?
   ii. Do I accept that I cannot do another person's loving?

9. Where, in all my affairs, do I still find difficulty in being fully
   i. honest?
   ii. open-minded?
   iii willing?

10. i. Do I see the Twelve-Step programme as a burden or a gift?
    ii. How do I show my recovery in taking full responsibility for my life?

11. Are spiritual values (acceptance, tolerance, forgiveness, love, tenderness, gentleness, hope, trust, honour, happiness, peace of mind, confidence, ease and grace) now an important part of my life?

12. Does my way of life illustrate characteristics of recovery:
    i. Do I still expect other people or the State to provide for me and bail me out of my problems?
    ii. Do I now contribute to society?
    iii. Are my relationships mature and stable?
    iv. Am I as sensitive to the needs and wants of others as I hope they will be of mine?

v.   Do I now have peace of mind despite living with unsolved problems?

vi. Am I now creative and enthusiastic?

vii. Do my words now match my actions?

Step XII for Compulsive Helping

Step XII: Having had a spiritual awakening as the result of these steps we try to carry this message to compulsive helpers who still suffer, and to practise these principles in all our affairs.

Spiritual awakening after a lifetime of addiction of any kind is glorious. For compulsive helpers the relief of no longer having to run everyone else's lives as well as our own is especially glorious. We have got our own lives back from the clutches of our addiction!

What shall we now do with our lives? The great risk for compulsive helpers is that we promptly ask ourselves how we can be truly helpful to others – and off we go into the pit again. But in fact we can be helpful to others, as specifically required in this Step. The beneficiaries of our help, however, should be other compulsive helpers who still suffer.

Our tendency on learning about the processes of addictive disease and recovery will be to want to become professional counsellors so that we can be helpful to addicts. The risks of that process should be obvious but, as compulsive helpers, we tend to be oblivious to risks of that nature: our cause of helping others is good and great and any risk is worthwhile!

Conversely, our attitude towards other compulsive helpers tends to be that they are a bit pathetic. We may even believe that they have not yet found out how to be really helpful, as we were and can certainly now be. Back comes the arrogance; off goes the disease again.

But it need not be like that if we remember our own journey through the Steps and focus on reaching out to help other compulsive helpers on an anonymous basis, remembering one golden rule and spiritual principle in all our affairs: leave other people (especially addicts) alone to get on with their own lives, while we get on with our own.

Step XII Work-sheets for Compulsive Helping

1. Do I acknowledge my continuing need for working a Twelve-Step programme or do I imagine that now I understand compulsive helping, I can simply shrug it off?

    i.   What regular ("family") Anonymous Fellowship meetings do I attend? (i.e. not "primary" Fellowships such as AA, NA, OA etc.)

    ii. What commitments do I have to those meetings or to the Fellowship as a whole?

    iii. What regular relationship do I have with my Fellowship sponsor?

    iv. What Fellowship literature do I read each day?

    v.   What regular attention do I give to the Twelve Steps of Helpers Anonymous?

    vi. To which aspects of caretaking and self-denial do I still cling?

2.   What form has my spiritual awakening taken?

3.   i.   What professional therapy, and which professional therapists, do I credit with helping me and the addicts in my life?

    ii. What will happen to me and to the addicts and others in my life when I discover that these therapies and therapists have feet of clay?

4.   If I am a professional in a Twelve-Step treatment centre, what am I doing to ensure my continuing spiritual health and recovery from compulsive helping?

    i.   What regular ("family") Fellowships do I attend?

    ii. What independent professional supervision (with an understanding of compulsive helping) do I receive?

    iii. What personal therapy (with an understanding of compulsive helping and an awareness that "burnout" is primarily caused by untreated compulsive helping) do I receive?

5.   For all recovering compulsive helpers, professiona counsellors and otherwise:

    i.   When do I give away my experience, strength and hope anonymously to other compulsive helpers?

    ii. Do I avoid giving advice other than to follow the Twelve Steps?

6.   For all recovering compulsive helpers, professional counsellors and otherwise:

    i.   Can I let go graciously when someone does not want what I offer?

    ii.   Do I accept that I cannot do another person's loving?

7.   i.   Do I see that recovery from my own compulsive helping, through working a Twelve-Step programme, is a gift rather than a curse or punishment?

    ii. How does it show in my life that I am now in recovery from compulsive helping?

Relapse to mood-altering substances, behaviours and relationships and to compulsive helping

Relapse back to using mood-altering substances, behaviours and relationships or to compulsive helping, is always a personal tragedy. Nonetheless, it can be an experience from which we can learn and develop a deeper understanding and a happier life than before.

Theoretically, to say that we have relapsed implies that we were (at some time) in recovery. But this may be the problem: if our concept of recovery is no more than physical abstinence from a particular addictive substance or process, then that recovery was superficial and relapse was inevitable.

True recovery is characterized by peace of mind despite unsolved problems, happiness, creativity, acceptance of personal responsibility, mutually respectful and successful personal and professional relationships, absence of resentment and the presence of gratitude. Anything less is not recovery. However, it says in the *Big Book* of Alcoholics Anonymous (p. 60), referring to the Twelve Steps, "No one among us has been able to maintain anything like perfect adherence to these principles". Nonetheless, we can certainly try.

We therefore refer to ourselves as recovering rather than recovered. We remember that addiction simply sleeps; it does not go away. This is precisely what we discover to such cost when we relapse: our addiction never went away – and it came back with a vengeance into our lives.

We have addictive disease. We are addicts. This problem is inside us, whatever other problems there may be in the world outside. This is the first and foremost acknowledgement that we need to make in coming to terms with our relapse. Addiction is not like a cold: it doesn't go away on its own in time. Nor is it like appendicitis; there is no operation (nor psychological treatment) that will get rid of it once and for all.

The grief reaction that sets in with a relapse is therefore not simply the sadness over what we may have thrown away, but more the full acceptance of Step I: we really are addicts and our lives really are unmanageable. However determined we were, and however hard we tried, our way of doing things simply doesn't work.

But what was it that went wrong? The answer to that question is depressingly simple: it went wrong because the foundation of our recovery was inadequate. The castle was built on sand.

The most common fundamental errors are as follows:
i.   We didn't believe that we really are addicts. We thought our problems were simply the result of disturbed relationships or things that have gone wrong in our lives. We believed that if we could change other people, places and things, then everything would be fine with us.
ii. We still carried deep resentments, most often towards our parents or others who had wronged us in childhood or towards people who have (as we saw it) treated us badly in more recent relationships.
iii. We continued to use addictive substances or processes. Nicotine addiction is the most commonly denied cause of relapse in any addiction but some drug addicts refuse to accept that they have a problem with alcohol or cannabis, and some sufferers from eating disorders refuse to accept that the refined carbohydrates (sugar and white flour) have specific mood-altering effects, until relapse knocks

them flat. We discover that the addictive substances and processes that affect us do affect us – and that's that.

iv. We continue to indulge ourselves in addictive relationships, using other people as if they were drugs. We hang on to old friendships, environments and habits, forgetting that they got us into trouble in the first place or, at least, that they tend to stimulate our own addictive disease.

v. We have tried to convince ourselves that black is white in our perceptions and actions, blaming other people for difficulties and disorders in our own thoughts, feelings and behaviour.

vi. We treated compulsive helping (using ourselves as drugs for other people, denying our own needs, and caretaking rather than caring for others) as a joke rather than a serious addictive disease in its own right, requiring its own Steps and its own Fellowship.

vii. We got caught up in guru worship with a counsellor or therapist, particularly one who, subtly and almost apologetically, fuels our resentment towards our parents or other childhood figures, and makes out that, with appropriate therapeutic treatment, all our problems – and perhaps even our addiction itself – will go away.

viii. We remained dishonest in our personal and professional relationships, playing psychological games, lying, cheating, stealing (time if not money), defrauding, posturing, pretending and rationalizing – while still reciting the Serenity Prayer!

ix. We have continued to focus on one particular issue or person, believing that if everything goes right in that area of life, then everything else will slot into place and we shall be happy.

x. We stopped doing the basic activities of recovery: working the Steps (rather than nodding in their general direction), reading the Fellowship literature, maintaining active contact with a Fellowship sponsor, and – most importantly of all – going regularly to Fellowship meetings and giving service to the Fellowship, taking our minds off ourselves and reaching out to help others.

xi. We have believed that life in recovery should be free of problems, that happiness should come to us on a plate, and that our problems are due primarily to the behaviour of others. We may blame God, other people or the programme, saying that it is not working. We may believe that our own lives should be special and different simply because we have put down an addictive substance, behaviour or relationship.

Recovery is a process, not a state. The same is true for relapse. From the moment we stop working on our recovery on a continuing daily basis, we are technically relapsing: we are moving backwards rather than forwards. Our addictive disease gains progressively more control over our thoughts, feelings and actions. When finally we pick up an addictive substance, process or relationship, it is almost a relief as well as a personal tragedy: But our relapse began long ago…

Work-sheets on Relapse

1. Which of the following characteristics did I achieve in my "recovery"? Answer Yes, No or Some to the following:

    i.   Peace of mind in spite of unsolved problems
    ii. Happiness
    iii. Creativity
    iv   Acceptance of personal responsibility
    v.   Respectful and successful personal and professional relationships
    vi. Absence of resentment
    vii. Presence of gratitude

Describe what happened to each of these personal characteristics when I took my mind off the recovery programme.

2. i.   Did I believe that my addiction had gone away or that I was never really an addict in the first place?
    ii. What did I therefore believe to be the cause of my problems?
    iii. Do I now accept that my addiction goes with me, wherever I go, whoever I am with, whatever I may possess, whatever happens to me and whatever I do?

3. i.   Which addictive substances, processes or relationships did I continue to use despite my awareness, from my cross-addiction questionnaires, that I am addicted to them?
    •   Alcohol
    •   Nicotine
    •   Recreational drugs
    •   Caffeine
    •   Gambling
    •   Work
    •   Addictive relationships
    •   Sex and love
    •   Shopping/spending/stealing
    •   Exercise
    •   Prescription drugs
    •   Food (sugar and white flour) bingeing/starving/vomiting/purging
    •   Compulsive Helping

    ii. Describe my rationalizations for continuing to use these addictive substances, processes and relationships, despite knowing from my cross-addiction questionnaires that I am addicted to them.

4. What addictive relationships have I continued (in the hope that they would not affect my recovery)?

    i.   "Using" (or risky) personal relationships.
   ii. "Using" (or risky) environments.
  iii. "Using" (or risky) habits.

5. How have I tried to convince myself that black is white in my perceptions, blaming others for difficulties in my own thoughts, feelings and behaviour?

6. If I know from my cross-addiction questionnaire that I am a compulsive helper,
    i.   how significant a problem do I believe this to be?
   ii. what Steps for Compulsive Helpers have I worked?
  iii. what Helpers Anonymous meetings have I attended?
  iv. do I have a Helpers Anonymous sponsor?

7. i.   What one-to-one counselling or therapy have I been having in the hope that this would solve all my problems or even cure my addiction?
   ii. What issues were examined?
  iii. Did I get caught up in guru worship with a particular counsellor or therapist, particularly one who, subtly and almost apologetically, fuels my resentment towards my parents or other childhood figures and who may even make out that, with appropriate therapeutic treatment, all my problems – and perhaps even my addiction itself – will go away?

8. In which areas of my life, and in what way, have I been dishonest, playing psychological games, lying, cheating, stealing (time if not money), defrauding, posturing, pretending or rationalizing?
    i.   Close personal relationships.
   ii. Family.
  iii. Professional relationships.
  iv. Other relationships.

9. i.   On which particular issue or person have I focused, believing that if everything goes right in that area of my life then everything else will slot into place and I will be happy?
   ii. What are my particular concerns and preoccupations over that particular issue or person?

10. Describe what happened to each of the following recovery activities:
    i.   working the Steps (rather than nodding in their general direction).
   ii. reading the Fellowship literature.
  iii. maintaining active contact with a Fellowship sponsor.
  iv. going regularly to Fellowship meetings and giving service to the

Fellowship, taking my mind off myself and reaching out to help others.

11. i.   Have I expected life in recovery to be free of problems and have I been   resentful when it is not, blaming God, the programme or other people rather than my own unrealistic belief that my life should be special and different and free from trouble simply because I have put down one or another addictive substance, behaviour or relationship?

  ii.   In what ways have I believed that the world in general, and some other people in particular, have let me down so that I blamed my behaviour on them?

12. Describe when and how my addictive disease began to gain control over my thoughts, feelings and actions from long before I eventually picked up an addictive substance, process or relationship.

Appendices

Appendix I. Original book reviews of the *Big Book* of Alcoholics Anonymous in the medical press

i. *Journal of the American Medical Association*, 10th April 1939.
Alcoholics Anonymous: The Story of How More Than One Hundred Men Have Recovered from Alcoholism. Cloth. Price, $3.50. Pp. 400. New York: Works Publishing Company, 1939.

The seriousness of the psychiatric and social problem represented by addiction to alcohol is generally underestimated by those not intimately familiar with the tragedies in the families of victims or the resistance addicts offer to any effective treatment.

Many psychiatrists regard addiction to alcohol as having a more pessimistic prognosis than schizophrenia. For many years the public was beguiled into believing that short courses of enforced abstinence and catharsis in "institutes" and "rest homes" would do the trick, and now that the failure of such temporizing has become common knowledge, a considerable number of other forms of quack treatment have sprung up.

The book under review is a curious combination of organizing propaganda and religious exhortation. It is in no sense a scientific book, although it is introduced by a letter from a physician who claims to know some of the anonymous contributors who have been "cured" of addiction to alcohol and have joined together in an organisation which would save other addicts by a kind of religious conversion. The book contains instructions as to how to intrigue the alcoholic addict into the acceptance of divine guidance in place of alcohol in terms strongly reminiscent of Dale Carnegie and the adherents of the Buchman ("Oxford") movement. The one valid thing in the book is the recognition of the seriousness of addiction to alcohol. Other than this, the book has no scientific merit or interest.

ii. *American Journal of Nervous Mental Disorders.* September 1940.

Alcoholics Anonymous. How More Than One Hundred Men Have Recovered from Alcoholism (New York: Works Publishing Company, Church St. Annex P.O. $3.50)

As a youth we attended many "experience" meetings more as an onlooker than as a participant. We never could work ourselves up into a lather and burst forth in soapy bubbly phrases about our intimate states of feeling. That was our own business rather than something to brag about to the neighbours. Neither then nor now do we lean to the autobiographical, save occasionally by allusion to point a moral or adorn a tale, as the ancient adage puts it.

This big book, i.e. big in words, is a rambling sort of camp-meeting confession of experiences, told in the form of biographies of various alcoholics who had been to a certain institution and have provisionally recovered, chiefly under the influence of the "big brothers get together spirit." Of the inner meaning of alcoholism there is hardly a word. It is all on the surface material.

Inasmuch as the alcoholic, speaking generally, lives a wish-fulfilling infantile regression to the omnipotency delusional state, perhaps he is best handled for the time being at least by regressive mass psychological methods, in which, as is realized, religious fervors belong, hence the religious trend of the book. Billy Sunday and similar orators had their successes but we think the methods of Forel and of Bleuler infinitely superior.

Appendix II. Addictions Anonymous suggested format for meetings
(reproduced in full with kind permission of the Addictions Anonymous Service Office)

Welcome to the .... meeting of Addictions Anonymous.

Shall we introduce ourselves by first names only?

My name is .... and I am a ....
(other members introduce themselves).

We ask that there shall be no eating, drinking, smoking or use of any mood-altering substance during the meeting.

Addictions Anonymous is for those who suffer from any form of primary addictive disease. We make the distinction between primary addicts, who use mood-altering substances, behaviours or relationships to relieve an inner sense of emptiness, and compulsive helpers (sometimes referred to as Co-addicts or Co-Dependents) who may be addicted to addicts and who may try to help the emptiness of others. Some of us may be both addicts and compulsive helpers but, in order to avoid confusion, we ask that at meetings of Addictions Anonymous we focus only upon our primary addictive disease and recovery.

Shall we begin our meeting with a period of silence in which we remind ourselves of our reasons for being here?

(silence)

We have learned that addiction is an illness in many forms. We have been saddened to see individuals recovering from one form of addiction, through one Anonymous Fellowship, suddenly or gradually relapse into another addiction. We have learned that any mood-altering substance or process may be used addictively and undermine our recovery. We believe that in order to free ourselves from addiction and gain the full physical, mental, emotional and spiritual benefits of recovery, we need to be increasingly aware of our basic addictive nature and of all our addictive tendencies.

Addictions Anonymous has basic readings that are read by different members at each meeting:

1. Recovering from Addiction
2. Twelve Steps
3. Twelve Traditions
4. Five Fatal Flaws
5. Am I addicted?

In the *Big Book* of Alcoholics Anonymous it states (p. 64) that "resentment is the number one offender". Therefore we do not come to meetings in order to cry over the injustices of our childhood or compete with each other in telling fearful stories of our past lives and present miseries, focusing upon our own needs instead of those of other people, and blaming others while pitying ourselves. Rather, in this meeting, we take our own inventory and we share our experience (both good and bad), strength and hope in such a way as to encourage newcomers and set a positive example of recovery.

Anything you hear in the meeting is strictly the opinion of each individual speaker. If any member says something with which you disagree or with which you feel upset, please remember that he or she is speaking only from his or her own experience and not on behalf of Addictions Anonymous.

We have a list of telephone numbers of members who are happy to be contacted between meetings. Please take such numbers as you may wish and add your own number if you wish to do so.

Announcements.

Do we have any announcements?

Introduction to the Step study, topic for discussion, or guest speaker.

* * * * *

Closing.

The principles of Addictions Anonymous are found in our Twelve Steps and Twelve Traditions.

Our seventh Tradition states that each group should be fully self-supporting. While no dues or fees are required for membership, and especially not from newcomers, our voluntary contributions are used to pay for rent and literature, as well as allowing us to carry the message of our programme to others through the continued support of the Addictions Anonymous Service Office.

(wait until all contributions are collected)

Our ninth Step states that we made direct amends wherever possible to those we had harmed except when to do so would injure them or others. The *Big Book* of Alcoholics Anonymous (p. 83) in dealing with this ninth step makes the following promises:

"If we are painstaking about this phase of our development, we will be amazed before we are half way through. We are going to know a new freedom and a new happiness. We will not regret the past nor wish to shut the door on it. We will comprehend the word serenity and we will know peace. No matter how far down the scale we have gone, we will see how our experience can benefit others. That feeling of uselessness and self-pity will disappear. We will lose interest in selfish things and gain interest in our fellows. Self-seeking will slip away. Our whole attitude and outlook upon life will change. Fear of people and of economic insecurity will leave us. We will intuitively know how to handle situations which used to baffle us. We will suddenly realize that God is doing for us what we could not do for ourselves."

(reprinted with permission of Alcoholics Anonymous World Services Inc.)

Shall we close our meeting with the Serenity Prayer?

God grant me the serenity
To accept the things I cannot change,
Courage to change the things I can
And the wisdom to know the difference.

Recovering from addiction

We tried will-power: it let us down.
We sought knowledge and understanding: we became confused.
We craved control: we lost it.
We looked for political or religious solutions: they solved nothing.
We demanded social change: we sometimes got it but it made no difference.
We ran away: our addiction came with us.

Despairing and dispirited, we came to Addictions Anonymous – and ran away again, determined to solve our own problems in our own way rather than share our private thoughts and feelings with a group of strangers. We feared losing our individuality, our sense of fun, and our few remaining sources of personal comfort. We may in practice have had little or no time for God, nor for other men and women, because our experience showed that they were unreliable: we could depend only upon ourselves.

In this final arrogant isolation we ruled our own kingdom: spiritually bankrupt. The sweetness of life had turned sour.

But we remembered the stories we had heard in Addictions Anonymous. Certainly they were similar to our own. Yet these people, by following the Twelve-Step programme first used by Alcoholics Anonymous, were clearly getting better from their addictions and gradually finding a way to live constructively and happily in spite of many unsolved problems. By doing what at times appeared to be almost the opposite of all the things that we had tried, their lives appeared to be improving while ours got worse. Gradually, step by step, we tried for ourselves the principles that seemed to work for them.

In place of will-power, we acknowledged that addiction had us in its grip and that we needed a power greater than ourselves to help us out of it. Instead of seeking yet more knowledge and intellectual understanding, we tried to practise for ourselves the suggested steps that apparently worked for others. Where once we had tried to control our feelings in one way or another, to such an extent that our lives became chaotic, we now learnt to share our experience, strength and hope with others in Addictions Anonymous so that we could regain peace of mind in place of preoccupation. Instead of looking for change in other people, places and things, we looked at our own feelings, thoughts and behaviour.

Gradually we ventured on a journey of the human spirit, discovering whether the Twelve Steps that apparently worked for others might also, in our own time and in our own way, progressively work for us.

Addictions Anonymous Twelve Steps
1. We admitted we were powerless over addiction and that our lives had become unmanageable.
2. Came to believe that a power greater than ourselves could restore us to sanity.
3. Made a decision to turn our will and our lives over to the care of God *as we understood Him*.
4. Made a searching and fearless moral inventory of ourselves.
5. Admitted to God, to ourselves and to another human being the exact nature of our wrongs.
6. Were entirely ready to have God remove all these defects of character.
7. Humbly asked Him to remove our shortcomings.
8. Made a list of all persons we had harmed, and became willing to make amends to them all.
9. Made direct amends to such people wherever possible, except when to do so would injure them or others.

10. Continued to take personal inventory and when we were wrong promptly admitted it.

11. Sought through prayer and meditation to improve our conscious contact with God, *__as we understood Him,__* praying only for knowledge of His will for us and the power to carry that out.

12. Having had a spiritual awakening as the result of these steps we tried to carry this message to addicts who still suffer and to practise these principles in all our affairs.

Addictions Anonymous Twelve Traditions

1. Our common welfare should come first; personal progress for the greatest number depends upon unity.

2. For our group purposes there is but one authority – a loving God, as He may express Himself in our group conscience. Our leaders are but trusted servants – they do not govern.

3. Individuals concerned with addiction, when gathered together for mutual aid, may call themselves an Addictions Anonymous group provided that, as a group, they have no other affiliation. The only requirement for membership is a desire to stop using addictive substances and processes.

4. Each group should be autonomous, except in matters affecting other groups or Addictions Anonymous as a whole.

5. Each group has but one primary purpose, to carry its message to the addict who still suffers.

6. Addictions Anonymous groups should never endorse, finance, or lend our name to any outside enterprise, lest problems of money, property and prestige divert us from our primary purpose.

7. Every group should be fully self-supporting, declining outside contributions.

8. Addictions Anonymous Twelfth Step work should remain forever non-professional, but our service centres may employ special workers.

9. Our groups, as such, should never be organized, but we may create service boards or committees directly responsible to the groups they serve.

10. Addictions Anonymous has no opinion on outside issues; hence our name should never be drawn into public controversy.

11. Our public relations policies are based on attraction rather than promotion; we should always maintain personal anonymity at the level of press, radio, films and TV. We need to guard with special care the anonymity of our members, as well as those of other recovery programmes.

12. Anonymity is the spiritual foundation of all our Traditions, ever reminding us to place principles before personalities.

Addictions Anonymous: Five fatal flaws

Addictive disease is cunning, baffling and powerful:Anonymous Fellowships are fragile. If our meetings and our Fellowship of Addictions Anonymous are to survive and flourish, they need the life of recovery breathed into them and we should beware of five fatal flaws:

The first is arrogance. We make no rules on how any individual member should work his or her programme of recovery. Even the Twelve Steps are merely suggested. We avoid any discussion of religion, politics, or therapeutic programmes, remembering that these are outside issues as far as Addictions Anonymous is concerned.

The second is betrayal. We share our thoughts, feelings and experiences in confidence and in anonymity.

The third is dominance. All members of Addictions Anonymous, including newcomers, have equal status. Any form of service to the groups or to the Fellowship itself is a privilege and a position of trust rather than authority.

The fourth is the use of therapeutic jargon. For example, we avoid the use of words or phrases such as "co-dependency", "Inner child" or "anger work" that may mean different things to different people and hence cause confusion and divert us from our goal of spiritual recovery. Many members of various Twelve-Step Programmes have individually benefited from specific ideas or therapies of one kind or another. Other members have not benefited and may even have been discouraged. Therefore, in order to maintain the cohesion of our groups, we refer during meetings only to the ideas and principles of the Twelve Steps.

The fifth is insensitivity. We avoid eating, drinking, smoking or using any other mood-altering substance or process during meetings. This use may be insensitive to other members. It may also blunt our own feelings and therefore damage our full capacity to benefit from any message of recovery. In Addictions Anonymous we believe that dependence upon mood-altering substances or processes is best acknowledged and helped through the Twelve-Step Programme in this Fellowship, or other appropriate Anonymous Fellowships, rather than accommodated.

Am I addicted?

We have learned that the tendency towards addiction is an illness that goes with the person rather than simply with particular substances or processes. Each one of us who suffers from this illness may become addicted to any mood-altering substance or process.

Examples of addictive substances are alcohol, recreational drugs, prescription drugs, nicotine, caffeine, sugar and other refined carbohydrates.

Examples of addictive behaviours are compulsive gambling or risk-taking; compulsive overeating, vomiting or starving; compulsive overspending, shopping or stealing; compulsive exercising; compulsive overworking on our basic occupations or on hobbies and interests, cults or sects; compulsive cleaning or other ritualization; compulsive sexual activity; compulsive relationships with other people, using them as if they were "drugs" whose purpose is to fill up our own emptiness.

All these and other substances and processes of addiction can undermine the recovery we work to achieve. They may cause great damage to our own lives and to the lives of those who are close to us.

Some of us also suffer from an addictive tendency towards compulsive helping or caretaking, being, as it were, addicted to addicts. For this we seek help through Helpers Anonymous or another appropriate family Fellowship.

To identify an addictive tendency we listen to the stories of others who acknowledge that they themselves suffer from addictive disease.

To further identify and clarify our own addictive tendencies, we look for the following addictive characteristics with respect to any potentially addictive substance or behaviour:

1. Preoccupation with use or with non-use.
2. Preference for, or contentment with, use alone.
3. Use as a medicine, to help relax or sedate or to stimulate.
4. Use primarily for mood-altering effect.
5. Protection of supply, preferring to spend time, energy or money in this way.
6. Repeatedly using more than planned so that the first use tends to trigger the next.
7. Having a higher capacity than other people for using the substance or process without obvious initial damaging effects, although in time this tolerance is lost.
8. Continuing to use despite progressively damaging consequences.
9. Drug-seeking behaviour, looking for opportunities to use and progressively rejecting activities that preclude use.
10. Drug-dependent behaviour, needing the addictive substance or behaviour in order to function effectively.
11. The tendency to cross-addict into other addictive substances or processes when attempting to control use.
12. Continuing to use despite the repeated serious concern of other people.

We take special care to bear in mind that we ourselves, in a central feature of our addictive disease, may try to defend our use of particular addictive substances or processes; the more determined our defence – in all its guises – the more likely it is that we are indeed addicted. For example, we may try to defend our use of drinks with low alcohol content, while overlooking our continued resentment at giving up the real thing and denying our risky dependence upon an alcohol-using environment; our use of cannabis, Methadone, antidepressants, tranquillizers or sleeping tablets, saying that they are not so bad as other drugs or that they are medically prescribed; our use of compulsive exercise, saying that it is healthy, or overworking, saying that it is necessary and that other people benefit; our use of nicotine, disregarding that its principal purpose is to alter our mood; our continued use of sugar and refined carbohydrates in the hope that working a spiritual programme of recovery for an eating disorder will enable us to continue using these addictive substances; our use of other addictive relationships, substances or behaviours, saying that they are not real addictions and that we have to be addicted to something.

If you find that you have an addictive tendency towards any or even all addictive substances or processes, then you are welcome in Addictions Anonymous.

Here, through progressively putting down all addictive substances and processes that affect you, and through working the Twelve-Step programme of recovery, with the aid of a Higher Power, greater than self, as each of us may choose to understand this, you will find that the sense of confusion and insecurity will gradually fade and you will develop, one day at a time, the confidence, ease and grace of life in continuing recovery.

Appendix III. Helpers Anonymous suggested format for meetings (reproduced in full with kind permission from the Helpers Anonymous Service Office)

Welcome to the .... meeting of Helpers Anonymous.
Shall we introduce ourselves by first names only?
My name is .... and I am a compulsive helper.
(other members introduce themselves.)

We ask that there shall be no eating, drinking, smoking or use of any mood-altering substance during the meeting.

Shall we begin our meeting with a period of silence in which we remind ourselves of our reasons for being here?

(silence)

Helpers Anonymous is for those who have known a feeling of despair in finding that being concerned for another person, or for many others, becomes compulsive so that it may become an obsession, never-ending and even destructive to ourselves and others.

We have learned that this compulsion is relieved by a change in our own thoughts, feelings and behaviour, through the continued working of our Twelve-Step programme of recovery, with the aid of a Higher Power, greater than ourselves, as each one of us may choose to understand this.

Here we learn to live comfortably in spite of unsolved problems and we learn to be genuinely helpful to others and to ourselves.

Helpers Anonymous has basic readings that are read by different members at each meeting:

Appendices

1. Twelve Steps
2. Twelve Traditions
3. Five Fatal Flaws
4. Helping others
5. The willingness to be helped ourselves

In the *Big Book* of Alcoholics Anonymous it states (p.64) that "resentment is the number one offender".Therefore we do not come to meetings in order to cry over the injustices of our childhood or compete with each other in telling fearful stories of our past lives and present miseries, blaming others and pitying ourselves. Rather, we take our own inventory and we share our experience (both good and bad), strength and hope in such a way as to encourage newcomers and set a positive example of recovery.Anything you hear in the meeting is strictly the opinion of each individual speaker. If any member says something with which you disagree or with which you feel upset, please remember that he or she is speaking only from his or her own experience and not on behalf of Helpers Anonymous.

We have a list of telephone numbers of members who are happy to be contacted between meetings. Please take such numbers as you may wish and add your own number, if you wish to do so.

Announcements.
Do we have any announcements?

Introduction to the Step study, topic for discussion, or guest speaker.

* * * * *
Closing.

The principles of Helpers Anonymous are found in our Twelve Steps and Twelve Traditions.

Our seventh Tradition states that each group should be fully self-supporting. While no dues or fees are required for membership, and especially not from newcomers, our voluntary contributions are used to pay for rent and literature, as well as allowing us to carry the message of our programme to others through the continued support of the Helpers Anonymous Service Office.

(wait until all contributions are collected)

Our ninth Step states that we made direct amends wherever possible to those we had harmed except when to do so would injure them or others. The *Big Book* of Alcoholics Anonymous (p.83), in dealing with this ninth Step, makes the following promises:

"If we are painstaking about this phase of our development, we will be amazed before we are half way through. We are going to know a new freedom and a new happiness. We will not regret the past nor wish to shut the door on it. We will comprehend the word serenity and we will know peace. No matter how far down the scale we have gone, we will see how our experience can benefit others. That feeling of uselessness and self-pity will disappear. We will lose interest in selfish things and gain interest in our fellows. Self-seeking will slip away. Our whole attitude and outlook upon life will change. Fear of people and of economic insecurity will leave us. We will intuitively know how to handle situations which used to baffle us. We will suddenly realize that God is doing for us what we could not do for ourselves." (reprinted with permission of Alcoholics Anonymous World Services Inc.)

Shall we close our meeting with the Serenity Prayer?

> God grant me the serenity
> To accept the things I cannot change,
> Courage to change the things I can
> And the wisdom to know the difference.

HELPERS ANONYMOUS TWELVE STEPS

1. We admitted we were powerless over other people's lives and our own compulsive helping and that our lives had become unmanageable.

2. Came to believe that a power greater than ourselves could restore us to sanity.
3. Made a decision to turn our will and our lives over to the care of God *as we understood Him*.
4. Made a searching and fearless moral inventory of ourselves.
5. Admitted to God, to ourselves and to another human being the exact nature of our wrongs.
6. Were entirely ready to have God remove all these defects of character.
7. Humbly asked Him to remove our shortcomings.
8. Made a list of all persons we had harmed, and became willing to make amends to them all.
9. Made direct amends to such people wherever possible, except when to do so would injure them or others.
10. Continued to take personal inventory and when we were wrong promptly admitted it.
11. Sought through prayer and meditation to improve our conscious contact with God *as we understood Him*, praying only for knowledge of His will for us and the power to carry that out.
12. Having had a spiritual awakening as the result of these steps we tried to carry this message to compulsive helpers who still suffer, and to practise these principles in all our affairs.

HELPERS ANONYMOUS TWELVE TRADITIONS

1. Our common welfare should come first; personal progress for the greatest number depends upon unity.
2. For our group purposes there is but one authority – a loving God, as He may express Himself in our group conscience. Our leaders are but trusted servants – they do not govern.
3. Individuals concerned with helping others in any way and concerned with their own compulsive helping, when gathered together for mutual aid, may call themselves a Helpers Anonymous group provided that, as a group, they have no other affiliation. The only requirement for membership is a desire to cease compulsive helping.
4. Each group should be autonomous, except in matters affecting other groups or Helpers Anonymous as a whole.
5. Each group has but one primary purpose, to carry its message to the compulsive helper who still suffers.
6. Helpers Anonymous groups should never endorse, finance, or lend our name to any outside enterprise, lest problems of money, property and prestige divert us from our primary purpose.
7. Every group should be fully self-supporting, declining outside contributions.
8. Helpers Anonymous Twelfth Step work should remain forever non-professional, but our service centres may employ special workers.
9. Our groups, as such, should never be organized, but we may create service boards or committees directly responsible to the groups they serve.
10. Helpers Anonymous has no opinion on outside issues; hence our name should never be drawn into public controversy.
11. Our public relations policies are based on attraction rather than promotion; we should always maintain personal anonymity at the level of press, radio, films and TV. We need to guard with special care the anonymity of our members, as well as those of other recovery programmes.
12. Anonymity is the spiritual foundation of all our Traditions, ever reminding us to place principles before personalities.

Helpers Anonymous: Five fatal flaws

Addictive disease is cunning, baffling and powerful: Anonymous Fellowships are fragile. If our meetings and our Fellowship of Helpers Anonymous are to survive and flourish, they need the life of recovery breathed into them and we should beware of five fatal flaws:

The first is arrogance. We make no rules on how any individual member should work his or her programme of recovery. Even the Twelve Steps are merely suggested. We avoid any discussion of religion, politics, or therapeutic programmes, remembering that these are "outside issues" as far as Helpers Anonymous is concerned.

The second is betrayal. We share our thoughts, feelings and experiences in confidence and in anonymity.

The third is dominance. All members of Helpers Anonymous, including newcomers, have equal status. Any form of service to the groups or to the Fellowship itself is a privilege and a position of trust rather than authority.

The fourth is the use of therapeutic jargon. For example, we avoid the use of words or phrases such as "co-dependency", "Inner child" or "anger work" that may mean different things to different people and hence cause confusion and divert us from our goal of spiritual recovery. Many members of various Twelve-Step Programmes have individually benefited from specific ideas or therapies of one kind or another. Other members have not benefited and may even have been discouraged. Therefore, in order to maintain the cohesion of our groups, we refer during meetings only to the ideas and principles of the Twelve Steps.

The fifth is insensitivity. We avoid eating, drinking, smoking or using any other mood-altering substance or process during meetings. This use may be insensitive to other members. It may also blunt our own feelings and therefore damage our full capacity to benefit from any message of recovery. In Helpers Anonymous we believe that dependence upon mood-altering substances or processes is best acknowledged and helped through Addictions Anonymous, or other appropriate Anonymous Fellowships, rather than accommodated.

Helping others

In Helpers Anonymous we learn through the Twelve Steps how to be genuinely helpful to others and avoid being compulsive helpers. We learn how to care and not caretake.

To help other people is a lovely thing. To be kind and considerate, supportive and generous, is beautiful.

These are the building bricks of a good life. In giving to others, we ourselves receive the gifts of happiness and contentment.

Yet this very process, the basis of honest and loving relationships, is corrupted by addictive disease. The more we give, the more the addict takes and demands, and then we feel we should give even more. Each of us, the addict and the helper, is hooked into the other's compulsive behaviour in a dreadful dance.

In Helpers Anonymous we learn to see the difference between helping the person and aiding and abetting his or her addictive disease by our own inappropriate action or inaction. We learn to take the risk of leaving the addict to take full responsibility for the consequences of his or her own decisions and behaviour. Throughout all the good times and bad, we respect the rights of the individual addict to make his or her own choices, regardless of how ill-advised or damaging we may perceive those choices to be. We recognize that addictive disease is not the fault of the sufferer and we continue to respect or love the individual regardless of the decisions and actions taken. While we reject addictive behaviour and we hold the addict to full account for all his or her actions, we still do not reject the human being from our minds or hearts.

We learn to encourage his or her steps towards recovery, not through believing promises or offering bribes for changes in future behaviour, but through responding to consistent and progressive change that is actually achieved. We learn to be deaf to the self-pity and blaming of addictive disease, while responding positively to genuine attempts at change in thoughts, feelings and behaviour through working a Twelve-Step programme of recovery. Yet at all times we continue our respect or love, even in the face of the very opposite of our own advice, belief or hope.

In Helpers Anonymous we also come to see that to be of real help to others we must first be willing to be helped ourselves by coming to understand our own addictive nature as compulsive helpers and treat this, one day at a time, through our own Twelve-Step programme of recovery.

The willingness to be helped ourselves

When we first come to Helpers Anonymous our concern is mostly for someone else. We search for new ideas on how to help the ones we love or for whom we are concerned. We want to understand new theories of addiction or of compulsive and destructive behaviour. We seek out new experts to advise us. In our desperation we will listen to anybody, go anywhere, and do almost anything.

Grabbing enthusiastically at each new solution, we become thrilled with the hope that at last we have found someone who really knows and something that really works. But each time, when the honeymoon period wears off, we become sad and disillusioned; until the next time; until we find the next idea and the next expert. Then off we go yet again in our exhausting and determined search.

But then even this new idea turns out to be no good and even this new expert is no wiser than the last. Certainly there are times – perhaps lasting weeks, months or even more – when things seem to be working out really well. We try to be calm, confident, hopeful and encouraging but inside there may still be the same old fears: "Is he going to go back to it one day?" "Is she in trouble again?" "Why did he do that?" "What is that so-called friend of hers doing now?" "Suppose it all goes wrong again?"

We learn from painful experience not to ask these questions out loud. But we say to ourselves that surely it is too much to ask that we shouldn't think these things. Anyway, surely it's our responsibility as a family member or friend, employer or counsellor, to be concerned about these things. Isn't it?

Then, at last, when we hear the stories told in Helpers Anonymous, we know one thing for certain: these people have been where we have been; they know our fears and hopes from the inside.

But the more we listen, the more we are struck by one particular feature: in Helpers Anonymous the members talk little about the addicts in their lives and they talk much about their own behaviour. They openly acknowledge that they work the Twelve-Step programme of recovery from addiction for themselves and not simply because they want to understand it for someone else.

Reflecting on our own behaviour, many of us recognize two things:

i.   We have been caretaking for other people, wanting them to need us, for as long as we can remember, certainly for longer than we have been trying to help the particular person who brought us to Helpers Anonymous.

ii. We may have neglected other people and other responsibilities, and we have damaged ourselves and the quality of our own lives.

These two characteristics - caretaking and self-denial - have been dominant features of our lives and, in truth, they have not helped in the way we wished and they have certainly led to a lot of damage in our own lives.

At first we may be angry at having the spotlight turned on our own behaviour - just as any addict reacts in exactly this way. In time we come to ask ourselves "Did my hive of activity really help? Was it really true, as I thought, that I did not try hard enough? However hard I tried, wasn't there always one more idea and one more expert?"

We come to see that we have ourselves been caught up in our own addictive behaviour. Caretaking and self-denial have become progressive and destructive in just the same way and to the same extent as any other addictive process is progressive and destructive. Here in Helpers Anonymous, just as in any other Anonymous Fellowship for any other form of addictive disease, we learn to look at our own behaviour and we gradually learn to be helped ourselves.

Appendix IV. The Twelve Steps and Twelve Traditions of Alcoholics Anonymous

THE TWELVE STEPS OF ALCOHOLICS ANONYMOUS

1. We admitted we were powerless over alcohol – that our lives had become unmanageable.
2. Came to believe that a power greater than ourselves could restore us to sanity.
3. Made a decision to turn our will and our lives over to the care of God *as we understood Him*.
4. Made a searching and fearless moral inventory of ourselves.
5. Admitted to God, to ourselves and to another human being the exact nature of our wrongs.
6. Were entirely ready to have God remove all these defects of

character.

7. Humbly asked Him to remove our shortcomings.
8. Made a list of all persons we had harmed, and became willing to make amends to them all.
9. Made direct amends to such people wherever possible, except when to do so would injure them or others.
10. Continued to take personal inventory and when we were wrong promptly admitted it.
11. Sought through prayer and meditation to improve our conscious contact with God, *__as we understood Him__*, praying only for knowledge of His will for us and the power to carry that out.
12. Having had a spiritual awakening as the result of these steps we tried to carry this message to alcoholics, and to practise these principles in all our affairs.

The Twelve Steps are reprinted with kind permission of Alcoholics Anonymous World Service, Inc. Permission to reprint and adapt the Twelve Steps does not mean that AA is in any way affiliated with this programme (publication). AA is a programme of recovery from alcoholism - use of the Twelve steps in connection with programmes and activities which are patterned after AA but which address other problems, does not imply otherwise.

THE TWELVE TRADITIONS OF ALCOHOLICS ANONYMOUS

1. Our common welfare should come first; personal recovery depends on AA unity.
2. For our group purpose, there is but one ultimate authority – a loving God as He may express Himself in our group conscience. Our leaders are but trusted servants: they do not govern.
3. The only requirement for AA membership is a desire to stop drinking.
4. Each group should be autonomous except in matters affecting other groups or AA as a whole.
5. Each group has but one primary purpose – to carry its message to the alcoholic who still suffers.
6. An AA group ought never endorse, finance, or lend the AA name to any related facility or outside enterprise, lest problems of money, property and prestige divert us from our primary purpose.
7. Every AA group ought to be fully self-supporting, declining outside contributions.
8. Alcoholics Anonymous should remain forever non-professional, but our service centres may employ special workers.
9. AA, as such, ought never be organized; but we may create service boards or committees directly responsible to those they serve.
10. Alcoholics Anonymous has no opinion on outside issues; hence the AA name ought never be drawn into public controversy.

11. Our public relations policy is based on attraction rather than promotion; we need always maintain personal anonymity at the level of press, radio and films.
12. Anonymity is the spiritual foundation of our traditions, ever reminding us to place principles before personalities.

The Twelve Traditions are reprinted with the kind permission of Alcoholics Anonymous World Service, Inc. Permission to reprint and adapt the Twelve Traditions does not mean that AA is in any way affiliated with this programme (publication). AA is a programme of recovery from alcoholism - use of the Traditions in connection with programmes and activities which are patterned after AA, but which address other problems, does not imply otherwise.

Acknowledgements

To my secretary, Sarah Oaten, my editor, Dr Harriet Harvey Wood and my agent, Natasha Fairweather, for their professionalism.

To my wife, Meg, and son, Robin, for their encouragement.

To my staff and to Meg and Robin for their understanding and hard work alongside me in the treatment centre and counselling centre.

To my friends for their enthusiasm.

To our staff and patients, illustrated herein, for their example and inspiration.

Index

253

Notes